SOLID GOLD

Eva Hedencrona
Karin Smed-Gerdin
Peter Watcyn-Jones

ENGELSKA 5

Studentlitteratur

Illustrationer
Ingrid Frölich
Fotografier
23 IBL Bildbyrå/Mint Digital/Rex Features
30 Doug MacLellan
33 Todd Pierson/shutterstock.com
47 i359702/shutterstock.com
92–93 IBL Bildbyrå
252 IBL Bildbyrå/Rex Features
270 Joe Seer/shutterstock.com
Övriga fotografier
Shutterstock

Studentlitteratur har både digital och traditionell bokutgivning. Studentlitteraturs trycksaker är miljö-anpassade, både när det gäller papper och tryckprocess.

Art.nr 36446
ISBN 978-91-44-08417-6
Upplaga 1:3

studentlitteratur.se
Studentlitteratur AB, Lund

Formgivning: Werner Schmidt
Omslagslayout: Jens Martin, Signalera
Omslagsbild: Masterfile

Printed by Interak, Poland 2017

Congratulations on choosing *Solid Gold!*

Solid Gold 1 will improve your English in a variety of ways and first and foremost help you meet the course requirements for English 5. You can access *Solid Gold 1* from your computer, iPad or mobile phone, whichever suits the occasion best. The *Quick Guide to Solid Gold* on pages 4–5 will show you what there is and how everything works.

Solid Gold 1 covers the core content of English 5. The focus in the nine units is mainly on living conditions, social issues and cultural features in the English-speaking world. *Solid Gold* also aims to make you aware of how culture influences communication. There are a variety of texts in different genres such as fiction, non-fiction, extracts from biographies, newspaper articles, reviews, songs, etc. *Some Names Worth Knowing* updates you on some famous people in your fields of study.

In the *Resource Section* you will be introduced to different strategies to use when learning English. There is also advice on how to become a better speaker or writer. For example, you will learn how to adapt your language according to the purpose, recipient and situation. Your ability to narrate, instruct, summarise, explain, discuss and argue will all be practised in *Solid Gold.*

The *Exercises* deal with the language and subject matter of the texts. Many of the exercises can be done either in the printed book or digitally and there are additional digital exercises, including intensive vocabulary practice.

The *Vocabulary Bank* section will help you expand your vocabulary further. There is an extensive *Grammar* section backed up by interactive grammar exercises. *Want Some More?* in the digital material provides additional reading with exercises.

We hope that *Solid Gold* will help you move ahead in your English studies, improving your communication skills and broadening your knowledge and understanding of the world where English is used.

The *Solid Gold* team

Quick Guide to Solid Gold

'ALL-IN-ONE' BOOK – TEXTS, EXERCISES, RESOURCES AND MORE

Solid Gold provides a complete base for your English course, offering a wide range of printed and digital materials. You may not have time to use everything in *Solid Gold* but we hope you will find all you need.

Reading

Nine chapters, each with a theme, containing a variety of texts from different countries. The authors of the texts are also presented and the illustrations are intended to provide extra food for thought.

Some Names Worth Knowing

In *Some Names Worth Knowing* a number of well-known people from the 19th century to the present are described. This is linked to a section of exercises with thematic questions focusing on aspects of your school work: social science, humanities, natural science, technology and economics.

Resource Section

An invaluable handbook on how to improve your language skills. You can look up critical reading and reviewing of sources, letter writing, how to work with different genres and much more.

Exercises

In the exercise section of *Solid Gold 1* there is an extensive body of exercises on each of the texts, as well as listening and grammar exercises.

WSM (Want Some More?)

Under this heading there is a selection of extra texts for further reading, some of them printed in the book and others appearing as extra texts in the digital material.

Vocabulary Bank

Here is an opportunity to learn/revise important words which do not necessarily occur in the nine chapters. The exercises are divided into three groups: Useful verbs, Useful adjectives and Useful nouns.

Grammar
In *Solid Gold 1* you will find a comprehensive grammar guide that covers the various aspects of grammar.

Word lists
Word lists for all the texts and listening exercises.

DIGITAL MATERIAL

Recorded texts and word lists
All the texts in *Solid Gold 1* are recorded with native voices from different English-speaking countries. The word lists are also recorded, both English and Swedish.

Listening comprehension
The listening comprehension passages are recorded with native voices from different English-speaking countries.

Recorded Resource Section, Exercises, Vocabulary Bank and Grammar
All pages are recorded with authentic voices, to provide extra support when reading.

Digital exercises
Throughout the exercise section there are a number of links ↗ that give access to digital exercises as well as the listening exercises. Here you will find different kinds of exercises on vocabulary, comprehension, grammar and a great deal more.

Contents

GET DOWN TO IT 1

THE RIGHT LEVEL?

BY ELIZABETH GILBERT

ELIZABETH GILBERT was born in Waterbury, Connecticut in 1969. From a very early age, all she ever wanted to do was write.

Elizabeth Gilbert attended New York University, where she studied Political Science by day and worked on her short stories by night. She is best known for her 2006 memoir *Eat, Pray, Love*, which depicts her journey alone around the world, after a difficult divorce.

In 2010, the follow-up to *Eat, Pray, Love* called *Committed: A Love Story* was published – a memoir which explored her ambivalent feelings about the institution of marriage.

First, though, I must get settled into school. My classes begin today at the Leonardo da Vinci Academy of Language Studies, where I will be studying Italian five days a week, four hours a day. I'm so excited about school, I'm such a shameless *student.* I laid my clothes out last night, just like I did before my first day of first grade, with my patent leather shoes and my new lunch box. I hope the teacher will like me.

We all have to take a test on the first day at Leonardo da Vinci, in order to be placed in the proper level of Italian class for our abilities. When I hear this, I immediately start hoping I don't place into a Level One class, because that would be humiliating, given that I already took a whole entire semester of Italian at my Night School for Divorced Ladies in New York, and that I spent the summer memorizing flash cards, and that I've already been in Rome a week, and have been practicing the language in person, even conversing with old grandmothers about divorce. The thing is, I don't even know how many levels this school has, but as soon as I heard the word *level,* I decided that I must test into Level Two – at *least.*

So it's hammering down rain today, and I show up to school early (like I always have – *geek*!) and I take the test. It's such a hard test! I can't get through even a tenth of it! I know so much Italian, I know *dozens* of words in Italian, but they don't ask me anything that I know. Then there's an oral exam, which is even worse. There's this skinny Italian teacher interviewing me and speaking way too fast, in my opinion, and I should be doing so much better than this but I'm nervous and making mistakes with stuff I already know (like, why did I say *Vado a scuola* instead of *Sono andata a scuola?* I know that!).

In the end, it's OK, though. The skinny Italian teacher looks over my exam and selects my class level:

Level TWO!

Classes begin in the afternoon. So I go eat lunch (roasted endive) then saunter back to the school and smugly walk past all those Level One students (who must be *molto stupido,* really) and enter my first class. With my peers. Except that it becomes swiftly evident that these are not my peers and that I have no business being here because Level Two is really impossibly *hard.* I feel like I'm swimming, but barely. Like I'm taking in water with every breath. The teacher, a skinny guy (why are the teachers so skinny here? I don't trust skinny Italians), is going way too fast, skipping over whole chapters of the textbook, saying, "You already know this, you already know that ..." and keeping up a rapid-fire conversation with my apparently fluent classmates. My stomach is gripped in horror and I'm gasping for air and praying he won't call on me. Just as soon as the break comes, I run out of that classroom on wobbling legs and I scurry all the way over to the administrative office almost in tears, where I beg in very clear English if they could please move me down to a Level One class. And so they do. And now I am here.

This teacher is plump and speaks slowly. This is much better.

Questions and exercises on the text are on page 150.

LOSING MY VIRGINITY

BY RICHARD BRANSON

RICHARD BRANSON is chairman of the Virgin Group. He was born in 1950 and educated at Stowe School. He founded Virgin in 1970 as a mail order record retailer and today the Virgin Group has around 300 companies in over 30 countries. *Losing My Virginity* is Branson's autobiography.

'You're going to be trouble, Branson.'

'Yes, sir. I mean, no, sir.'

I was trouble – and always in trouble.

Aged eight I still couldn't read. In fact, I was dyslexic and short-sighted. Despite sitting at the front of the class, I couldn't read the blackboard. Only after a couple of terms did anyone think to have my eyes tested. Even when I could see, the letters and numbers made no sense at all. Dyslexia wasn't deemed a problem in those days, or, put more accurately, it was only a problem if you were dyslexic yourself. Since nobody had ever heard of dyslexia, being unable to read, write or spell just meant to the rest of the class and the teachers that you were either stupid or lazy. And at prep school you were beaten for both. I was soon being beaten once or twice a week for doing poor classwork or confusing the date of the Battle of Hastings.

My dyslexia was a problem throughout my school life. Now, although my spelling is still sometimes poor, I have managed to overcome the worst of my difficulties through training myself to concentrate. Perhaps my early problems with dyslexia made me more intuitive: when someone sends me a written proposal, rather than dwelling on detailed facts and figures I find that my imagination grasps and expands on what I read.

However, my saving grace was outside the classroom: I was good at sports. It is difficult to overestimate how important sport is at

English public schools. If you are good at sports, you are a school hero: the older boys won't bully you and the masters won't mind you failing all your exams. I was intensely keen to succeed at sports, possibly because it was my only opportunity to excel. I became captain of the football, rugby and cricket teams. Every sports day I won a series of cups for sprinting and hurdling. Just before my eleventh birthday, in 1961, I won all the races. I even decided to go in for the long jump. I had never done a good long jump before, but this time I decided to just have a go. I sprinted down the track, took off from the wooden plank and soared through the air. After I landed in the sand the master came up to me and shook me by the hand: it was a new Scaitcliffe School record. That summer day I couldn't put a foot wrong, and my parents and Lindi sat and clapped in the white marquee afterward as I went up to collect every cup. I won the Victor Ludorum. Who cared if I couldn't spell? Not me.

The next autumn term I was playing in a football match against another local school. I was running rings round the defender and had already scored one goal. I put my hand up and yelled for the ball, which was booted upfield and bounced over both of us. I turned and sprinted after it, controlled it and was bearing down on the goal when the defender caught up with me and floored me with a sliding tackle. My leg was caught beneath him as he fell across me. I heard a ghastly scream and for a split second I thought that he was hurt until I realised that it was me. He rolled off me and I saw my knee twisted at a horrible angle. My parents had always told us to laugh when we were in pain, so half laughing but mainly screaming I was carried off the field to the school matron, who drove me to hospital. My agony stopped only after they gave me an injection. I had badly torn the cartilage in my right knee and they were going to have to operate.

I was given a general anaesthetic and fell unconscious. I awoke to find myself out in the street. I was still in my hospital bed, and a nurse was holding a drip above my head, but my bed, together with several others, was parked outside. I thought I was dreaming, but the nurse explained that there had been a fire in the hospital during my operation and all the patients had been evacuated on to the street outside.

I went home for a few days to recover. Lying in bed, I looked at my silver cups on the mantelpiece. The doctor told me that I would not play sports again for a very long time.

'Don't worry, Ricky,' my mother said as she swept into the room after the doctor had gone. 'Just think of Douglas Bader. He hasn't got any legs at all. He's playing golf and flying planes and everything. You don't want to be lying there in bed doing nothing all day, do you?'

Questions and exercises on the text are on page 152.

PHENOMENAL WOMAN

BY MAYA ANGELOU

Pretty women wonder where my secret lies.
I'm not cute or built to suit a fashion model's size
But when I start to tell them,
They think I'm telling lies.
I say,
It's in the reach of my arms
The span of my hips,
The stride of my step,
The curl of my lips.
I'm a woman
Phenomenally.
Phenomenal woman,
That's me.

Born on April 4th, 1928, in St. Louis, Missouri, Maya Angelou was raised in St. Louis and Stamps, Arkansas. As a teenager, Dr. Angelou's love for the arts won her a scholarship to study dance and drama at San Francisco's Labor School. At 14, she dropped out to become San Francisco's first African-American female cable car conductor. Dr Maya Angelou was a poet, educator, historian, best-selling author, actress, playwright, civil rights activist, producer and director. She died on May 28th, 2014.

Questions and exercises on the text are on page 155.

ROCK WHAT YOU'VE GOT

BY KATHERINE SCHWARZENEGGER

Rock What You've Got **is KATHERINE SCHWARZENEGGER'S first book. She was born in 1989 and has a communication degree from the University of Southern California's Annenberg School. She writes for various websites on the issue of body image and other women's matters.**

"I hate myself!" I cried to my mother.

"I'm fat, I'm ugly, I'm stupid, and I feel totally disgusting!"

Both of my parents grew up feeling very confident, with a strong sense of self-worth, gifts they were doing their best to pass on to my three younger siblings and me. A self-defeating attitude, pity parties, and self-loathing aren't a part of their worlds, and it wasn't how they were raising their children.

Whenever I told my mom I didn't feel smart, she assured me that I was a bright and intelligent girl. If I told her I felt ugly, she'd tell me I was beautiful. When I told her I was miserable, she'd remind me how blessed I am. My mom had a way of knowing how to turn my negative statements into positive ones, something I had yet to learn. I knew she said things like that to comfort me, but it didn't always make me feel better because, well, let's face it, *she* is *my* mom. She's *supposed* to say those things to me, right? I actually believed it was her responsibility to tell me stuff like I am beautiful when I feel unattractive or that I am not fat when I think I am. I thought all moms did and said things like that to get their daughters through the awkward years. After all, they were once young like us too. But I realize now that not all mothers say these things to their daughters, and it *is* a big deal.

When my younger sister, Christina, and I were babies, my mother constantly reminded us that we had to be more in life than just a pretty face. My father took a videotape of us sitting in our high chairs

saying aloud, "I'm beautiful, smart, nice, and kind ..." over and over with hand motions to go along with it. It's a little embarrassing to look at now, but it was the start of building our self-confidence and self-esteem.

With that kind of support and positive reinforcement growing up, it may seem strange that I was suddenly feeling so much doubt and insecurity. Admittedly, I consider fourth grade to be one of my "chubby" years as a kid. I felt overweight, and looking back at old pictures of myself, I can honestly say I wasn't fat, but I certainly felt that way.

Up until then, I was always pencil thin. Without warning and with little awareness that it was happening, my body had changed. I was no longer the skinny little girl I had always been. In fact, the changes were so unexpected that I thought something must be wrong because I was inexplicably gaining weight.

I wasn't eating any differently than I used to.

I wasn't going through puberty ... yet.

My body just changed, which I wasn't ready or properly prepared to face.

As we reached our cruising altitude on the flight to Idaho that day, I was now all out sobbing. Instead of comforting me, my mom took out a pad of paper and a pen. She drew a line down the center of the paper and wrote "Likes" and "Don't Likes" at the top of each column. She asked me to list all of the things I liked about myself and then the things I didn't. I had to really stop and think about the things I liked.

I paused.

And then I yelled, "I don't like anything!" My sobs turned into uncontrollable weeping – you know the kind of crying where you can't catch a breath.

"I hate myself and I feel ugly all the time." I could barely get the words out of my mouth.

My mom continued to calmly walk me through a series of questions, focusing on all of my assets instead of my perceived flaws.

"Do you like your hair or hate your hair?" Mom asked.

"I like my hair, I guess," I replied in between breathless gasps and streaming tears.

"Do you like your eyes or hate your eyes?"

"I like those too," I said.

She made me write each of these attributes in the "Likes" column. One by one, we made a list of all the things I actually felt good about instead of what made me feel insecure. It was obvious there was more bothering me than just my looks. I was just too young to articulate all of the conflict I was feeling at the time.

After I calmed down, I was able to explain to my mother that I was angry because I didn't think I was as smart as the other kids in school. The classes in my school were divided up into slow, average, and advanced groups. When it came to math, I was in the slow class. This distinction and separation from most of my friends was eating away at my self-esteem. It made me feel isolated and "different." Looking back, I now realize the system our school implemented wasn't in the students' best interests, but at the time, it solidified my self-belief that I was not smart – and that really hurt.

I explained to my mother that math was the class I felt worst about. I told her how the teacher made me feel like a complete idiot for not understanding the problems.

"I was never very good at math, Katherine, but that didn't make me stupid or stop me from achieving my goals. You're not stupid, honey, you're really smart," my mother reassuringly said. "I became successful without being perfect at math, and you can too."

By the time the pilot announced we were landing, I remarkably realized that there were a lot more "Likes" about myself than "Dislikes" on the lists my mom and I had made during the flight. I felt better about myself than I had in months and actually began to look forward to a couple of days away from the pressures of school and life, not to mention spending some quality time skiing with my family.

Questions and exercises on the text are on page 155.

CHEAT!

Some American university students are using new methods to cheat in exams: using hand-free cell phones to get answers from friends outside the classroom, or hiding cameras in pens to snap online exams, then pass them on.

Now university officials are fighting back with their own high-tech strategies. Here, a special *New York Times* report gives you the "cheat shocker."

The frontier in the battle to defeat student cheating may be at the testing center of the University of Central Florida. No gum is allowed during an exam: chewing can disguise a student's speaking into a hands-free cell phone to an accomplice outside.

The 228 computers that students use are recessed into desk tops so that anyone trying to photograph the screen – using, say, a pen with a hidden camera to help a friend who will take the test later – is easy to spot. Scratch paper is allowed – but it's stamped with the date and must be turned in later.

When a proctor sees something suspicious, he records the student's work at the computer and directs an overhead camera to zoom in: images are burned onto a CD for evidence.

Taylor Ellis, an associate dean who runs a testing center at Central Florida – the U.S. university with the third largest number of enrolled students – says cheating has dropped to 14 suspected incidents out of 64,000 exams given in spring 2010. "It will never stop cheating completely, but I'll find out more about it," Ellis says.

CRACKDOWN

As the eternal temptation of students to cheat has gone high-tech – not just on exams, but also by cutting and pasting from the Internet and sharing homework online like music files – educators have responded with their own efforts to crack down.

The extent of student cheating appears widespread at American universities. In surveys of 14,000 undergraduates over the last four years, an average of 61 percent admit to cheating on assignments and exams.

Donald McCabe, a business professor at Rutgers University in New Jersey, suspects students no longer even think of certain acts as cheating at all – like copying a few sentences at a time from the

Internet. But anti-plagiarism services requiring students to submit papers to be checked for copying is a booming business. Fifty-five percent of universities now use such a service.

Questions and exercises on the text are on page 160.

2 MAKE IT HAPPEN

FRY AND JOBS – STEPHEN MEETS STEVE

BY STEPHEN FRY

STEPHEN FRY is an English writer, actor and broadcaster. His films include, among others, *Wilde, Gosford Park, V for Vendetta* and more recently *The Hobbit: There and Back Again*. He has also been the reader for the British versions of all the Harry Potter audio books. His first novel was *The Liar* (1995). Another novel is *The Stars' Tennis Balls* (2000) and with two volumes of autobiography, one called *The Fry Chronicles: An Autobiography* (2010) as well as various plays, screenplays and TV series he is an established writer.

I have met five British Prime Ministers, two American Presidents, Nelson Mandela, Michael Jackson and the Queen. My hour with Steve Jobs certainly made me more nervous than any of those encounters. I know what you are thinking, but it's the truth. I do believe Jobs to be a truly great figure, one of the small group of innovators who have changed the world. He exists somewhere between showman, perfectionist overseer, visionary, enthusiast and opportunist, and his insistence upon design, detail, finish, quality, ease of use and reliability are a huge part of Apple's success.

When I get to see Jobs, he is wearing the famous black turtleneck sweater and blue Levi's 501 jeans without which I would have cried, "Impostor!" Recent weight loss from his liver transplant has imparted a delicacy that reminds me, I can't think why, of the actor William Hurt. We meet in a conference room. On every spare shelf and ledge, at least a dozen iMacs are placed, each one playing a family slide show. Jobs leans back on his chair, feet up on the table, a welcoming grin on his face. My first question is a nervous babble that lasts five minutes. He listens with patient amusement and answers, "Yes." Or possibly, "No." I cannot remember what the question was. I had forgotten to turn on the recorder. I do so now, abashed.

A little calmer, I remind Jobs that at the product launch of the iPad in January, he had stood in front of two street signs, one reading "Liberal Arts," the other "Technology." "This is where I

have always seen Apple," he told the audience, "at the intersection of the Liberal Arts and Technology."

I suggest there's a bit more to it than that; surely Apple stands at the intersection of liberal arts, technology and commerce? "Sure, what we do has to make commercial sense," Jobs concedes, "but it's never the starting point. We start with the product and the user experience. You seen an iBook yet?" His pleasure in showing me the *Winnie the Pooh* iBook bundled with every iPad is unaffected and engaging. He demonstrates how the case can be used as a lectern and as a stand. "I think the experience of using an iPad is going to be profound for many people," he says. "I really do. Genuinely profound." That rings a bell. "I've heard it said that this is the device for you," I reply. "The one that will change everything." "When people see how immersive the experience is," Jobs says, "how directly you engage with it ... the only word is *magical.*"

In five years, Jobs has emerged from two serious health scares. His obituaries had been written, much as Apple's had been back in 1997. "Is this then the curtain dropping on your third act?" I ask. "Will you perhaps leave Apple on this high, a fitting end to your career here?" "I don't think of my life as a career," he says. "I do stuff. I respond to stuff. That's not a career – it's a life!"

After he leaves, I am finally left alone with an iPad. Finally I get some finger time. I peep under the slip holder, and there it is. When I switch it on, a little sigh escapes me as the screen lights up. Ten minutes later I am rolling on the floor, snarling and biting, trying to wrestle it from the hands of an Apple press representative.

Questions and exercises on the text are on page 166.

Steve Jobs died in 2011, the same year that he resigned as CEO of Apple Inc.

ENCOUNTERS

BY TERRI IRWIN

The name of the zoo was the Queensland Reptile and Fauna Park. As I crossed the parking area, I prepared myself for disappointment. *I am going to see a collection of snakes, lizards, and miserable creatures in jars, feel terribly sorry for them, and leave.*

It was October 1991. I was Terri Raines, a twenty-seven-year-old Oregon girl in Australia on an unlikely quest to find homes for rescued American cougars. A reptile park wasn't going to be interested in a big cat. I headed through the pleasant spring heat toward the park thinking pessimistic thoughts. *This is going to be a big waste of time.* But the prospect of seeing new species of wildlife drew me in.

I walked through the modest entrance with some friends, only to be shocked at what I found on the other side: the most beautiful, immaculately kept gardens I had ever encountered. Peacocks strutted around, kangaroos and wallabies roamed freely, and palm trees lined all the walkways. It was like a little piece of Eden.

After I paid my admission fee, I saw that the reptile enclosures were kept perfectly clean – the snakes glistened. I kept rescued animals myself at home. I knew zoos, and I knew the variety of nightmares they can fall into. But I saw not a sign of external parasites on these animals, no old food rotting in the cages, no feces or shed skin left unattended.

So I enjoyed myself. I toured around, learned about the snakes, and fed the kangaroos. It was a brilliant, sunlit day.

"There will be a show at the crocodile enclosures in five minutes," a voice announced on the PA system. "Five minutes."

That sounded good to me.

I noticed the crocodiles before I noticed the man. There was a whole line of crocodilians: alligators, freshwater crocodiles, and one big saltie. Amazing, modern-day dinosaurs. I didn't know much about them, but I knew that they had existed unchanged for millions of years. They were a message from our past, from the dawn of time, among the most ancient creatures on the planet.

Then I saw the man. A tall, solid twentysomething (he appeared younger than he was, and had actually turned twenty-nine that February), dressed in a khaki shirt and shorts, barefoot, with blond flyaway hair underneath a big Akubra hat and a black-banded wristwatch on his left wrist. Even though he was big and muscular, there was something kind and approachable about him too.

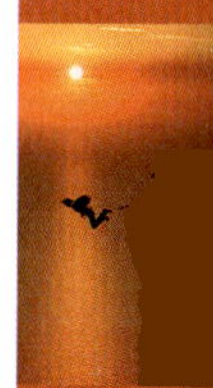

I stood among the fifteen or twenty other park visitors and listened to him talk.

“They can live as long as or even longer than us,” he said, walking casually past the big saltwater croc’s pond. “They can hold their breath underwater for hours.”

He approached the water’s edge with a piece of meat. The crocodile lunged out of the water and snapped the meat from his hand. “This male croc is territorial,” he explained, “and females become really aggressive when they lay eggs in a nest.” He knelt beside the croc that had just tried to nail him. “Crocodiles are such good mothers.”

Every inch of this man, every movement and word exuded his passion for the crocodilians he passed among. I couldn’t help but notice that he never tried to big-note himself. He was there to make sure his audience admired the crocs, not himself.

I recognized his passion, because I felt some of it myself. I spoke the same way about cougars as this Australian zookeeper spoke about crocs. When I heard there would be a special guided tour of the Crocodile Environmental Park, I was first in line for a ticket. I had to hear more. This man was on fire with enthusiasm, and I felt I really connected with him, like I was meeting a kindred spirit.

What was the young zookeeper’s name? Irwin. Steve Irwin.

Questions and exercises on the text are on page 170.

3

CROSSING LINES

SO WHERE YOU FROM?

BY IVA R. SKOCH

AMERICANS ARE SO NICE. It's a shame, really. It wouldn't be so bad if nice people didn't like small talk so much, but they seem to love it. If you're an immigrant with an accent, your days will be filled with conversations with nice people.

It goes like this: I utter a simple "thank you" to a grocery store cashier, prompting an immediate "Where are you from?" "Czech Republic," I say. "Really? My aunt went to Russia last year," she responds. What do I say to that? Do I go with the pointless, "That's nice" and beat a hasty retreat? Or do I say what I'm actually thinking: "What does that have to do with anything?" But that's rude. I try not to be rude – partly because I am an immigrant here (and there are few things more insufferable than ungrateful immigrants) and partly because being nice is contagious. I usually opt for the pointless.

Don't get me wrong, I haven't quite become a nice person. I often long for the rude anonymity of Europe. Back in 2000, when I was "fresh off the boat," as the not-so-nice folks say, I worked on the 24th floor of an office building in Seattle. How I dreaded those long 9 a.m. elevator rides. They were filled with the nicest people you'll ever meet. To make matters worse, they had all just spent an hour cooped up alone in their cars and were just dying to talk. "Could you press 24 for me, please?" I ask an elderly man. "Do I detect an accent?" he asks, all proud of himself. "Where are you from?"

Here we go. "Czech Republic," I say. "Ah, Czechoslovakia," he says. "It's actually the Czech Republic now," I explain politely. "The country split up in 1993." Undeterred, he continues, "My friend's grandfather was from Czechoslovakia." "That's nice," I say and watch the elevator stop on the fifth and sixth floors. Please, I beg quietly, don't let him ask any more questions.

"So what brings you here?" he, of course, asks. "My husband is American," I say, knowing what's coming next. "What does your husband do?" "He is a lawyer. Don't hold it against me," I say, trying to soften the blow, since even nice people love to hate lawyers. It also buys time. He chuckles for a floor or two. "How long have you been here?" he asks. "Just a year," I respond. "Well, your English is fantastic," he says. And this, I must admit, is very nice to hear. "Thank

you," I say – but what I'm thinking is: "Clearly, it isn't fantastic enough to allow me to be anonymous."

He gets out on the 18th floor. Now it's only me and three other people, with six floors still to go. "Where do you live in Seattle?" a young woman asks. "Belltown," I say. "No way! Me too," she exclaims. "What building?"

I've just told a group of complete strangers where I'm from, what got me here, how long I've been here, my husband's occupation and where I live. Now they want me to reveal my address. "I'm sorry," I say "I don't feel comfortable telling you that." "I didn't mean to offend you," she says, stiffly. "You didn't," I assure her. Finally, there is silence. But it isn't the anonymous silence I grew up with in Europe. Why do nice people have to ruin everything?

Questions and exercises on the text are on page 180.

WATCH YOUR STEP

BY PETINA GAPPAH

PETINA GAPPAH is a Zimbabwean writer who has law degrees from Cambridge University, Graz University and the University of Zimbabwe. *Watch Your Step* is an extract from *The Maid from Lalapanzi* in her debut collection of short stories titled *An Elegy for Easterly*. She shares her views on the world, etc. on her blog.

‘You should not play outside in the rain when you are wearing red,’ *Sisi*Blandina said to Munya and me.

‘Lightning likes things that are red and it will hunt you out and strike you down and burn you from inside out.

‘And you must not sit out on the road, otherwise you will grow festering boils on your bottoms.

‘You should never cut your hair out of doors, because if even the smallest fluff is left in the open, *varoyi* will find it, and put a spell on you, and you know how powerful their sorcery is.

‘And you must not peek at each other while you dress, because boys and girls who spy on each other’s nakedness get styes in their eyes.’

She told story upon story of the fates that awaited us if we did things we were not supposed to do, and she had the proof, for these things had happened to people she knew in Lalapanzi.

‘You must not walk over a person’s legs,’ *Sisi*Blandina said. ‘If you do so, you must walk back the other way to reverse the action, and if you don’t, the one who has been walked over won’t grow.’

I made Munya lie on his back. I jumped over his legs and out of the house to play. He ran to find *Sisi*Blandina and wailed, ‘Chenai jumped me. She always jumps me, and now I won’t grow.’

*Sisi*Blandina marched out of the house, with Munya sniffling beside her. Her nails dug into my flesh as she grabbed me above my right elbow and dragged me from my play.

‘You will not go outside until you walk back over him,’ she said.

I obeyed, jumping over him, but making sure that I crossed my fingers on both hands behind my back.

‘She had nings on,’ my brother cried. ‘It won’t work because Chenai crossed her fingers, she had nings on.’

Questions and exercises on the text are on page 186.

OCD

Why do some people suffer from thoughts and actions they can't control? Here are the hard facts on a condition called Obsessive Compulsive Disorder - or OCD.

Imagine if you had to know exactly how many cans of fizzy drinks are in your fridge. You need to order the drinks in pairs – two cans of cola, say. You need to put a third can out of sight in a cupboard. Inside the fridge, the can labels have to face outwards in the exact same way.

The ritual may sound very strange to you, but it isn't for the world's most famous footballer – David Beckham. He suffers from a psychological condition called Obsessive Compulsive Disorder (OCD). People with OCD experience obsessive thoughts they can't control, or acts or rituals they need to repeat over and over again.

"Beckham spends hours straightening furniture at home, buys exactly 20 packets of Super Noodles at the supermarket, and wears a new pair of football boots for every match," says *The Daily Mail*. Though the disorder causes high anxiety for Beckham – and can eat up his time, it hasn't stopped his success or a normal life. But for many OCD sufferers, the condition is unbearable.

Gregg first noticed signs of OCD at 18. "At first I just thought I was being paranoid," he says. "But it got worse. I'd go mental if people touched my DVDs. I had to wash my hands at certain times of the day. I'd always played lots of sports, but suddenly I stopped."

So just what is OCD, and why can it be so crippling? Read our Q&A to find out more.

WHAT DOES IT FEEL LIKE TO HAVE OCD?

"Everyone worries sometimes," says psychiatrist Dr Eve Wood at the University of Arizona. "But people with OCD have brains that get stuck on particular thoughts and behaviours." If you get a bit obsessive over an exam or a romance, it doesn't at all mean you have OCD. But genuine sufferers experience uncontrollable thoughts that are unwelcome and constantly repeated – they're called compulsions, and take two forms:

• **COVERT COMPULSIONS** are mental thoughts rather than physical actions. One example: every time a person with OCD thinks something negative, they feel compelled to repeat a series of words in their head, such as a prayer. Or a sufferer might become obsessed they are going to accidentally harm a loved one.

• **OVERT COMPULSIONS** are rituals acted out as the result of disturbing thoughts. Actress Cameron Diaz admits to opening doors with her elbows to avoid touching germs, and scrubbing clean her Hollywood home every day. Common overt compulsions include constant hand washing, continually checking on something – like if a front door is locked, or *hoarding* – keeping every piece of clothing, for instance, for fear of not having something one might need.

Most sufferers know their thoughts and behaviour are irrational, yet feel incapable of controlling them. As David Beckham says, "I've tried to change my behaviour and I can't stop."

WHAT CAUSES OCD?

"In spite of many theories and research, scientists can't yet identify a definite cause of OCD," says the charity *OCD UK*. Many researchers think certain people are born with a biological tendency to develop

OCD – and life experiences or disturbing events then trigger the condition.

Another theory: some young people learn negative thoughts and behaviour patterns in response to certain situations, which later lead to OCD. And some scientists think OCD results from an imbalance in the brain chemical *serotonin,* which controls either a person's feelings of well-being or anxiety, and plays a role in memory and sleep.

Experts do know that OCD affects up to 3 per cent of UK teens, around 350,000 under 16. Boys tend to develop it before the age of 15, while girls often develop OCD in their late teens.

HOW DOES SEVERE OCD AFFECT ONE'S LIFE?

Severe OCD can cripple a sufferer's life. "Some people can't go to school or keep a job," says Diana Wilson at *OCD UK.* Greg's condition reached its worst just after he started university: "I couldn't go to a bar without thinking I'd set my house on fire before I left. It made it really hard to make friends because some people thought I was so weird." Severe OCD causes people like Greg extreme anxiety, guilt and shame.

WHAT HELP IS THERE FOR SOMEONE WITH OCD?

"The first thing to do is to talk to somebody – so you don't feel so alone," says Diana Wilson, "because there is help out there." If you can, try to explain what you're going through to a parent or close friend. "But ideally a family doctor is the person you really want to speak to. And teenagers can see their doctor alone."

A support organisation like *OCD UK* is also very useful, Wilson explains: "We provide a phone information line and online forums. We also produce booklets for teens."

Some sufferers are psychologically assessed and receive Cognitive Behavioural Therapy (CBT), while others receive both therapy and medication like anti-depressants.

Greg claims a circle of friends he finally met at university helped him as well. "When everyone around me realised how bad it was, they talked to me for hours. They made me analyse ways I could ignore my rituals, starting with small things: they made me mess up my DVDs and CDs – and live with more disorder. They made me leave the house for as long as I could."

It took Greg a year to mostly gain control of his OCD, and he got his social life back on track. He still experiences obsessive thoughts and rituals but says, "I'm able to ignore them for now. I know OCD is more serious than most people think. It can really screw up your whole life."

Questions and exercises on the text are on page 188.

SEXY

BY JOYCE CAROL OATES

JOYCE CAROL OATES is a highly productive American author who has published more than fifty novels. She has also written many volumes of short stories, poetry and non-fiction. Two of her most famous novels are *Blonde* (2000), a fictional story about Marilyn Monroe, and *The Falls* (2004). Oates has also written books for children and young adults. Oates has taught Creative Writing at Princeton University, New Jersey for many years.

Soon as he turned sixteen, put on weight and began to get attention for his looks, things began to turn weird.

Being a swimmer, advanced to the varsity team at the end of his sophomore year at North Falls High, also a promising diver, what Coach called "up-and-coming," he got more attention.

People began to say how good-looking he was. In the street, older girls and even women in their twenties would turn to watch him. Even some teachers, teasing: "Darren Flynn could pass for Brad Pitt's younger brother."

Oh, sure! Darren went red in the face, glowered and turned his lower lip inside out to look as ugly as possisble.

To hide his odd silvery-gold hair, he wore a grungy Red Sox cap reversed on his head. A grungy NFH purple-and-cream sweatshirt frayed at the cuffs. Rotted old salt-stained Nikes on his size-eleven feet.

In a hot mood, his skin erupted at his hairline. And across his upper back, flaring and itching like hives.

Girls liked to say about Darren Flynn that he was sexy, but shy. Or he was shy, but sexy.

Darren was a guy's guy, basically. Unmistakably a jock. Laughing and relaxed with his friends, but with girls this weird kind of light would come into his face as if his mind were struck blank. Like he could see how girls were drawn to him like those sad little moths drawn to the light, beating their wings and crowding one another desperate for the light, and when it's switched off, the little moths are like, *What? What happened? Where is –?*

Darren Flynn would light you up from inside, just the way he looked at you. Make you feel like you were somebody special. Then suddenly he backs off, blushes and mumbles something and walks away and you're standing there blinking as if the light has gone – where?

Thinking, *Next time I won't fall for it. Let Darren try!*

Next time, same damn thing happens.

The way Darren Flynn had of getting inside a girl's head.

2
3

Inside his head, oh, man, was it strange! He hated it, some days.

Sexy was how he felt, a lot. Like he was charged up and ready to explode.

Hot. Hard-on.

And the word *fuck* intruding into his thoughts like a floating virus he couldn't control. Say he's talking to someone, a girl, a teacher, his own mother, and *fuck* floats in, or some really raw porn-type picture, and Darren goes hot in the face, stammers and mumbles and walks away.

Fuck was a word you heard on cable TV and lots of other places but were forbidden to say at home (at least when Darren's mother might overhear) because it was vulgar, "lowlife" and "trashy." *Fuck suck cock* were similar words Darren and his older brother, Eddy, were not supposed to say at home. (Their father wasn't so fussy, how his sons spoke. Walt Flynn worked construction for the county; his speech was what you'd call casual.)

"Boys, we are not trailer trash. You will be judged by your language and your manners. Watch your mouths!"

Edith Flynn tried to speak lightly and playfully, but her sons heard the quaver in her voice, almost a kind of fear. Exchanging a glance over her head, Eddy with a shrug, grinning as if to say, *Poor Mom, better humor her.*

Strange to Darren, his mother was so upset by words. She'd been a nurse before marrying Walt Flynn. You'd think a nurse would be experienced and no-nonsense about some things.

Sex, sexy. Sexual. "Man is a sexual being," Darren had read on the Internet, and these words ran through his head, a strange way of thinking, but wasn't it true? In biology class, sophomore year, they'd learned that everything was "reproduction of the species" – "adaptation and survival of the species" – so why did people try to pretend they were ninety-percent spiritual beings? Religious people, most adults in fact, but it was obvious that "Man is a sexual being," wasn't it? Darren wasn't the kind of student who waves his hand in class and asks questions, he wasn't even the kind of student who lingers after class to ask questions, but one day, blushing and stammering, he waited until the others had left the room to ask the teacher, Mrs. Robley, what was the point of it, just reproducing the species, over and over passing on DNA, was that all it was? what did it add up to? and Mrs. Robley looked at him kind of startled, as if Darren Flynn had begun speaking in a foreign language, and smiled and said that was a good question she could answer for him at another time, this wasn't an ideal time, maybe tomorrow, Darren?

Next day, Darren Flynn was one of the first out of the classroom.

Questions and exercises on the text are on page 191.

MOVING ON

Leaving Home

Beijing to London

LISTENING

Tapas & Tears

Singapore and Back

4

LEAVING HOME

BY ROSE TREMAIN

ROSE TREMAIN was born in 1943 in London and graduated from the University of East Anglia in 1965, where she also taught Creative Writing. She is an historical novelist who approaches her subjects from unexpected angles, concentrating her attention on unglamorous outsiders. In June 2008, she won the Orange Prize for fiction. *The Road Home* is the story of an Eastern European immigrant in the UK. Her other novels include *Restoration* and *Sacred Country*.

‘My name is Lev,’ said Lev.

‘My name is Lydia,’ said the woman. And they shook hands, Lev’s hand holding the scrunched-up kerchief, and Lydia’s hand rough with salt and smelling of egg, and then Lev asked: ‘What are you planning to do in England?’ and Lydia said: ‘I have some interviews in London for jobs as a translator.’

‘That sounds promising.’

‘I hope so. I was a teacher of English at School 237 in Yarbl, so my language is very colloquial.’

Lev looked at Lydia. It wasn’t difficult to imagine her standing in front of a class and writing words on a blackboard. He said: ‘I wonder why you’re leaving our country when you had a good job at School 237 in Yarbl?’

‘Well,’ said Lydia. ‘I became very tired of the view from my window. Every day, summer and winter, I looked out at the school yard and the high fence and the apartment block beyond, and I began to imagine I would die seeing these things, and I didn’t want this. I expect you understand what I mean?’

Lev took off his leather cap and ran his fingers through his thick grey hair. He saw Lydia turn to him for a moment and look very seriously into his eyes. He said: ‘Yes, I understand.’

Questions and exercises on the text are on page 196.

BEIJING TO LONDON

BY XIAOLU GUO

XIAOLU GUO was born in a fishing village in south China in 1973. She studied film and published six books in China before she moved to London in 2002. *Beijing to London* is an extract from *A Concise Chinese-English Dictionary for Lovers* (2007), her third novel and the first one to be written in English. *UFO in Her Eyes* (2009) and *Lovers in the Age of Indifference* (2010) are other novels by Guo. Guo is also active making films and has received a number of film awards.

Now.
Beijing time 12 clock midnight.
London time 5 clock afternoon.

But I at neither time zone. I on airplane. Sitting on 25,000 km above to earth and trying remember all English I learning in school.

I not met you yet. You in future.

Looking outside the massive sky. Thinking air staffs need to set a special time-zone for long-distance airplanes, or passengers like me very confusing about time. When a body floating in air, which country she belonging to?

People's Republic of China passport bending in my pocket.

Passport type	P
Passport No.	G00350124
Name in full	Zhuang Xiao Qiao
Sex	Female
Date of birth	23 JULY 1979
Place of birth	Zhe Jiang, P. R. China

I worry bending passport bring trouble to immigration officer, he might doubting passport is fake and refusing me into the UK, even with noble word on the page:

The Ministry of Foreign Affairs of the People's Republic of China requests all civil and military authorities of foreign countries to allow the bearer of this passport to pass freely and afford assistance in case of need.

China further and further, disappearing behind clouds. Below is ocean. I from desert town. Is the first time my life I see sea. It look like a dream.

As I far away from China, I asking me why I coming to West. Why I must to study English like parents wish? Why I must to get diploma from West? I not knowing what I needing. Sometimes I not even caring what I needing. I not caring if I speaking English or not. Mother only speaking in village dialect and even not speaking official Mandarin, but she becoming rich with my father, from making shoes in our little town. Life OK. Why they want changing my life?

And how I living in strange country West alone? I never been to West. Only Western I seeing is man working in Beijing British Embassy behind tiny window. He stamp visa on brand new passport.

What else I knowing about West? American TV series dubbing into Chinese, showing us big houses in suburb, wife by window cooking and car arriving in front house. Husband back work. Husband say Honey I home, then little children running to him, see if he bringing gift.

But that not my life. That nothing to do with my life. I not having life in West. I not having home in West. I scared.

I no speaking English.

I fearing future.

Questions and exercises on the text are on page 199.

SINGAPORE AND BACK

BY PETER CROUCH

My story begins in earnest a long way from Liverpool, or Macclesfield, where I was born on 30 January 1981, or Ealing, in west London, where I grew up and first felt a ball at my toes. As a baby, I took my first steps around a courtyard in Singapore – and if my mum and dad had decided to take one of the options offered to them when they lived in the Far East all those years ago, I wouldn't have been playing for England at the last World Cup finals. I'd have been Australian. We lived in Singapore for three years and we nearly didn't come back. Dad had done well in his job there and had been offered another job in Australia. But he was a London boy, from Fulham in south-west London originally, and he wanted the same for his son. Even so, I certainly didn't have the average English kid's start to life.

I don't remember much about Singapore – even from the photographs we still have at home – but Mum and Dad say it was a great time, and the stories about it that have been told over the years are a big part of Crouch family history. Apparently, the first words I spoke were not in English – they were in Japanese. No joke. Not for me anything as simple as 'Mummy' or 'Daddy'. I picked it up at play-school when I was about eighteen months old. I'd be brought home babbling away. Mum and Dad say they didn't pay much attention until it became obvious that the little Japanese kid from next door, Tohru, was answering me back. We were having a conversation. The trouble is, no one in the family can say with any certainty what my first words were – just that they weren't in English. I also picked up a bit of Mandarin from watching the telly. I can't remember a word of it now.

Maybe it's a result of those early days spent abroad but I have always wanted to see the world. I love travelling and in the summers I head off to America with my old gang of mates from Ealing and get off the tourist trail. Even when you're a 6ft 7in. England international, most Americans couldn't care less who you are. As a footballer you do travel quite a bit, but you don't see a lot of the countries you visit. Take the average Champions League away trip – airport, hotel, stadium, hotel, stadium, airport, home. I've been to a lot of interesting places with Liverpool and England, but I can't say I've actually seen much of them.

My father Bruce and my mother Jayne always wanted to travel, too, so when Dad was offered a job at a Singapore advertising agency in 1982, they decided that having a one-year-old kid shouldn't stop them going to the Far East. By today's standards, they were both young when I was born, 21, but they were still determined to see the world. I was simply taken along for the ride.

Dad moved around a lot when he was a kid – his dad was a salesman for Rowntree's. He met my mum in Cheshire when he was in his first job – copywriter at an advertising agency, writing commercials. He has worked in the same business ever since, moving up the career ladder. Somehow, along the way, he has been to just about every single football match I have ever played in, and I don't just mean at Anfield or with England. He helped to run my first serious boys' team, West Middlesex Colts. He's been there with Queens Park Rangers on the away trips to Grimsby and Crewe. He's been there on the worst times of all, the crap Tuesday evenings playing for Southampton reserves when Steve Wigley had struck me out of the first team reckoning.

The same goes for my mum. She has sat on the sidelines in gyms and parks where I played as a kid. She has ferried me around after school, taking me to games or training. She has sat in the car with the heater on, waiting for me to finish playing on cold winter nights. When I moved clubs – and I've done that a few times – she helped me pack up my stuff in one city and unload it in another. My sister Sarah has always been a real support, too. Sarah has had to put up with a lot, including people wanting to know her because her brother is a professional footballer. It sounds crazy but it does happen, and Sarah has learned how to spot a fake. She has her own career and we are very close. I confide in her a lot.

When I think of Mum, Dad and Sarah parking the car outside Anfield and making their way through the crowds, it makes me feel good to know that my success is theirs too. To the other supporters going to Liverpool or England games, they must look like any other normal family going to the match, but the three of them know what a long journey it has been for me to get there.

Before my parents moved to Singapore they were, my dad says, pretty skint. They lived at my mum's parents' place in Stockport and, when they arrived in Singapore, they didn't have enough money to live in the plush area of the city where the expat businessmen lived – not for my mum and dad the swimming pools and servants of the Brits abroad. The Crouchs had to live on Dad's wages, and that meant living among the ordinary local people in a 'walk-up' apartment.

They say that, as far as I was concerned, there was always a willing babysitter, or 'amah' as they call the local girls who do the childminding in Singapore. I wasn't a particularly big baby – I weighed 7 1/2 pounds when I was born. What made me unusual in Singapore was my blond hair. I'm told that I was quite a novelty in our little apartment community, and that led to a big panic one day when Mum came home to discover me and the amah gone and our flat empty. There was no note, no explanation. Mum was beside herself. Dad got a search party organised but he admits now that he thought they'd lost me for good.

The whole neighbourhood was on the look-out for a small blond English boy by the name of Peter who had a very basic understanding of Japanese and Mandarin. Dad says they finally found me in a local market where I was causing a great deal of interest. My amah that day had been so overcome with the pride of being asked to look after this strange blond kid that she had taken me on a publicity tour around the neighbourhood.

Questions and exercises on the text are on page 204.

John Logie Baird (1888–1946) is the inventor of the first television system and also the world's first colour television tube. This Scottish engineer has a prominent place in the history of television and is considered one of the 10 greatest Scottish scientists in history. He attended the University of Glasgow but never graduated since World War I interrupted his studies.

Amelia Earhart (1897–1937) became the first woman to fly as co-pilot across the Atlantic Ocean, in 1928. In 1932, Earhart set out on her next flight across the Atlantic, this time flying solo. Bad weather and mechanical problems forced her to land her red Lockheed Vega 58 in Ireland instead of mainland Europe. These early flights were followed by many more.
In 1937, she made her second attempt to fly around the world with her navigator, Fred Noonan. But the plane went missing. Neither the plane, Earhart nor Noonan were ever found.

Walt Disney (1901–1966) was an American film producer, animator, and entrepreneur. He had a major influence on the field of entertainment during the 20th century and, together with his brother, co-founded Walt Disney Productions, which nowadays is called The Walt Disney Company. He and his staff created some of the world's best-known fictional characters including Mickey Mouse, and during his lifetime he received more awards and nominations than any other filmmaker in history.

Indira Gandhi (1917–1984) was the Prime Minister of India from 1966 to 1977 and also from 1980 up to her death. She was the leader of the Congress Party. Politically, Indira Gandhi had close relations with the Soviet Union, seeking its support in the long-standing conflict with Pakistan. In the early 1980s, several states sought more independence from central government. Sikh separatists used violence and, in response, the Indian army attacked the Sikhs' holy Golden Temple killing 450 Sikhs in June 1984. The Sikhs took their revenge five months later when Indira Gandhi was assassinated in her garden by her own Sikh bodyguards.

Nelson Mandela (1918–2013) was president of South Africa from 1994 to 1999 and the first to be elected in a fully representative democratic election. He had previously been imprisoned for 27 years for his anti-apartheid activities. Most of these years were spent on Robben Island outside Cape Town. He was finally released in 1990. During his time in jail he became known as the most significant black leader in South Africa. In 1993, he was jointly awarded the Nobel Peace Prize, along with President F. W. de Klerk.

Henrietta Lacks (1922–1951) was a poor African-American woman who, in 1951, made one of the greatest contributions ever to medical science. She was suffering from terminal cervical cancer and was treated at the Johns Hopkins Hospital in Baltimore. It was discovered that her cancer cells could be kept alive and reproduced infinitely. This was the 'miracle cell' long awaited by the scientific community. These cells were named 'HeLa' (**He**nrietta **La**cks). They were put into mass production and sent to scientists all over the world and have been used in medical and biological research ever since.

Elizabeth II (1926–) became Queen in 1952 at the age of only 25. She's the Head of State of the UK and of the 16 'Commonwealth realms'. These are all part of the Commonwealth of Nations, made up of 54 nations – mostly countries of the old British Empire. In 1947, Elizabeth married Prince Philip. They have four children – Charles, Anne, Andrew and Edward. The Queen celebrates two birthdays – her actual birthday on 21 April and her 'official' birthday on a Saturday in June. The Queen is an animal lover and is particularly interested in horses and dogs. In 2012 she celebrated her Golden Jubilee – 60 years on the throne.

Bob Geldof (1951–) is an Irish singer, songwriter, writer and political activist. He started his career as the lead singer of the Irish rock band The Boomtown Rats and one of their hits was *I Don't Like Mondays*. Along with singer Midge Ure he founded Band Aid with the purpose of raising money for starving people he had seen during a visit to Ethiopia. He also organised the charity concert 'Live-Aid' on July 13th 1985 which was one of the largest-scale satellite link-ups and television broadcasts of all time with an estimated global audience of 1.9 billion people across 150 nations. He has received several awards for his work.

Barack Obama (1961–) was the 44th President of the United States and the first African American to hold the office. Obama is a graduate of Harvard Law School and, before becoming President in 2009, he was senator for the state of Illinois.
As President he initiated patient protection and affordable care for people of limited means, to ensure that medical care is available to all. He also openly supported same-sex marriage. In 2009 he was awarded the Nobel Peace Prize. He served as president from 2009–2017.

Russell Crowe (1964–) is an Australian actor and film producer born in New Zealand. In 2000 he received international attention for his role in the film *Gladiator* for which he won an Academy Award for Best Actor. His role in *A Beautiful Mind* also brought him numerous awards and he has a star on the Hollywood Walk of Fame. In 2014 he played the lead in the film *Noah*. Apart from being an actor Crowe also has a career as a musician.

Waris Dirie (1965–) was born into a nomad family in Somalia. When she was only 13 years old, she ran away to escape marriage to a man old enough to be her grandfather.
At the age of 18 she was discovered by one of Britain's leading fashion photographers and she quickly became an international celebrity. Waris Dirie has worked hard to stop female genital mutilation by working both for the UN and also through her own Desert Flower Foundation. In 1998 she published her biography *Desert Flower* which has sold more than 11 million copies worldwide. The book has been followed by, among others, *Desert Dawn* and *Desert Children.*

Cathy Freeman (1973–) started competing at an early age. She won her first gold medal at a school championship when she was only eight. Being an Australian Aboriginal did not stop her from dreaming of becoming the world's greatest female athlete and Olympic Champion. In 1992, she became the first Australian Aboriginal to represent Australia at an Olympics. In Atlanta 1996, she won a silver medal. At the Sydney Olympic Games in 2000 she was invited to light the flame at the opening ceremony. She also won the gold medal in the 400m. Her dream had come true!

Read up on the 20th Century.

Questions and exercises on the text are on page 209.

IN REAL LIFE?

Movie Review – The Hunger Games

LISTENING

The Reaping

Bollywood People and Plots

Instant Millionaire

Public, Private

5

MOVIE REVIEW – THE HUNGER GAMES

JACKIE K COOPER

The much anticipated film "The Hunger Games" has finally arrived in theaters. The movie based on Suzanne Collin's first novel of a trilogy has fascinated readers and created much excitement as to who would play the lead characters and how would the story be presented on film. As one who has not read the book on which the movie is based, the entire presentation of the film was a letdown.

The story involves a futuristic society where most of the population is kept confined to Districts. In the nation of Panem there are twelve districts. Two children, one boy and one girl, between the ages of twelve to eighteen are chosen from each district to take part in "the hunger games." These twenty-four will fight to the death on a reality type show. Only one will emerge alive.

In District 12, Katniss Everdeen's much younger sister Prim (Willow Shields) is the girl selected. Katniss (Jennifer Lawrence) volunteers to take her place. The boy chosen to compete is Peeta (Josh Hutcherson). These two are taken to the Capitol where they are groomed for the contest. Katniss' best friend Gale (Liam Hemsworth) must stand by helplessly and watch from District 12.

The rest of the movie focuses on the competition and how the contestants kill each other. The violence of these acts is not specific in many cases, but the psychological impact of what is occurring is intense. It all boils down to children killing other children for the entertainment of the elite.

The subject matter is off-putting and for those who have not read all three novels the impact of this first story is diluted. Audiences are watching a violent movie that seems to have no direction or moral. It is just a story about a fight to the death and how it occurs.

The most brilliant part of the movie is the casting of Lawrence. She is one talented actress and she gives depth to a storyline that does not deserve it. If there is one factor contributing to the success of the movie it is her performance. Hutcherson is one-dimensional as Peeta and Hemsworth is almost non-existent as Gale. Elizabeth Banks, Stanley Tucci, Wes Bentley and Toby Jones are annoying in their roles as eccentrics who facilitate and comment on the "games."

More effective is Woody Harrelson as a former winner and now mentor in the games. Lenny Kravitz also has some good moments as costumer Cinna. He manages to create an emotional bond with the audience in just a few scenes.

The movie is rated PG-13 for profanity and violence.

In years past violence directed towards children was more or less off limits. Now, as this movie proves, they are fair game. Watching a movie about children killing each other for the pleasure of adults seems a little sick.

There are still two more movies at least with this cast of characters. Perhaps they will prove to be more enjoyable and entertaining than this one.

I scored "The Hunger Games" a non-playful 5 out of 10.

***The Hunger Games* is the first book in a trilogy by SUZANNE COLLINS, a television scriptwriter and novelist, who published the book in 2008. Her inspiration came partly from the Greek myth about Theseus and the Minotaur but also from her father's experiences of the Vietnam war. The book has become an international bestseller and has been on the New York Best Seller List for 60 weeks.**

Questions and exercises on the text are on page 214.

BOLLYWOOD PEOPLE AND PLOTS

BY NASREEN MUNNI KABIR

The most efficient way of showing a hero's true courage is to set him up against an evil villain. The greater the hero, the greater his opponent. This pairing of good and evil forces is a well-established pattern in Hindi films; the villain becomes the hero's partner in carrying forward the film's narrative, and provides the reasons for a good old punch-up. The lively and charismatic stunt director Mahendra Varma believes that no matter how many great lines a hero may speak, he is not a hero until he flattens the villain.

> **MAHENDRA VARMA**: Since I first started watching Hindi films, they have followed a tradition. This tradition means that at the end of the film there has to be a fight, and this is the climax of the movie. The public wait for the end. Until the hero beats the villain to a pulp, the audience doesn't enjoy the film. At the end of the film, the public must cheer and leave the cinema satisfied.

The villain isn't only an essential character in action movies. He also has an important role to play in the love story – the most recurrent subject of Hindi cinema. The love story usually follows the Romeo and Juliet pattern: two people meet, they fall in love and want to marry and live happily ever after. But there are obstacles aplenty in their path. An outside force (a jilted admirer of the heroine, or an envious friend of the hero, for example) is introduced into the plot. This villain stops the lovers from being together in some devious and dreadful way. And until the hero vanquishes the villain, the lovers cannot be united. The need to vary the traumas and obstacles gives the villain myriad ways of keeping the lovers apart. He can be the land-owning rapist *(Madhumati),* the hero's scheming cousin *(Virasat),* the heroine's evil brother *(Aan),* a bandit *(Awaara)* or a lecherous landowner *(Gunga Jumna).* In the older films, instead of having to contend with a plotting villain who is always waiting on the sidelines of the story, the lovers are thwarted by a repressive society in which, for example, differences in caste keep them apart.

However, since the 1960s, increasing social intermingling,

especially in the cities, has resulted in issues of caste difference more or less disappearing from Hindi cinema. Social obstacles have more recently taken the form of class differences, exemplified by the theme of rich-girl-falls-in-love-with-poor-boy. In this scenario, the girl's parents are unwilling to accept that the penniless, jobless boy is genuinely in love with their daughter, and see the young hero as nothing but an unscrupulous gold-digger. In countless films we see the parents of the heroine offering the boy a considerable sum to leave their daughter alone. Such a scenario ends with the hero proving his worth and ultimately winning the approval of the girl's family.

Questions and exercises on the text are on page 218.

INSTANT MILLIONAIRE

BY VIKAS SWARUP

In 2005, VIKAS SWARUP, an Indian writer and diplomat, published his debut novel *Q&A* about a penniless waiter from Mumbai who makes a fortune from winning a quiz show. *Q&A* was an immediate success, translated into 43 languages and filmed as *Slumdog Millionaire*. The film won eight Oscars in 2009. Swarup's second novel is called *Six Suspects* and was published in 2008.

The studio lights have been dimmed. I can hardly see the audience sitting around me in a circle. The hall is illuminated by one spotlight in the centre, where I sit in a leather revolving chair opposite Prem Kumar. We are separated by a semicircular table. There is a large screen in front of me on which the questions will be projected. The studio sign is lit up. It says 'Silence'.

'Cameras rolling, three, two, one, you're on.'

The signature tune comes on and Prem Kumar's booming voice fills the hall. 'Here we are once again, ready to find out who will make history today by winning the biggest prize ever offered on earth. Yes, ladies and gentlemen, we are ready to find out Who Will Win A Billion!'

The studio sign changes to 'Applause'. The audience begins clapping. There are some cheers and whistles, too.

The signature tune fades out. Prem Kumar says, 'We have three lucky contestants with us tonight, who have been selected at random by our computer. Contestant number three is Kapil Chowdhary from Malda in West Bengal. Contestant number two is Professor Hari Parikh from Ahmedabad, but our first contestant tonight is eighteen-year-old Ram Mohammad Thomas from our very own Mumbai. Ladies and gentlemen, please give him a big round of applause.'

Everyone claps. After the applause dies down, Prem Kumar turns to me. 'Ram Mohammad Thomas, now that's a very interesting name. It expresses the richness and diversity of India. What do you do, Mr Thomas?'

'I am a waiter in Jimmy's Bar and Restaurant in Colaba.'

'A waiter! Now isn't that interesting! Tell me, how much do you make every month?'

'Around nine hundred rupees.'

'That's all? And what will you do if you win today?'

'I don't know.'

'You don't know?'

'No.'

Prem Kumar scowls at me. I am not following the script. I am supposed to 'vibe' and be 'entertaining' during the 'small talk'. I should have said I will buy a restaurant, or a plane, or a country. I could have said I will host a big party. Marry Miss India. Travel to Timbuktu.

'OK. Let me explain the rules to you. You will be asked twelve questions, and if you answer each one correctly, you stand to win the biggest jackpot on earth: one billion rupees! You are free to quit at any point up until question number nine and take whatever you have earned up to then, but you cannot quit beyond question number nine. After that, it is either Play or Pay. But let's talk about that when we come to that stage. If you don't know the answer to a question, don't panic, because you have two Lifeboats available to you – A Friendly Tip and Half and Half. So I think we are all set for the first question for one thousand rupees. Are you ready?'

'Yes, I am ready,' I reply.

'OK, here comes question number one. A nice easy one on popular cinema, I am sure everyone in the audience can answer. Now we all know that Armaan Ali and Priya Kapoor have formed one of the most successful screen pairings of recent times. But can you name the blockbusting film in which Armaan Ali starred with Priya Kapoor for the very first time. Was it a) *Fire,* b) *Hero,* c) *Hunger,* or d) *Betrayal*?'

The music in the background changes to a suspense tune, with the sound of a ticking time bomb superimposed over it.

'D. *Betrayal*,' I reply.

'Do you go to the movies?'

'Yes.'

'And did you see *Betrayal*?'

'Yes.'

'Are you absolutely, one hundred per cent sure of your answer?'

'Yes.'

There is a crescendo of drums. The correct answer flashes on the screen.

'Absolutely, one hundred per cent correct! You've just won one thousand rupees! We will now take a quick commercial break,' declares Prem Kumar.

The studio sign changes to 'Applause'. The audience claps. Prem Kumar smiles. I don't.

Questions and exercises on the text are on page 221.

PUBLIC, PRIVATE

BY DANNII MINOGUE

Having a baby: joyful, a quiet celebration with family. An intimate and magical moment of discovery shared with your partner. Hmmm .... I wish!

Tuesday, 24 November 2009
The car is stuck in rainy London traffic and, as usual, I'm running on what some of my closer friends would call 'Minogue Time', which basically means I'm late. For most of the afternoon, I'd been hurtling around Somerset House on ice skates, filming a segment for *The X Factor* with one of my contestants, Stacey Solomon. It was all good fun, but now I'm tired, and I'm wilting into the soft leather back seat of a very slow moving Jaguar.

My friends, Sam and George, are due to arrive at my apartment in Battersea at any minute for supper and I'm not even close to home. What's worse is that I've recklessly opted to make my much-lauded veggie lasagne tonight, which, as the cooks among you know, takes some time to prepare and then an hour or so on top of that to bake, so I'll almost certainly have to rustle up a hearty salad as soon as I get in to keep us going in the meantime.

Damn! My BlackBerry is ringing again and it's a work call. I feel too tired to talk. I just want to get home and chop vegetables.

'Hello!'

At least the car is moving now.

'Hi, D.'

It's Nathan, who works for my management, and he's chuckling. 'You're gonna laugh at this,' he says, cautiously.

Something tells me I won't.

'Simon from our PR company has just called to say that a national newspaper is claiming that you're three months pregnant and that you went for a scan at the weekend. They're running it front page tomorrow and want us to comment – isn't that ridiculous?'

I don't answer. I'm numb and I feel slightly faint.

'Obviously, need to confirm with you that it's a load of rubbish before I get back to them,' Nathan says.

I still don't answer and now I can hear my own breath.

'D?'

'Er... can I call you when I'm out of the car?' I ask him flatly.

'Oh!'

When I usher Sam and George into my apartment, minutes after I get in myself, I settle them in the lounge and tell them I have to make a quick business call before I start dinner.

'Guys, pour yourselves a glass of wine,' I say. 'I won't have one. No, it's fine – really. I'm too tired. I need to be fresh for work tomorrow. I'll just pop some music on ... Sorry about this ... Won't be long.'

I wonder if I got away with that. Do they think it's odd I'm not having a glass of wine with them?

Now quite flustered, I dash into my bedroom, which is next to the lounge, and call Nathan and tell him the truth. He tries to calm me down, then puts me on to Simon, my publicist, who informs me that the newspaper is going to print with the pregnancy story. Front cover. In thirty minutes. It's literally sitting on the press waiting for the editor to give the go-ahead to run it.

'Simon,' I whisper urgently. 'You've got to help me. How can we stop them running this story? Yes, I'm pregnant, but only about six weeks. Kris knows, of course, but we haven't even told our parents yet. I want to tell my mum and dad face to face when I go back to Australia, not like this, not splashed across the papers ... I can't breathe, hang on a sec ...'

My face feels flushed and my palms are sweating and shaking – so much that I almost drop the phone. I pop my head around the bedroom door.

'Sorry, guys. Won't be long,' I call out to Sam and George. 'I'm doing a lasagne for dinner. Nice?'

Back to the call.

'Seriously, is there a way we can stop this?'

It turns out that the only way we can stop it is by admitting to the newspaper that I am, in fact, pregnant, but just six weeks. Simon informs me that it's an infringement of a woman's rights for any media to make a pregnancy public knowledge before the three-month scan. If the newspaper knows for sure I'm only six weeks pregnant, then they can't print the story.

'But I have to call Kris and ask him if it's OK first,' I say, now brimming over with tears. 'I'll try to get hold of him now and get back to you.'

'We have to do it soon, Dannii, or they'll run the story anyway,' Simon says, solemnly. 'Call me straight back.'

I try calling Kris, but it's 5:30 a.m. in Australia and his phone is off. I text him and then try calling him again but still there's no

answer. The clock is ticking. My blood is running hot and cold. What do I do?

I stick my head out of the bedroom again.

'Won't be long now, boys. Help yourselves to more wine. Chat among yourselves and all that!'

Right. I'm going to have to make this decision all on my own, aren't I? I've already had to tell my management and my PR company that I'm pregnant before I was ready to; now I'm going to have to tell a national newspaper too, just in time to stop the whole world from finding out – even before Kris and I have had a chance to tell our families and friends the happy news, and while cooking a veggie lasagne. This isn't how it was supposed to be.

Questions and exercises on the text are on page 223.

CITY LIFE

6

he Big Apple

LISTENING

Which City?

Vertical Living

If My Dad Were Still Here

The Ballad of Sonny Payne

New York, New York

THE BIG APPLE

Almost everyone knows New York from films. Skyscrapers, Central Park, Brooklyn Bridge and yellow cabs are some of the common ingredients. New York City is also known as 'The Big Apple'. The name derives from a sports journalist called John FitzGerald, working for the *New York Morning Telegraph* in the 1920s, who heard stable boys in the South say that participating in a horse race in NYC was "a big apple" for all horses.

ONE CITY - FIVE BOROUGHS

NYC really consists of five boroughs – Manhattan, Queens, The Bronx, Brooklyn and Staten Island. However, Manhattan is the cultural and financial center which attracts most tourists. In fact, NYC is visited by about 50 million tourists, domestic and international, every year. In other words, tourism is an important source of income for the city.

THE STATUE OF LIBERTY AND ELLIS ISLAND

The Statue of Liberty, 93 meters high and given to US by the French in 1886, has become a symbol of freedom and hopes for a better life. More than 17 million immigrants saw the statue when arriving to the US and Ellis Island between 1892 and 1954. Today you can visit the statue and the Immigration Museum by ferry from Battery Park on Manhattan.

MANHATTAN

Manhattan is surrounded by water and to the west is the Hudson River and to the east is the East River with Brooklyn Bridge. It is fairly easy to find your way around Manhattan since the avenues run from south to north beginning with 1st Avenue on the east side and ending with 12th Avenue on the west side. Then there are the streets that cross from west to east with numbers from 1st up to 220th as you reach the very north of Manhattan. The avenue that divides the streets in Manhattan between east and west is 5th Avenue. So the famous Grand Central Station is found at 87 East 42nd Street.

DOWNTOWN

The lower part of Manhattan is known as downtown. The Twin Towers which used to be part of the skyline were destroyed on 9/11 in 2001. The space it occupied is now called 'Ground Zero' and the 9/11 Memorial and the 9/11 Memorial Museum have been built to commemorate all the people who died in the terrorist attack there in 2001.

In downtown you'll find Chinatown where Chinese people live and run shops and restaurants. There you can have a good meal at a good price. A bit of Asia in NYC! Little Italy is another area dominated by Italian immigrants. Interested in art? Then go to SoHo and TriBeCa for exhibitions and art galleries. Quite a contrast to these places is Wall Street – New York's famous Financial District and home to the New York Stock Exchange. The dress code here is a suit and a tie.

MIDTOWN

Walking up Fifth Avenue you come across many places you have seen in movies.

The Empire State Building offers from its 86th floor a magnificent view of NYC. The public gained access to the office block in 1931 and in 1933 came the film where King Kong climbed all the way up to the top at 443 meters.

Grand Central Station in 42nd Street, with its famous clock as a popular meeting place, was nearly demolished in the 1970s but protests initiated by Jackie Kennedy-Onassis rescued the beautiful building from 1913. Many commuters make use of the restaurants and shops at the station. A good place to eat is the Oyster bar.

At the end of 42nd Street by East River is the headquarters of the United Nations with its 193 member states.

In midtown you also find the theater district and Times Square where you can buy cheap tickets for shows on Broadway. The square got its name after the newspaper, the *New York Times* which built an office there in 1904.

UPTOWN

Central Park is a place for recreation. Here you can go jogging, walking, biking, riding, skateboarding and skating or skiing in the winter. Strawberry Fields is an area dedicated to the memory of John Lennon. It is named after The Beatles song, *Strawberry Fields Forever*. On the east side of the park there are some famous museums such as The Metropolitan Museum of Art and the Guggenheim Museum.

North of Central Park is Harlem where the inhabitants are predominately African-American. Harlem has a much better reputation today than a few decades ago, when it was run down, poverty-stricken and crime-ridden.

SHOPPING IN NYC

Macy's, in Herald Square, is a huge department store – one of the largest in the world. Along Fifth Avenue there are some more luxurious shops like Gucci, Prada and Tiffany's but also trendy ones for the younger generation such as Abercrombie & Fitch and Juicy Couture. Another shop attracting customers is the Apple Store just by Central Park. Downtown 21 Century is the shop for designer products sold at a reduced price.

Questions and exercises on the text are on page 230.

VERTICAL LIVING

The manufacture of stronger, lighter steel combined with the development of lifts that could carry people safely made possible the first high-rise buildings in the 1880s. By the year 2000, improvements in technology and design brought skyscrapers to almost 460 m (1,500 ft) in height, with the promise of even taller megastructures using superframes in the near future.

A skyscraper needs to be strong, stable, and able to withstand natural forces, such as wind and earth tremors. The weight of the building is carried by the foundations, which are set firmly in the soil or bedrock. Types of foundation include spread footings, which spread the weight of the building over a wide area, and caisson piles, which transmit the load to stable bedrock.

Above ground, a skyscraper is constructed round a frame made of steel or concrete, which bears the load of walls, roof, and floors, and so supports the building. The design of skyscrapers has evolved to make them taller or lighter or more specifically geared to the conditions in the local environment. The steel frames of the early skyscrapers in Chicago and New York were followed in cities throughout the world by frames attached by cables to a central concrete core. Many modern skyscrapers are built around the steel-framed tube design, in which the load is borne by steel columns.

Transamerica Pyramid ■ The 260 m (853 ft) Transamerica Pyramid, built in San Francisco, is designed to withstand earthquakes. During the 1989 Loma Prieta earthquake, which measured 7.1 on the Richter scale, the building swung by more than 30 cm (one foot) but sustained no damage. The two windowless abutments rising from the 29th floor house the lifts and stairwells.

FRAMES

Skyscraper frames provide the main structural support for the building and are composed of materials that are designed to withstand the force of the wind. Although there are many variations, most frames fall into two categories – skeleton and cable hung. Skeleton skyscrapers, which include steel-framed tube designs, use a structural frame to support the walls and floors. In a cable-hung skyscraper the main support is provided by a central concrete core, which acts as a wind brace and as a shaft for lifts and other utilities.

Skeleton frame

A compact lattice of columns and girders, often supported by cross-bracing, spreads the load of the overall structure throughout the building.

❶ Girder

❷ Column
Evenly spaced columns form the vertical component of the skeleton frame.

❸ Cross-bracing
Steel cross-bracing provides added rigidity.

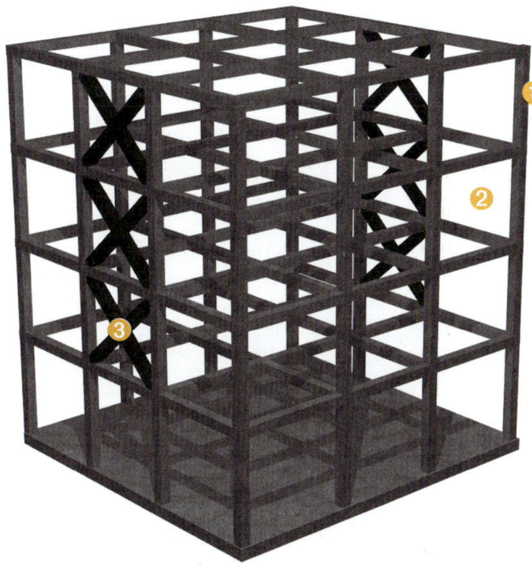

Cable hung

The floors of each storey are supported by the central core and by cables that are attached to the roof of the frame at the top of the structure.

❹ Roof

❺ Central core
The concrete core forms the mainstay of the cable-hung frame.

❻ Cables
Cables round the perimeter support the floors.

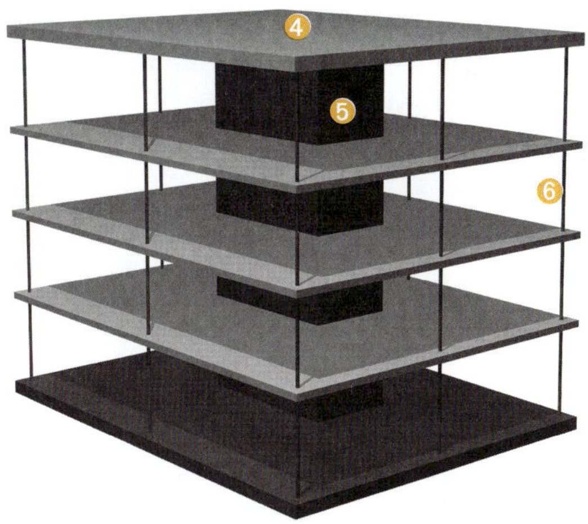

Questions and exercises on the text are on page 233.

IF MY DAD WERE STILL HERE

BY MAX GIACCONE

I was 10 years old on 9/11, when the towers fell and I lost my father. Here's what Osama bin Laden's death means to me.

I WAS IN the fifth grade when it happened. I had just arrived at school. My teacher picked up the phone in our classroom, and I could tell something wasn't right. He hung up and told me to go to the office. My mom was there, hysterically crying. That was 10 years ago, but I still remember her face. She said someone had flown a plane into the World Trade Center and we hadn't heard anything from Dad. By the time we got home, Tower Two had just fallen.

My dad worked on the 103rd floor of the first tower. He was the director of global infrastructure at Cantor Fitzgerald. The day before he died, I remember, we had a really good night. He was quoting from the Pink Panther movies that we used to watch and chasing me around the house. Then he had to pick up my sister from somewhere, so I went to bed. That was the last time I ever saw him.

It took me a while to accept he was gone. It was all so surreal. At 10 years old you don't understand that much. My mom said the thing she'll never forget was when, about two weeks after the towers fell, she finally came to me and said we're going to start preparations for a memorial service. I told her, "Absolutely not. I know where Dad is: he's walking home." She said that broke her heart.

After Dad died, I kind of started latching onto things. Baseball was my thing, because it was one of the sports my dad and I did together. He coached me from when I was little. He came home from work every day to see me play. After 9/11, my mom begged the coach not to hesitate to let me play. I was back playing a few days later. That helped tremendously.

I also latched onto music. That was one of my dad's other passions. His favorite band was Yes, and my parents grew up listening to them, the Rolling Stones, the Who, Led Zeppelin. I started a band with my friends last year, and I write a decent number of songs. Writing has helped. I have a tattoo on my back of my dad holding me as an infant, and another on my forearm that says "Sowing Season," which is the name of a song by the band Brand New. The song goes, "Nothing gets so bad, a whisper from your father couldn't fix it."

I couldn't have asked for a better father. We played golf. He took me to the movies. Sundays were our big day together. He'd make pasta. We would sit down in the living room and watch Jets games together. That's one of my biggest memories. After the game, he'd turn off the lights and have his glass of wine and listen to Andrea Bocelli. He was definitely the best dad.

Over the years, I've always found myself thinking what life would be like if my dad were still here. It's something that I try not to dwell on, but this is how my life has gone. The lows are extremely low, but it's just something that you learn to live with and accept. Graduating high school was so bittersweet for me. It was a huge accomplishment in my life, but there was only one parent there. The holidays are difficult, too. You're happy, but you always know someone is missing. My birthday is on Father's Day this year, which is the second time that's happened: all you want to do is celebrate both, but you can celebrate only one.

I had a dream about my father recently. It was nice to see him, but he wouldn't talk to me. I don't remember his voice anymore. There are home videos, but I can't bring myself to watch them. In a few months, I'll have lived as long without my father as I did with him. I learned at a really young age how valuable life can be, and how quickly it can all go away.

I was sitting in my bed when I turned to CNN and heard that Osama bin Laden was dead. I jumped up and ran into my mom's room and told her. We hugged. We rejoiced. I don't even know how to describe the feeling. I don't like to say I am celebrating someone's death. I don't know what closure is – I don't know how it's supposed to feel. But it feels like something has been lifted. Knowing the person who plotted to kill my father is off the face of the earth, that's a good feeling.

Questions and exercises on the text are on page 235.

THE BALLAD OF SONNY PAYNE

BY STEVEN KURUTZ

I first saw Sonny five years ago, while riding the F train. I was living in Park Slope, writing nightclub reviews, and I would run into him some evenings on my way into Manhattan. Whenever I saw him, he brightened my day, and I always made it a point to give change. Eventually, quarters no longer seemed adequate, and I upgraded to dollar bills. [...]

Sonny's daily goal is to bring in $30, enough to buy that evening's dinner and the next morning's breakfast. On average, he makes $7 a trip panhandling between Avenue X and Jay Street, and he keeps the change in separate pockets, using his front left pocket for quarters, his front right for dimes and nickels, and his backpack for pennies. By night's end, he said, he can tell by the weight of his pack how much money is inside.

When he has collected enough loose change, he generally goes to a Pathmark in Brooklyn, where a Coinstar machine turns the coins into bills. Two or three nights a week, he exchanges his quarters at a Popeye's at Stillwell and Surf Avenues, where he also eats. This particular morning, as Sonny finished his breakfast and took a big drink of milk, he looked as if he could consume three meals and still not be filled up. I asked if he wanted a cup of coffee. "I can't have coffee," he said. "Gives me the shakes."

Although his sleepy, gracious manner suggests a childhood in the South, Sonny said he was born in Trinidad and came to Washington as an infant. "My father was named Howard Augustine Payne, and my mother was Georgetta Payne," he said. "I was born St. Augustine Des Sales Payne. They divorced when I was young, and I lived with my mother in Corona, Queens. I used to ice skate right where Shea Stadium is now. But I haven't been to Queens in nine months now. In Queens, if you don't have access to public transportation, it's rough."

Sonny said that before he was laid off, he worked for 23 years as a printer. For the past year, he added, he has stayed at the Church of the Greater God on Neptune Avenue in Coney Island. "The reverend, we call him Brother Jack," he said. "You can almost feel him when you talk to him, he's so real."

The conversation lasted a while longer, ranging over sports, cellphones, which Sonny called leashes, and the coming of warmer weather, about which he had mixed feelings. "I like this time of year," he said, "but you have to be careful. All the kids are coming out of school. They tease homeless people. You can't respond. If you respond, then you have to debate. Then they gang up on you." He sighed, "When you're homeless, there's a lot of stress."

Sonny became homeless, he said, after a string of bad luck; he was laid off, his apartment caught fire, he didn't want to bother friends. Early on, he stayed in city-run shelters, but he stopped, he said, after he was robbed. Now he prefers to stay in small churches where he can secure a safe bed. [...]

I found it strange that someone as seemingly intelligent and personable as Sonny has remained homeless for so long. I asked him if he would stay homeless if he had the chance to get off the street. "I want to be back living in an apartment," he said. "I know some homeless people prefer the street because they're afraid of responsibility. But that goes against how I was raised. When I was in the shelters, I saw a lot of young guys in there. If I was 30, there's no way I'd be homeless. I'd find a job. I know how to do a lot of different things."

Questions and exercises on the text are on page 237.

NEW YORK, NEW YORK

BY FRED EBB AND JOHN KANDER
AS PERFORMED BY FRANK SINATRA

Start spreadin' the news, I'm leavin' today
I wanna be a part of it, New York, New York
These vagabond shoes are longing to stray
Right through the very heart of it, New York, New York

I wanna wake up in a city that doesn't sleep
And find I'm king of the hill, top of the heap

These little town blues are melting away
I'll make a brand new start of it, in old New York
If I can make it there, I'll make it anywhere
It's up to you, New York, New York

I wanna wake up in a city that never sleeps
And find I'm A-number-one, top of the list,
King of the hill, A-number-one …

These little town blues are melting away
I'm gonna make a brand new start of it
in old New York
And if I can make it there, I'm gonna
make it anywhere
It's up to you, New York, New York

New York!

Questions and exercises
on the text are on page 241.

GET (DIS)CONNECTED

7

Childhood Memories

LISTENING

The Story of the Makgabe

Can You See Me?

Playing the Enemy

LISTENING

After the Game

CHILDHOOD MEMORIES

BY GARETH EOIN STOREY

GARETH EOIN STOREY was born in Dublin. He started writing poetry and short fiction at eighteen and graduated in Creative Writing at Kingston University. His story *Grainne* features in *Born in the 1980s*.

We spent the afternoon messing around by the stream and talking until I asked her if she liked kites. She said she did, so we went back to the house and I asked my da if we could play with the kite because he seemed more interested in it than I did until now. He looked at me and laughed. I could see empty bottles of wine on the kitchen table and the rest of the adults were smoking. He took it from the shelf in the coat cupboard near the front door and said: 'Have fun, son.' He only called me son when he was drunk, or when he picked me up or dropped me off at the airport. But when he said it I felt more like his son than I usually did.

We took the kite down the hill to the stream then walked up another hill. It was windy and looked like it would rain but it didn't rain until about an hour after – when we were at home and bored by the kite already. Grainne was great with the kite and I had way more fun with her than with my da. She looked happy controlling this thing flying in the air and always laughed when the kite crashed to the ground, unlike me or my da. When it happened with us I had to run and pick it up and be careful not to get it tangled up. With her I didn't mind, I liked running to pick it up.

We got back to the house and the rain poured. The sky that was a bright blue most of the day had now turned a dull grey. I was glad to be inside. We ate dinner with the adults who were still drinking wine and smoking. They were listening to a band called Talking Heads which I thought was a cool name. After dinner Grainne and I went to my room so I could show her my video cases. She hadn't seen *Nico* or *Marked for Death*, my Steven Segal films or *The Terminator*. I wanted her to see them. I wanted to know if she would like them as much as I did. I told her to ask her parents if they would rent or buy them for her when she got back to Dublin and she said she would.

We played board games that were left in the house by someone else until around ten thirty when my da's wife came into my room and said we had to go to bed. There were two beds in my room and she said that Grainne would sleep in the spare one. We were told to go straight to sleep. She closed the door.

We were both excited. We had become good friends throughout the day and we were happy to have met each other. We brushed our teeth together and then jumped into our separate beds. In the dark we talked in whispers. Grainne said she wanted to move her bed closer to mine so I got out of my bed and she got out of hers and we pushed the beds together. We were quiet because no one came in to check on us. I had never kissed a girl but I could sense it was coming. I reached my hand over to her bed and asked her to hold my hand. She did. Then she moved closer to me. I could smell her breath. She smelt of garlic and mint toothpaste and I'm sure I did as well – we had both eaten the same dinner and both brushed our teeth. We held hands and talked. I had no idea about love or sex. I was a naïve child of divorce on holiday in Wicklow. I told her I really liked her and she said the same to me. Our bodies met together and we kissed using tongues, we didn't touch each other though we kept holding hands. I wanted to tell her that I loved her. I wanted her to stay or for me to go with her when she left for Dublin. I didn't want to be left alone in this house for another week.

I asked her to wake me up before she left but when I woke up she was gone. I started crying and sat in my pyjamas in the moved-together beds. I pushed them apart and opened the curtains. It looked like it would rain. I counted the days I had left with my da before I was pushed on to one of my nanas and the tears kept coming. I missed my ma, I missed watching videos, I missed Grainne.

Questions and exercises on the text are on page 241.

CAN YOU SEE ME? BY NICOLE KRAUSS

NICOLE KRAUSS, born in 1974, is an American author best known for her novels *Man Walks Into a Room*, *The History of Love* and, most recently, *Great House*. She studied at Stanford University and later enrolled in a master's program at Oxford University. Her novels have been translated into around 35 languages. *The History of Love* weaves together the stories of Leo Gursky, an 80-year-old Holocaust survivor from Slonim, the young Alma Singer who is coping with the death of her father, and the story of a lost manuscript also called *The History of Love*.

I often wonder who will be the last person to see me alive. If I had to bet, I'd bet on the delivery boy from the Chinese take-out. I order in four nights out of seven. Whenever he comes I make a big production of finding my wallet. He stands in the door holding the greasy bag while I wonder if this is the night I'll finish off my spring roll, climb into bed, and have a heart attack in my sleep.

I try to make a point of being seen. Sometimes when I'm out, I'll buy a juice even though I'm not thirsty. If the store is crowded I'll even go so far as dropping my change all over the floor, the nickels and dimes skidding in every direction. I'll get down on my knees. It's a big effort for me to get down on my knees, and an even bigger effort to get up. And yet. Maybe I look like a fool. I'll go into the Athlete's Foot and say, *What do you have in sneakers?* The clerk will look me over like the poor schmuck that I am and direct me over to the one pair of Rockports they carry, something in spanking white. *Nah,* I'll say, *I have those already,* and then I'll make my way over to the Reeboks and pick out something that doesn't even resemble a shoe, a waterproof bootie, maybe, and ask for it in size 9. The kid will look again, more carefully. He'll look at me long and hard. *Size 9,* I'll repeat while I clutch the webbed shoe. He'll shake his head and go to the back for them, and by the time he returns I'm peeling off my socks. I'll roll my pants legs up and look down at those decrepit things, my feet, and an awkward minute will pass until it becomes clear that I'm waiting for him to slip the booties onto them. I never actually buy. All I want is not to die on a day when I went unseen.

Questions and exercises on the text are on page 248.

PLAYING THE ENEMY

BY JOHN CARLIN

JOHN CARLIN is senior international writer for *El Pais*, the world's leading Spanish-language newspaper. He has also written for numerous other publications and is the author of *Playing The Enemy*.

In 1994, Nelson Mandela won the presidency in South Africa in the nation's first free election. At that time the country was dangerously divided as a result of almost fifty years of apartheid. Mandela needed a cause that all South Africans could share. He picked the Springboks, the national rugby team, who would host the Rugby World Cup in 1995. Their chances of victory were remote and their chances of capturing the hearts of the South Africans were even more remote. However, Mandela succeeded in uniting the people by wholeheartedly supporting the team.

When you enter the story, the Springboks are about to play the championship match against New Zealand's heavily-favoured squad.

Mandela sat in his presidential box wearing a Springbok jersey, while 62,000 fans – mostly white – chanted "Nelson, Nelson!" Millions more gathered around TV sets, whether in dusty black townships or leafy white suburbs.

"I couldn't sing the anthem," François Pienaar admitted. "I dared not." He had been desperate to rise to the occasion, to set an example, not to let Mandela down. He had rehearsed the scene over and over in his mind. But when the time came, when the two teams lined up on the side of the pitch before the game and the band struck up the first strains of "Nkosi Sikelele," he couldn't open his mouth.

"Because I knew that if I did, I'd fall apart. I'd just crumble, right there. I was so emotional," the Springbok captain said, "that I wanted to cry. Sean Fitzpatrick [the All Black captain] told me later that he looked over and saw a tear roll down my cheek. But that was nothing compared to what I was feeling inside. It was such a proud moment in my life and I stood there and the whole stadium was reverberating. And it was just too much. I tried to find my fiancée, to focus on her, but I couldn't find her. So I just bit my lip. I bit it so hard I felt the blood rolling down my throat."

What had brought Pienaar to the emotional brink was Mandela's visit to the Springboks' dressing room ten minutes before. Between the jumbo jet flyover and stepping out onto the field in his green jersey, Mandela had asked Louis Luyt to take him down to the bowels of the stadium to say a few words to the players.

Pienaar recalled the scene. "I had just got strapped up and there we all were, in a state of tension like we'd never known, and so much was going through my mind, knowing that this was the biggest thing ever – one shot, one opportunity to seize everything you've always wanted. And I was just thinking about all that, but at the same time with so much attention to all the details of the game, and then, suddenly, there he was. I didn't know he was coming, and even less did I know that he was going to wear the Springbok jersey. He was saying 'Good luck,' and he turned around and on his back there was this number 6, and that was me ...

"You know, the passionate supporters, they're the ones who wear the jersey of their team. So now here I am seeing him walking into the dressing room, in this moment of all moments, dressed like another passionate fan, but then I see that it is my jersey he is wearing. There are no words to describe the emotions that ran through my body."

Questions and exercises on the text are on page 250.

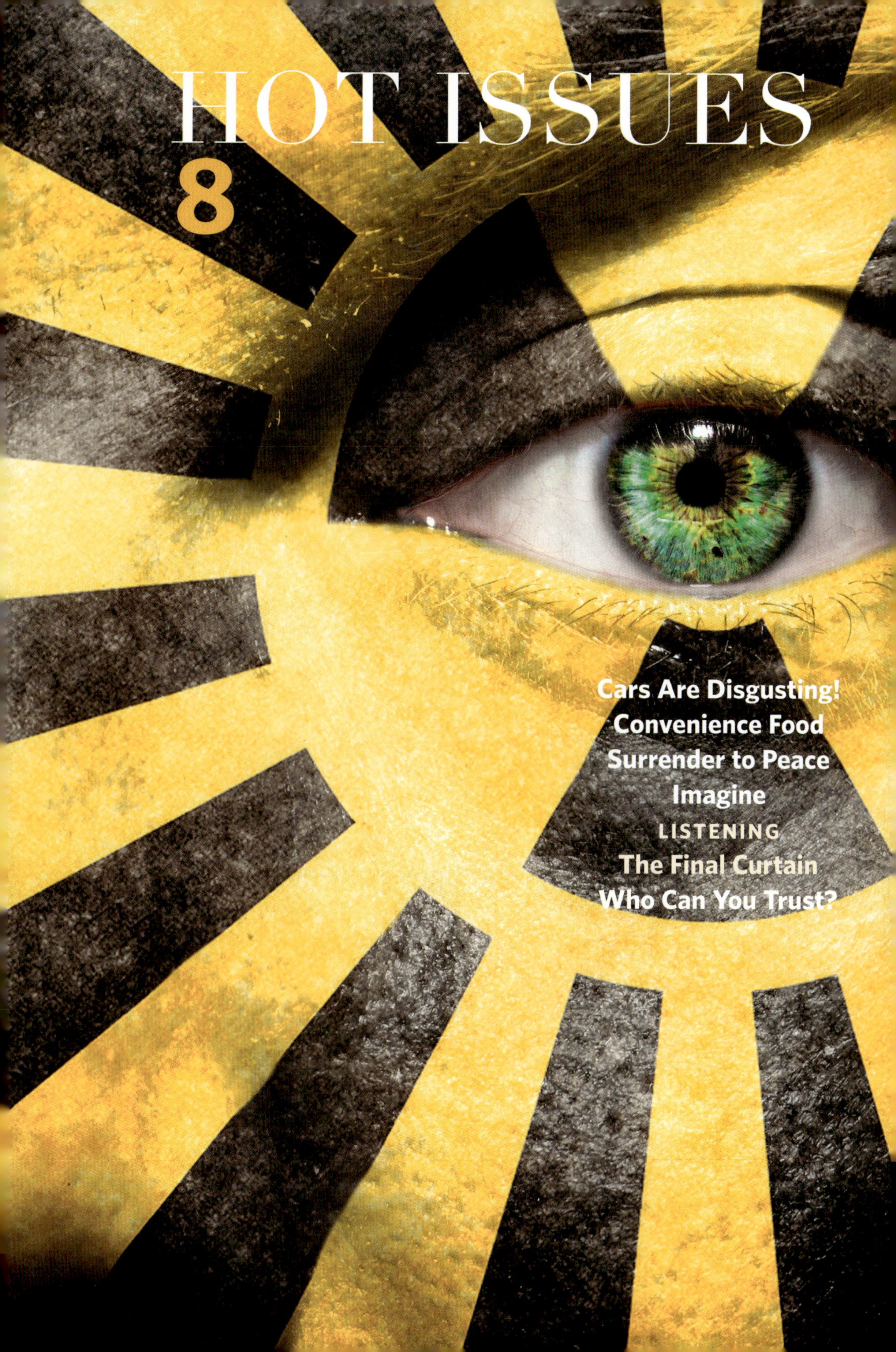
HOT ISSUES
8
Cars Are Disgusting!
Convenience Food
Surrender to Peace
Imagine
LISTENING
The Final Curtain
Who Can You Trust?

CARS ARE DISGUSTING!

BY BLAKE NELSON

James Hoff
Junior AP English
Mr. Coqweiller
ASSIGNMENT: *four-page persuasive essay*

DESTROY ALL CARS!

We stand at the edge. We stand at the brink. We have come to a final point in history. Greenhouse gases are heating our oceans, choking our atmosphere, changing our entire planet. Toxins and pollutants threaten not only our lives, but all life on earth. If action is not taken, all will be lost!

We can no longer chip away at the edges of our problem with meaningless "feel good" solutions. Recycling, buying "green" products, Take the Bus to Work Day – none of these will save our atmosphere or slow down the disastrous heating effects of air pollution. Organic salad bars are not going to refreeze the North Pole. Instead we must fearlessly strike at the root of the problem.

We must destroy all cars.

We must destroy all cars for what they do.

We must destroy all cars for what they stand for.

We must destroy all cars to break the mind-set that makes it impossible to see beyond our own most immediate and selfish needs.

We must destroy all cars because if we don't, they will destroy us!

A world without cars is possible. But how can we imagine such a thing the way we live now?

PRIMITIVE MACHINE

The car is a primitive machine. It is not complicated. You put gas in it and poison comes out. It's pretty damn simple.

Is it a good idea to start your car in your garage and sit beside it, reading the paper, while your garage fills up with exhaust? No. Then why would that be a good idea on a global level?

I AM SO SICK OF CARS

I am sick of cars idling in my school parking lot. I am sick of the endless river of them that forms every morning on the main road by my house. I am sick of sitting on the bus and watching them

packed all around me, ninety percent of them containing A SINGLE INDIVIDUAL. I am sick of that one woman sitting there in her cocoon of false safety, with her Poland Spring water and her Healthy Choice granola bar, polluting the world outside while inside, in her air-conditioned insulation pod, she deludes herself into thinking that drinking fake mineral water and eating fake candy bars is going to purify her body. I reject that person. I reject the falsity of this belief system.

THE LAMENESS OF PEOPLE IN GENERAL

I understand that people are lame and they cannot do without a luxury item once they possess it. I denounce their lameness.

I understand that people are weak and cannot walk to the mall once they have driven there. I denounce their weakness.

I understand that it is the nature of Consumer Americans to constantly drive their vehicles to different stores so they can buy endless amounts of useless crap. I denounce their simplicity of mind.

I understand that our entire economy is based on the production and consumption of USELESS CRAP. I denounce it all: TARGET, WAL-MART, ROSS DRESS FOR LESS, SEARS, MACY'S, KMART, MERVYNS. It is crap! All of it! Crap!

CALL TO ARMS

Young people, students, future citizens and leaders, I ask you to CLEARLY SEE where our present course is taking us. The automobile is the foundation upon which our unsustainable lifestyle is based. They must be DESTROYED. All of them. Even the cute ones. Even the little Mini Cooper that Daddy bought you for your birthday, Ashley.

Cars keep the present political system in place. They keep lower-class people going to war. They keep upper-class people in their mansions and their private jets.

By sitting in our gas-guzzling minivans in traffic, moving at three miles an hour, burning fuel pointlessly, we are keeping the whole car-based social system afloat. Every day OIL COMPANIES make BILLIONS of dollars because we lazy-ass Americans cannot ride a bike to school or work.

The End

Questions and exercises on the text are on page 259.

CONVENIENCE FOOD

BY GILL HOLCOMBE

The funny thing about convenience food – at least it would be funny if we weren't the fattest nation in Europe and getting bigger all the time – is it's not even that convenient. Once you've removed the packaging, read the instructions, pierced the film lid (or not), waited, taken the tray out halfway through the cooking time to stir the food, waited again, let it stand for two minutes, scalded yourself on the steam, searched in vain for a piece of meat amongst the gunk, wolfed the lot in four minutes flat and wondered what else there is to eat because you're still hungry, it might occur to you that the little bit of effort you saved by not cooking your own dinner wasn't really justified by the end result. And the same can be said about so-called fast food, as anyone who has ever been served a burger at the counter in a fast food restaurant, then waited at the table (dirty, usually) for the fries to be brought over ten minutes later, will know.

The other food myth that often gets repeated is that the unhealthiest foods are necessarily the least expensive, and that some people, especially families on very low incomes, only resort to eating them because they have no choice. But this is nonsense. A week's worth of good quality meat and fish with lots of potatoes, rice, pasta, vegetables, fruit and other whole foods costs no more than the same

amount of cheap chicken, burgers, pies, reconstituted potatoes, instant microwave meals and fizzy drinks.

I know cooking isn't everyone's idea of fun, and some people through no fault of their own are never going to enjoy it, which is why this book isn't about learning to cook complicated meals that take hours to prepare and only minutes for your kids to reject. You don't have to like cooking; you don't have to be a great cook, or even a particularly good one. You don't have to go shopping more often than you want to, or spend more money than you can afford. There's nothing here that you can't buy from any of the big supermarkets – assuming that's where you do your shopping because, like me, you're not lucky enough to have anything better where you live – and no expensive ingredients with unfamiliar names. Some of the recipes can be thrown together in minutes and a few don't involve any cooking at all. They all contain a certain amount of fat, sugar and salt, but nowhere near as much as you'd find in commercially prepared food – and at least the nutrients are there as well. [...]

When I was a child growing up in the 1970s, a healthy meal was meat and three veg followed by a fruit pudding; a takeaway meant the occasional trip to the fish and chip shop, and for something continental there was Batchelor's Savoury Rice and Vesta Curry. Now we can laugh, but people worried a lot less about food in those days; no one obsessed about their five portions a day, far more people stayed effortlessly slim, women apparently had smaller waistlines, obesity and obesity-related diseases were a lot less common, if not virtually unheard of, and a seriously overweight child was rarer than a white Christmas.

Much has been made in the past about the history of our unhealthy British diet, but it doesn't seem to me to have been too bad for what was, traditionally, a skinny population inhabiting a chilly little island off the North Sea. We may have had something to learn about the way we cooked our vegetables (like how to steam instead of boiling them to death), but what's wrong with potatoes, puddings and pies, as long as you're eating your greens? For my money, a proper home-cooked meal – with or without chips – is worth a dozen fast food hits that leave you with nothing but a craving for something sweet and a raging thirst.

Miracle foods come and go, but whether the current flavour of the month is wheat grass, alfalfa sprouts or Goji berries, the secret of feeding good food to your family without chaining yourself to the kitchen, depriving your children of the things they like to eat and driving yourself round the bend is that really there *is* no secret. The answer was here all along.

Questions and exercises on the text are on page 262.

YOKO ONO is a successful Japanese artist born in Tokyo. She was married to ex-Beatle, John Lennon. She is both an author and a peace activist. Together with Lennon she protested against the Vietnam War by spending their honeymoon in a week-long Bed-in for peace in Amsterdam. Ono has also had her own musical career and been active as an artist with many award-winning art exhibitions. Since 1980 – when Lennon was shot – she has commemorated him in various ways. Yoko Ono funded the construction and maintenance of the Strawberry Fields Memorial in Central Park in New York City.

BY YOKO ONO

SURRENDER TO PEACE

In the summer of '72 in New York City, John and I invited the press to announce the founding of a conceptual country called Nutopia. Anybody could be a citizen of this country. Citizens were automatically the country's ambassadors. The country's body was the airfield of our joint thoughts. Its constitution was our love, and its spirit, our dreams. Its flag was the white flag of surrender. A surrender to peace. We wished that one day we would take the flag to the United Nations and place it alongside the other flags as Nutopia was just another concept, as were concepts such as France, United States, and the Soviet Union. It was not a concept founded to threaten any other. At this time, the idea of "surrender" did not go down too well. A radical friend of ours expressed that he, too, disliked the

term. "Surrender sounds like defeat," he said. "Well, don't you surrender to love, for instance?" I looked at him. "No, he wouldn't," I thought. "Are women the only people to know the pride and joy of surrender?" I wondered. "It's a waste of time to explain to a macho radical, didn't I tell you?" said John; a man who surrendered to the world, life, and finally to the Universe. "Anyway, don't worry, Yoko. One day we'll put it up there. You and I. I promise." I still believe we will. /- - -/

Questions and exercises on the text are on page 265.

IMAGINE

BY JOHN LENNON

Imagine there's no heaven
It's easy if you try
No hell below us
Above us only sky
Imagine all the people living for today

Imagine there's no countries
It isn't hard to do
Nothing to kill or die for
And no religion too
Imagine all the people living life in peace

You may say
I'm a dreamer, but I'm not the only one
I hope some day you'll join us
And the world will be as one

Imagine no possessions
I wonder if you can
No need for greed or hunger
A brotherhood of man
Imagine all the people sharing all the world

You may say
I'm a dreamer, but I'm not the only one
I hope some day you'll join us
And the world will live as one

Questions and exercises on the text are on page 267.

IMAGINE

WHO CAN YOU TRUST?

BY CHIMAMANDA NGOZI ADICHIE

CHIMAMANDA NGOZI ADICHIE was born and grew up in Nigeria. At the age of nineteen she left for the United States where she continued with her studies. She is famous for her novels *Purple Hibiscus* (2003) and *Half of a Yellow Sun* (2006) both of which describe life in Nigeria. She says her next major literary project will focus on the Nigerian immigrant experience in the United States. Her time is now divided between Nigeria – where she regularly teaches writing workshops – and the USA.

You thought everybody in America had a car and a gun; your uncles and aunts and cousins thought so, too. Right after you won the American visa lottery, they told you: In a month, you will have a big car. Soon, a big house. But don't buy a gun like those Americans.

They trooped into the room in Lagos where you lived with your father and mother and three siblings, leaning against the unpainted walls because there weren't enough chairs to go round, to say goodbye in loud voices and tell you with lowered voices what they wanted you to send them. In comparison to the big car and house (and possibly gun), the things they wanted were minor – handbags and shoes and perfumes and clothes. You said okay, no problem.

Your uncle in America, who had put in the names of all your family members for the American visa lottery, said you could live with him until you got on your feet. He picked you up at the airport and bought you a big hot dog with yellow mustard that nauseated you. Introduction to America, he said with a laugh. He lived in a small white town in Maine, in a thirty-year-old house by a lake. He told you that the company he worked for had offered him a few thousand more than the average salary plus stock options because they were desperately trying to look diverse. They included a photo of him in every brochure, even those that had nothing to do with his unit. He laughed and said the job was good, was worth living in an all-white town even though his wife had to drive an hour to find a hair salon

GAS

that did black hair. The trick was to understand America, to know that America was give-and-take. You gave up a lot but you gained a lot, too.

He showed you how to apply for a cashier job in the gas station on Main Street and he enrolled you in a community college, where the girls had thick thighs and wore bright-red nail polish, and self-tanner that made them look orange. They asked where you learned to speak English and if you had real houses back in Africa and if you'd seen a car before you came to America. They gawped at your hair. Does it stand up or fall down when you take out the braids? They wanted to know. All of it stands up? How? Why? Do you use a comb? You smiled tightly when they asked those questions. Your uncle told you to expect it; a mixture of ignorance and arrogance, he called it. Then he told you how the neighbors said, a few months after he moved into his house, that the squirrels had started to disappear. They had heard that Africans ate all kinds of wild animals.

You laughed with your uncle and you felt at home in his house; his wife called you *nwanne,* sister, and his two school-age children called you Aunty. They spoke Igbo and ate *garri* for lunch and it was like home. Until your uncle came into the cramped basement where you slept with old boxes and cartons and pulled you forcefully to him, squeezing your buttocks, moaning. He wasn't really your uncle; he was actually a brother of your father's sister's husband, not related by blood. After you pushed him away, he sat on your bed – it was his house, after all – and smiled and said you were no longer a child at twenty-two. If you let him, he would do many things for you. Smart women did it all the time. How did you think those women back home in Lagos with well-paying jobs made it? Even women in New York City?

You locked yourself in the bathroom until he went back upstairs, and the next morning, you left, walking the long windy road, smelling the baby fish in the lake. You saw him drive past – he had always dropped you off at Main Street – and he didn't honk. You wondered what he would tell his wife, why you had left. And you remembered what he said, that America was give-and-take.

Questions and exercises on the text are on page 274.

HORROR
9
The Collector
Dead Men Talk
Counterfeit Protection
LISTENING
The Year We Disappeared
Hush, Hush

THE COLLECTOR

BY JOHN FOWLES

JOHN FOWLES studied at Oxford where he received a degree in French in 1950. After several years of teaching jobs abroad in France and Greece and then finally in London, he completed the first draft of *The Collector* in just four weeks in 1960. After some years of revision it was published in 1963 and was an immediate bestseller. Another famous work by him is *The French Lieutenant's Woman* which was later turned into a film starring Meryl Streep in the title role.

SCENE 1
FIRST CONVERSATION

The cellar

Miranda comes round and is violently sick over the side of the bed. She gasps for breath. Clegg backs away and goes behind the screen and returns with a bucket

CLEGG *(very tentatively; this is the moment his fantasy becomes reality, for better or worse)* Hello. How are you? I'm sorry – I didn't realize it had that effect on people. Well, this is your room, I hope you find it comfortable. I'm just upstairs so I'll make sure you have everything you need. There's all sorts of books there for you and clothes. Just ask for anything you want. Oh yes, what would you like for breakfast? I've got most things – cereal, eggs, toast, you can even have French croissants, if you like.

MIRANDA Where am I?

CLEGG I'm afraid I can't tell you that.

MIRANDA Who are you? Why have you brought me here?

CLEGG Don't start worrying about all that now. Get some rest. Have some water. It's just there, and the Ladies is just behind the screen – I'm sorry it's so basic – I couldn't get any pipes down here. *(He turns to leave the cellar)*

MIRANDA I demand to be released at once. Do you hear me? *(She moves towards the cellar door)*

Clegg blocks her and throws her back on to the bed forcefully

CLEGG You can't go yet. Please don't oblige me to use force again. *(He backs away)* We'll talk tomorrow. Good-night.

Clegg exits from the cellar, locking the door behind him

MIRANDA Wait! Come back, come back!

After a pause, Miranda starts to look around the room, discovering all Clegg's preparations; the wardrobe is full of clothes her size and underwear. She continues to look as –
Clegg enters DS *outside the cellar*

THE BEST THING I'VE EVER DONE

CLEGG *(to the audience)* Afterwards, she was always telling me what a bad thing I had done and how I ought to try and realize it more. I can only say that when she came to stay, that first evening I was so happy, happier than I had ever been in my life. My intentions were for the best, you see, that's what she never understood. It's the best thing I've ever done. It was like catching a Mazarine Blue or a Queen of Spain Fritillary – a dream come true.

Finally, Miranda sits in absolute horror
The Lights fade to Black-out

SCENE 2
MIRANDA GREY (DAY 1)

The cellar
There is a knocking on the cellar door, followed by the sound of keys in the lock
The Lights come up on Miranda standing in the middle of the cellar
Clegg enters

CLEGG Good-morning.
MIRANDA Where have you been? I've been waiting for ages.
CLEGG I hope you slept well.
MIRANDA What time is it?
CLEGG Just after eight.
MIRANDA Look, I don't know who you think I am. But if you think I'm from a rich family or something and you're going to get a lot of money, you're wrong.
CLEGG *(trying to reassure her)* Oh, don't worry, I know who you are. You're Miranda Grey. You live at No. 32 Kensington Crescent but at the moment you're studying at St Martin's School of Art in London. You won a scholarship. So you're sharing with other students in Muswell Hill. Your father's Dr Grey. You used to go to Ladymont School for girls. It's funny you trying to make out you're not rich – some would say you're very rich. But you needn't worry, it's not money.
MIRANDA Oh my God ...

CLEGG What?

MIRANDA I know you, don't I?

CLEGG *(completely thrown)* No.

MIRANDA Yes – you work at the Job Centre – I've seen you.

CLEGG I don't know what you mean.

MIRANDA Yes, you do. You were in the paper. The Lottery, you won it. We all said we had seen you about.

Clegg panics and quickly turns to leave

Wait! Don't go! Why am I here? If you know so much about me, why have you brought me here?

CLEGG *(improvising quickly)* I was forced to.

MIRANDA Forced to? By whom?

CLEGG *(turning)* I can't tell you that.

MIRANDA What are you talking about? Tell me why I'm here.

CLEGG I'm only obeying orders.

MIRANDA Whose orders?

CLEGG I can't tell you.

MIRANDA Whose orders?

CLEGG *(clutching at straws)* Mr Singleton.

MIRANDA What?

CLEGG I'm not meant to tell you, he'd kill me if he knew.

MIRANDA Mr Singleton? My old headmaster?

CLEGG It's not what you think.

MIRANDA Mr Singleton ordered you to kidnap me? Why?

CLEGG I don't know.

MIRANDA Of course you do – why?

CLEGG *(thinking quickly)* Do you remember the girl in Penshurst Road? The one that disappeared two years ago?

MIRANDA No ... What happened to her?

CLEGG I don't know, but he did it.

MIRANDA Did what?

CLEGG *(clumsily)* I don't know. I don't know what happened to her. But he did it ... Whatever it was. She's never been heard of since.

MIRANDA So Mr Singleton kidnaps girls and you help him?

Clegg nods

Why? Why do you help him?

CLEGG I have to – I can't tell you. I'm not meant to tell you anything. I'm not going to answer any more questions.

MIRANDA What's he going to do with me?

CLEGG I don't know.

MIRANDA Where is he now?

CLEGG He'll be coming – I expect.

MIRANDA Of course, this must be his house in Suffolk.

CLEGG Yes.

MIRANDA He hasn't got a house in Suffolk.

A stand off

CLEGG *(trying to change the subject)* I came to ask you what you'd like for breakfast. There's cereal, eggs, toast ...

MIRANDA I don't want any fucking breakfast ... This bloody room and that stuff you used – what the fuck was it?

CLEGG *(shocked by her language)* Chloroform. I didn't know it would make you sick. Honest.

MIRANDA *(sarcastically)* Mr Singleton should have told you.

CLEGG *(flustered)* You must want something?

MIRANDA How long are you going to keep me here?

CLEGG I don't know ... I mean, it's not up to me. *(Trying to regain control)* I'm going to the shops now. You must tell me what you want. I'll buy anything you need.

MIRANDA Anything?

CLEGG Well ...

MIRANDA Mr Singleton told you to?

CLEGG No, this is from me.

MIRANDA I just want to get out of here.

CLEGG Well – apart from that what would you like?

MIRANDA Look, we're going to start all over again. I don't believe what you've said about Mr Singleton. It's ludicrous. I know his daughter, he's not like that. And if he was, he certainly wouldn't have you working for him. He wouldn't have done all this either.

Questions and exercises on the text are on page 280.

DEAD MEN TALK

BY SANDRA MARA

"The most calculated and callous killing I've ever encountered" was how Judge Paul Carney described the murder of Mary Whelan.

Twenty-seven-year-old Mary Gough worked as a solicitor's clerk and, like any young woman in love, was excited about her forthcoming wedding. She had been with the man of her dreams, Colin Whelan, for almost seven years and she was finally planning her wedding.

Thirty-year-old Colin was a freelance computer analyst working for Irish Permanent – which would later turn out to be somewhat ironic. The couple were well set up as they already had their own home, having bought a house at Clonard Street, Balbriggan, from a relation of Colin's.

Mary and Colin married in March 2001. They were still newlyweds when, six months later, tragedy apparently befell Mary. As she made her way up to bed, she fell down the stairs, tripping on her dressing gown cord. Her distraught husband rang the emergency services, who arrived within minutes, but too late for Mary, who was already dead.

The ambulance crew were less than convinced about the manner in which Mary Whelan had met her death. When the investigating gardaí arrived on the scene, they too had concerns. They were not so sure that the grieving husband's tears were genuine. Following an investigation and an examination by the then Assistant State Pathologist, Dr Marie Cassidy, the "accidental death" was upgraded to murder. Mary Whelan had indeed died as a result of a cord, but not from her dressing gown. The cord came from her husband's pyjamas and her death was no accident – it was strangulation.

After choking the very life out of his young wife, Colin Whelan then dragged her body from the bedroom and threw her down the stairs, making it look as if she'd fallen. He had made sure there were no ligature marks on her neck, shielding it with a towel before he choked her – a trick he'd learned on his murderous trawl through the Internet. Only then, when he was satisfied she was dead and beyond help, did he phone the emergency services.

Investigations into Colin Whelan's background unearthed a murky past, one that his young wife had known nothing about; for if she had, she'd never have married him. While still a teenager, Whelan had been involved in a lengthy relationship with an older woman. He had a history of sexual and physical abuse towards her and she became terrified of him. To escape from his constant threats and violence, she had fled to England, leaving no trace of her whereabouts. Whelan didn't seem too worried, as he coolly moved on to his next victim, the innocent Mary Gough.

A full-scale investigation launched by gardaí revealed some interesting information. It seemed that Whelan had been planning to murder his wife since long before the wedding. He had played the long game, knowing his ultimate plan was to kill his new wife Mary, to reap the financial rewards. His prowess with a computer was, he believed, the key to realising his dream. A forensic investigation by the Garda Computer Investigation Unit examined Colin Whelan's work computer at the Irish Permanent Building Society. Forensic analysis of the computer's hard drive revealed he was doing more than his job. At least six months before the wedding, Colin Whelan had been trawling through Internet sites to find out the best way to asphyxiate someone, without leaving the telltale ligature marks usually found on a strangulation victim's neck. He had accessed sites advising the use of a thick towel to prevent ligature marks, and recommendations as to make a murder look like an accident.

Whelan had also scoured the Internet for stories about serial killers and their methods, what mistakes they'd made, how they evaded detection for long periods, and how they disposed of their victim. He was obsessed with the prospect of quick, easy money, and had the stomach to do whatever it took to achieve his dream, even if it meant killing his young wife.

Six months after the wedding, he put his grizzly plan into action, putting his new-found knowledge to use: killing his young wife and making it look like an accident.

They also discovered that Whelan was involved in yet another relationship with an older Welsh divorcee. Perhaps he was lining up yet another victim for when he disposed of his wife? Whelan's wasn't an unhappy marriage, but for him it was a marriage of convenience, a sure way to make easy money.

Mary Whelan was no heiress, but if his plan had worked Colin Whelan would have been a wealthy young man. He had taken out an insurance policy for £400,000 payable to the surviving spouse, should either of them die within ten years. They were both young, healthy and a good risk. Colin wasn't expecting his wife ever to collect on the policy, but he was already making plans for the money. The only

obstacle to his fortune was the now inconvenient matter of Mary, his bride of just six months, and that, he believed, had been sorted out.

But for the investigating detectives, it might well have been. Following the pathology report and the forensic computer evidence, together with the significant insurance policy on Mary's life, not to mention his previous history, detectives were in no doubt they had a killer on their hands.

Whelan was arrested and charged with his wife's murder and was due to stand trial at the Central Criminal Court, but he fled the jurisdiction while on bail in 2003. His car, together with his clothes, were found abandoned at the cliffs in Howth in Dublin, suggesting he had committed suicide. He disappeared from sight. No contact was made with any family members or friends and it looked like he just hadn't been able to face the impending trial.

Dogged detectives were more sceptical. They were proved right when, almost eighteen months later, he was spotted working in a bar in Majorca by an Irish tourist, who immediately reported the sighting to the gardaí. Spanish police confirmed he was well known in the area, spending his money on the local prostitutes and flirting with the female tourists. It later transpired that the day he disappeared, he had caught a flight to Spain, travelling on false documentation "stolen" from a friend.

Whelan's party was over as an extradition warrant was issued. Murder squad detectives brought him back from his island paradise to face charges for the murder of his wife. Whelan again sought bail but, not surprisingly, was refused by Mr Justice Paul Carney. Unexpectedly, when the case was called, Colin Whelan pleaded guilty, to the relief of Mary's family. He is currently serving a life sentence, convicted by his own stupidity and a trail of his intent on the Internet.

Questions and exercises on the text are on page 282.

COUNTERFEIT PROTECTION

Manufacturing paper money is a complex and secretive business, reflecting the fact that banknotes have always been an obvious target for thieves and counterfeiters. Most aspects of paper money design are aimed at rendering the notes as difficult as possible to forge. This means using special paper and inks, a range of different printing techniques, and innovative devices such as holograms.

Fully printed banknotes have only been in circulation since about 1850. Before then, part-printed notes, which had to be signed like cheques, circulated in some major financial centres. Banknote printing involves several stages, using different techniques. The first of these, used to print most features of each note, is offset printing – the same process used to print books and magazines. Next is intaglio printing, which involves pressing an engraved metal plate against the paper and is used to add the more finely detailed parts of the design, giving them a distinctive "raised" feel. Special features such as holograms may then be added, and finally the serial numbers are stamped on to the notes. In Australia, plastic bills, which last longer and are more difficult to copy, are issued.

Despite the sophistication of modern banknote protection technology, counterfeiting remains a problem – and it has become more of a threat in some countries since the introduction of high-quality colour photocopiers. Apart from trying to stay "one step ahead" of counterfeiters in technical terms, the principal weapon used by governments is to punish offenders with fines and heavy prison sentences.

Counterfeiting and skimming credit cards is another story.

US $100 BILL

The $100 bill shown above was first issued in 1996. In addition to the security devices depicted, the bill has fine-line printing in the background to the portrait and special "never-dry" ink is utilized. Viewed from the front a watermark is located at the far right of the bill.

Fluorescent feature When the front of the note is viewed under ultraviolet light, a fluorescent "20" can be seen in an area towards the lower left corner. This feature is not apparent in normal light.

Metallic thread A thread is embedded in the paper, showing as a series of silver dashes on the reverse of the note (left). When held up to the light, the thread shows as a solid dark line (right).

Thread A polymer thread is embedded vertically in the bill and indicates, by its position, the bill's denomination. The words "USA 100" can be seen on the thread when held up to a bright light.

Microprinting The words "THE UNITED STATES OF AMERICA" are printed in tiny capital letters along Benjamin Franklin's coat lapel, and "USA 100" is printed repeatedly within the "100" at bottom left.

Paper The paper for this bill is made of cotton and linen and has a strong but pliable feel. It has hundreds of tiny red and blue fibres embedded within it.

Colour shifting ink The "100" in the lower right corner appears green when viewed straight on but looks black when viewed from an angle.

Fine detail Most banknotes include portraits or natural objects as part of the design, providing ample opportunity for incorporating fine details, such as hair or moustaches, that are difficult to counterfeit.

ENGLISH £20 NOTE

The £20 note shown above was first issued in 1999. As well as the security features highlighted, the note contains a watermark; a holographic foil on the front that shows the figure "20" or an image of Britannia according to the angle of view; raised (intaglio) printing for words such as "Bank of England" and serial numbers that vary in size and colour.

DETECTING COUNTERFEIT NOTES

A small proportion of the banknotes circulating in most countries are counterfeit. Any counterfeit note presented to a bank is liable to be confiscated without compensation, so it pays to be on guard. Spotting a counterfeit in broad daylight is usually quite easy, but detection in an environment such as a darkened bar can be more difficult. The best solution is to be aware of all the security features on the notes you handle regularly, and check for those features in any notes you are handed. Also pay particular attention to the feel of the notes.

Questions and exercises on the text are on page 285.

HUSH, HUSH

BY BECCA FITZPATRICK

***Hush, Hush* is a young adult novel written by the American writer BECCA FITZPATRICK. It is written through the perspective of the main character, Nora Grey, who finds her life in danger when she becomes involved with a mysterious new student at her school named Patch, who is revealed to be a fallen angel with a dark connection to Nora herself. There are four books altogether in the *Hush, Hush* series: *Hush, Hush*, *Crescendo*, *Silence* and the final book *Finale*.**

"Stop the bus!" I called to the driver.

He applied the brakes, and I was thrown against the seat in front of me.

"Can you tell me which way to Highsmith?" I asked him once I'd made it to the top of the aisle.

He pointed out the windows paneling the right side of the bus. "West of here. You planning to go on foot?" He surveyed me up and down. "'Cause I should warn you, it's a rough neighborhood."

Great.

I had to walk only a few blocks before I knew the bus driver had been right to warn me. The scenery changed drastically. The quaint storefronts were replaced by buildings spray-painted with gang graffiti. The windows were dark, barred up with iron. The sidewalks were desolate paths stretching into the fog.

A slow, rattling noise drifted through the fog, and a woman pushing a cart of garbage bags wheeled into view. Her eyes were raisins, beady and dark, and they twitched their way over me in almost predatory evaluation.

"What we got here?" she said through a gape of missing teeth.

I drew a discreet step back and clutched my handbag against me.

"Looks like a coat, mittens, and a pretty wool hat," she said. "Always wanted me a pretty wool hat." She pronounced the word *pritee*.

"Hello," I said, clearing my throat and trying to sound friendly. "Can you please tell me how much farther to Highsmith Street?"

She cackled.

"A bus driver pointed me in this direction," I said with less confidence.

"He told you Highsmith is this way?" she said, sounding irritated. "I know the way to Highsmith, and this ain't it."

I waited, but she didn't elaborate. "Do you think you could give me directions?" I asked.

"I got directions." She tapped her head with a finger that strongly resembled a twisted, knotted twig. "Keep everything up here, I do."

"Which way is Highsmith?" I encouraged.

"But I can't tell you for free," she said in a chiding tone. "That's gonna cost you. A girl has to make a living. Nobody ever tell you ain't nothing in life free?"

"I don't have any money. Not much, anyway. Only enough for a bus fare home."

"You got a nice warm coat."

I looked down at my quilted coat. A chilly wind ruffled my hair, and the thought of peeling my coat off sent a flush of goose bumps down my arms. "I just got this coat for Christmas."

"I'm freezing my derrière off out here," she snapped. "You want directions or not?"

I couldn't believe I was standing here. I couldn't believe I was bartering my coat with a homeless woman.

I shucked off my coat and watched her zip into it.

My breath came out like smoke. I hugged myself and stamped my feet, conserving body heat. "Can you please tell me the way to Highsmith now?"

"You want the long way, or the short way?"

"Sh-short," I chattered.

"That's gonna cost you too. Short way's got an additional fee attached. Like I said, always wanted me a pretty wool hat."

I tugged the pink and white beanie off my head. "Highsmith?" I asked, trying to hold onto the friendly tone as I passed it over.

"See that alley?" she said, pointing behind me. I turned. The alley was a half block back. "You take it, you come out on Highsmith on the other side."

"That's it?" I said incredulously. "One block over?"

"Good news is, you got a short walk. Bad news is, ain't no walk feel short in this weather. 'Course, I'm nice and warm now I got me a coat and a pretty hat. Give me those mittens, and I'll walk you there myself."

I looked down at the mittens. At least my hands were warm. "I'll manage."

She shrugged and wheeled her cart to the next corner, where she took up a post against the bricks.

The alley was dark and cluttered with trash bins, water-stained cardboard boxes, and an unrecognizable hump that may have been a discarded water heater. Then again, it just as easily could have been a rug with a body rolled inside. A high chain-link fence spanned the alley halfway down. I could hardly climb a four-foot fence on a good day, let alone a ten-foot one. Brick buildings flanked me on both sides. All the windows were greased over and barred.

Stepping over crates and sacks of trash, I picked my way down the alley. Broken glass crunched beneath my shoes. A flash of white darted between my legs, stealing my breath. A cat. Just a cat, vanishing into the darkness ahead.

I reached for my pocket to text Vee, intending to tell her I was close and to watch for me, when I remembered I'd left my cell phone in my coat pocket. Nice going, I thought. What are the chances the bag lady will give you back your phone? Precisely – slim to none.

I decided it was worth a try, and as I turned around, a sleek black sedan sped past the opening to the alley. With a sudden glow of red, the brake lights lit up.

For reasons I couldn't explain beyond intuition, I drew into the shadows.

A car door opened and the crackle of gunfire broke out. Two shots. The car door slammed and the black sedan screeched away. I could hear my heart hammering in my chest, and it blended with the sound of running feet. I realized a moment later that they were my feet, and I was running to the mouth of the alley. I rounded the corner and came up short.

The bag lady's body was in a heap on the sidewalk.

Questions and exercises on the text are on page 290.

RESOURCE SECTION

Welcome to the Resource Section of Solid Gold. It's here to help you improve the way you learn and use English. It will help you build your vocabulary and sharpen up your grammar, as well as showing you ways to get better at understanding, speaking, reading and writing in English. There's no need to read the whole Resource Section from start to finish – just go straight to the section you need as you work through the book.

Three keys are the letters S, L and P:

Strategies. Don't just do your homework, think about the way you study and decide how to improve your spoken English and your ability to understand when other people speak English. Decide on ways to get better at writing.

Logbook. Keep a logbook and write down how you're progressing. Write a date next to each entry. Get into the habit of reflecting on how you learn. Keep a note of the different strategies you use and how well you think they work for you.

Portfolio gives you solid proof of what you've achieved. Tests, papers, recordings – anything you've produced in English should be kept in your portfolio. You'll be surprised how much you've collected at the end of the year.

Follow these links or go to the page:

1 STRATEGIES TO IMPROVE YOUR LANGUAGE SKILLS

How to become a better reader

SOME PRACTICAL ADVICE

Preparation: pen and paper

When reading, be prepared to make notes on paper or on your computer, mobile phone or other device. Try to be comfortable and if possible see that you're not disturbed.

BEFORE YOU START

Pre-reading: What's the purpose of your reading?

What are you expected to find out when reading? Are you looking for details or is your task to summarize a story or an argument? It's important to know before you start why you're reading this particular text.

?

Look for clues: headings, subheadings, pictures

Look first at headings, subheadings and illustrations. What conclusion can you draw from looking at these? What do they tell you?

LOOK FOR CLUES

Prior knowledge of the subject

Ask yourself 'What do I already know about this subject?'

WHAT DO I KNOW?

Read the text twice

Your first reading is to get a main overview of the text – a general idea of what the text is about. Your second reading is for you to pay closer attention to the text and to get a clearer idea of what the writer wants to say. If your aim is just to scan the text for specific information one reading might be enough. You'll know when you've found what you were looking for.

READ X 2

Take notes

Take notes when you're reading. Write down key words, important information and use a dictionary if necessary.

TAKE NOTES

What to do if you get stuck

If you get stuck and don't understand something, move on and then go back later to try to work out why this particular part was so tricky. A better grasp of the whole text can often help you understand parts.

Divide up the job of reading

If you have to read a long text, plan to read say a certain number of pages a day. Write a short summary of each part that you've read.

Look at a text in three ways

First of all, consider the basic information right there on the page. Make sure you understand the words and phrases. Next, try to read 'between the lines', that is, try to find out what the author really means or wants to say.
Finally, go beyond the text. What thoughts occur to you as you put the text in relation to your own knowledge, experience or previous reading?

What if you don't understand?

If you don't 'get' what part of a text means, ask a friend to help you.

How to become a better listener

Pre-listening: What's the purpose of your listening?

What are you interested in finding out? Before listening to a talk, for example, write at least three questions on the subject which you think may be answered. Think about what the answers to these questions might be.
Predict at least 10 words you might expect to hear in the talk and list them.

Prior knowledge of the subject

What do you already know about the subject? What would you like to know about it? What do you think the speaker will talk about? What form or genre do you expect the talk to take – a speech, a presentation, a lecture or just a plain announcement of information?

The main idea

When listening, focus on the main issue the speaker is talking about and don't pay too much attention to details. Focus on understanding the main topic or line of argument.

Identifying the main idea

A speaker often signals the main idea by using phrases such as:
The main point is....
What I'm going to talk about today is...
My purpose is to show....

A speaker will often repeat important words or phrases during a talk and may back up or clarify important points by using visual aids such as PowerPoint.

Take notes

When listening, take notes. Try not to get stuck on details. Just try to write down main points and what you think are key words and phrases. If you like using mind maps, try making one as you listen.

Identify what you need to know

What sort of information are you hoping to hear? Is it one piece of information or a whole process?

Listen out for linking words and phrases

When listening, pay attention to the speaker and his/her use of linking words.
'Firstly' will usually be followed by' secondly', 'thirdly' and so on.
'Finally' tells you the conclusion is coming.
'Because…', 'for this reason…' 'in this way' and so on will aim to explain something.

Summarizing

After you've listened to the talk, write down the main ideas. Do this as soon as you can after the talk. It'll be easier and will help you to remember later.

How to be become a better speaker

First of all, in order to develop as a speaker you need to take risks, i.e. not just saying things you're sure about and have said before. Don't worry about making mistakes. Mistakes are inevitable and the main thing is to make yourself understood.

Take every opportunity to speak English

Practice is the key. Speak only English during English lessons and why not find someone to skype with in English? It's only by using the language that you'll become fluent.

- You improve your speech by trying to speak rather than being silent.
- Nobody's perfect so believe that you're good enough!
- Everyone has the right to speak and make mistakes.

Taking part in a conversation

If you're having problems understanding what's being said, don't be afraid to interrupt with a question, for example:

- Excuse me, I'd like to ask something.
- Sorry, but I don't quite follow.
- Excuse me, could you repeat that please?
- Excuse me for interrupting, but could I ask…?
- Sorry, I don't quite understand.

Express yourself
If you can't think of the exact word, try to paraphrase, i.e. explain by using other words. Use gestures and body language.

Strategies for using new words.
Increasing your vocabulary will help you express yourself better and in more varied ways. So put some extra effort into learning and using new words and expressions you come across through listening or reading.

Listen and repeat
You learn a lot by listening and imitating. By using the *Wordmatch* and *Spelling* exercises you can listen to and repeat any words you're unsure of how to pronounce. And the great thing is that you can practise as many times as you want.

Make up your own sentences
Make up sentences using the new words you want to know. This will help you to remember the words and is a really effective way of learning them.

Summarize texts using new words
After reading a text find the main points and summarize them in your own words, using headings or key words. This will help you to speak at more length. Why not record yourself and listen carefully to how you express yourself?

- Write down some key words
- Retell the story to yourself
- Record yourself and listen

Dramatize a text
Work with some friends and pick a story to dramatize. Using the characters in the story, write dialogues and act them out. Another alternative is to find a play and rehearse a scene from it. Let your class be your audience!

Prepare a presentation in English
Finding information and preparing a speech to give to your class will challenge your speaking ability. You'll probably feel nervous – this is normal – but having done it a few times, you'll feel more confident and sure of yourself.

- Find information on your topic.
- Structure your speech: use a mind map or key words.
- Practise until you know your speech more or less by heart.
- Ask for peer response.

2 ASSESSMENT

Assessment is necessary in order to keep a record of your progress. Use the following questions when you need some feedback.

The statements match my level of English (choose 0–4)

0 = not at all 1 = a little 2 = fairly well 3 = very well 4 = perfectly

I can understand spoken English overall and in detail. ☐

I can take part in discussions and comment on general content and details. ☐

I can read and understand different genres of English. ☐

I can adjust my written and spoken English to the purpose, recipient and context as required. ☐

I can express myself orally and in writing in a clear, coherent and structured way using appropriate genres. ☐

I can discuss and comment on the content of written material. ☐

I know ways to improve my own writing. ☐

I can select and use different strategies to improve my interaction in English. ☐

I can choose material from different media and use it in my own written production as well as in oral interaction. ☐

I can check and critically evaluate spoken and written sources. ☐

I can discuss cultural differences and make references to my own knowledge and experience. ☐

3 HOW TO BECOME A MORE CRITICAL READER

When you look for information – especially on the Internet – it's very important that you evaluate the sources you intend to use. Anyone can publish articles on the net, as you well know, and therefore it's very important to pay attention to the work you're referring to. When you're looking for information you usually have an assignment that you're working on and finding facts is a big part of the working process which could be described as:

- Defining the assignment and finding research questions.
- Finding information. Where can it be found?
- Searching for information using different sources.
- Evaluating and analysing the information.
- Compiling a text.
- Reporting.

Critical reading and reviewing of sources

Who is the author?

Is it a well-known person? Someone who is an expert in the field? Does he or she have a title? Is there a presentation of this person to be found anywhere?
Does the author represent a particular standpoint or opinion?

Who lies behind the webpage?

Is it an organization that's well-known within this field?

Can you tell when the text was published and how up-to-date the information is?

It's important to check when the webpage was last updated and, if possible, when the information you're looking for was first published.

What is pure fact? And what are opinions or value statements?

You need to practise, preferably with a group of other students, your ability to tell facts from values and opinions. When you've done this you can of course refer to what people think – their opinions – but you need to be clear about this and it isn't always easy to do.

Are the facts consistent with information from other sources?

It's always useful to compare different sources to be on the safe side – to make sure that what you're using is credible. Be sure to discuss with classmates whether your material is credible.

For more information see Skolverket

http://www.skolverket.se/skolutveckling/resurser-for-larande/kollakallan/in_english

4 GENRES

When you speak or write you tend to adapt what you say or write according to who you're speaking or writing to, what you're speaking or writing about and to the situation you find yourself in. These different ways of speaking or writing are known as different genres or different text types.

Purpose

Every genre has a specific purpose. The purpose determines how the genre is constructed. Instructions, for example, are meant to explain a process and are constructed so that the information is given step by step.

Structure

Every genre has its own structure. A set of instructions starts by stating the goal – for example, how to make a delicious fudge cake. This is then followed by a list of ingredients and step-by-step instructions showing how to make the cake.

A news program can also be considered as a genre and has its own structure, often starting with the day's headlines, followed by details of the major news items, moving on to smaller news items and ending with the weather report. You would probably be surprised if it started with the weather report and ended with major international news.

Language

Every genre has a specific use of language. For example, many newspaper articles are written in the past tense, while a set of instructions will require action verbs in the imperative form.

This may at first seem confusing – 'English is always just English, isn't it?' you may ask. But if you think about it you will find that the structure and language of a bedtime story is completely different from that of a car manual telling you how to change a tyre. When writing in a particular genre you need to know how to structure the text and what type of language is required. In this course you will learn how to write **a formal letter, a letter to the editor, a set of instructions, a narrative, a review** and **a summary**. These different genres will mean differences in the grammar and vocabulary to be used.

The above are examples of written genres. But we also speak in different genres. For example, you may need to instruct someone how to do something or explain what a TV-program was about. In each case, you'll use different ways of expressing yourself. By paying attention to genres and learning about them you'll become a better writer and speaker.

The rhetorical process

When you're writing or preparing a speech you can make use of something called the rhetorical process. It helps you work in a more structured and methodical way. It will help you to understand the aim or purpose of the text, who you should address your writing to and the context, i.e. when, where and how the text is to be used.

1 Understand the aim and the context

Before writing a text or putting together a speech, start by asking yourself:
What's the aim? What do I want to achieve? What does the context demand?

If you tackle the following questions first it'll be easier to write your paper, letter, news item or speech:

What is the purpose? Do I want to write a story, an instruction, a review or what?
Who is the recipient? Friends of yours? Complete strangers? A potential employer?
Where is your text to be published? On Facebook, in a letter of application, as a paper, as a speech to be given?
How do I best convey the message? What's required for the genre I've chosen – formal/informal, step-by-step instructions, interest, suspense?
Why this means of communication? Is there a better way?

2 Find, collect and evaluate material

Find and collect ideas from books, the Internet, magazines, newspapers, radio/TV, etc. Go through the material and make a note of the sources. What can you use? Pick out what you need. Structure your material, i.e. see how different items can go together and decide what order to put things in.

3 Plan

Make a plan before you start to write an article or a speech. It will make your assignment much easier. Think of your work as having three parts:

Introduction Here your aim is to catch the reader's or listener's attention. Ask a question, make a statement or give a brief presentation of the subject. For example if you're going to write about the importance of recycling you can start by explaining *why* it's important.

Thesis This is where the main part of the subject is presented.

Conclusion Finish your text by explaining your conclusions or by summing up the text.

4 Language check

Go through what you've written. Have you made the right choices of formal or informal language? Did you use words and phrases that suit your purpose? When you've checked your work it's always a good idea to ask someone else to read through what you've written and to offer feedback.

And when giving a speech …

5 Memorise

When giving a speech make sure you know most of it by heart. Prepare yourself well. Use key notes or a mind map or cards with key words and phrases on them to trigger your memory. Don't forget to number the cards in case you drop them just before you're about to begin!

6 Act it out!

Use your voice well to create empathy and variation. For example, speak more quickly when showing enthusiasm about something or more slowly and quietly when referring to something sad. Also think about your body language. For example where you stand, how you dress and how you keep eye contact with your audience.

CHECKLIST FOR WRITING

When you've finished working on your text, check it over one last time – to see if there's anything you should or would like to change. Use the following as a guide.

1. Read the text to yourself. Does it make sense or is there anything missing?
2. Have you divided the text into separate paragraphs?
3. Is there an introduction, a thesis (the main body of the text) and a conclusion?
4. Does the title or heading match the text?
5. Do the structure and choice of vocabulary match the genre?
6. What does your text require – formal or informal language? Make sure not to mix the two.
7. Check the use of linking words. For example: *To begin with …, In addition …, In conclusion …*
8. Check the use of verbs. For example, the -s form, the use of tenses.
9. Check punctuation and capital letters.
10. Check spelling.
11. Check overall grammar. For example, the use of tenses, articles, prepositions, pronouns and adverbs.

Peer response – writing

Your peers are those around you who are involved in the same activities as you, in this case your classmates. When you're in the process of writing a text or when you've finished it, it's useful to **let someone else read what you've written**. What you actually mean can sometimes be difficult for a reader to understand. Therefore, get a classmate or a friend to read your texts and use the questions below as a basis for discussion. At first you might feel uncomfortable about hearing another person's opinion on what you've written, but you'll get used to it and your writing will gain by it. And don't forget that **the roles may later be reversed** and that you'll be the person giving feedback on what someone else has written.

Before you get peer response it's important that you check your own text and that you analyze it in order to make it better.

DISCUSS THE TEXT WITH THESE QUESTIONS AS A GUIDE:

1 What is the purpose of the text?
2 Does the message come across? How can you summarize the message?
3 Does the headline correspond to the text?
4 What genre is this? Is it well chosen?
5 How is the text structured? Does the introduction link with the conclusion?
6 What kind of linking words are used?
7 Does the choice of vocabulary and grammar correspond to the genre?
8 Is there a good variation of words?
9 Are the sentences grammatically correct?
10 What about paragraphing, spelling, punctuation?
11 Does anything need to be changed?
12 How can the text be improved? Make a few suggestions.

Peer response – speaking

For most people, making a speech in front of a group usually means feeling both anxious and nervous. It's therefore important that you, as a listener, do all you can to **encourage the speaker**. The speaker needs to get feedback but speaking in front of a group can be an awkward situation and the speaker may feel they're being criticized rather than helped. So giving your response in writing might be a better idea.

CHECKLIST WHEN RESPONDING TO A SPEECH

1. What was the purpose of the speech? Did it come across?
2. How did the speaker adjust his or her speech to the audience?
3. What kind of contact was made with the audience?
4. Did the opening of the speech link to the ending?
5. Did the speaker use any props, like pictures? How did that work out?
6. Did the person speak without a script?
7. Was it easy to understand? Was the speech clear, and loud enough to hear?
8. Comment on the use of body language.
9. What could be improved?
10. What were the best things about the speech?

How to write a narrative

When you write a story there are certain components that are usually included. The scene is set, something happens, a problem arises and finally the problem is solved. Let's look at an example.

Round Like a Shot ❶

Going to bed the other night I noticed people in my shed stealing things. ❷

I phoned the police but was told no one was in the area to help. They said they would send someone over as soon as possible. ❸

I hung up. A minute later I rang again. "Hello," I said, "I called you a minute ago because there were people in my shed. You don't have to hurry now, because I've shot them."

Within minutes there were half a dozen police cars in the area, plus helicopters and an armed response unit. They caught the burglars red-handed. ❹

One of the officers said: "I thought you said you'd shot them." To which I replied: "I thought you said there was no one available." ❺

1. The **heading** catches your attention immediately. It arouses your curiosity and makes you want to read the story. When you write something, always spend time on the heading. Try to find a good, catchy heading to get the reader's attention.
2. In this first sentence you're introduced to the **action** of the story. Someone is stealing something from the person in the text. You're also introduced to when and where the story takes place and to the main person in the story.
3. The **problem** is now introduced. The police don't seem to treat the man's call very seriously.
4. In this part of the story you get to know how the man solved the problem. He called the police and told them that he'd taken care of the problem himself – he'd shot the

burglars, thereby describing himself as a major criminal. This brought the police round immediately.

5 The **problem is solved.** The police do come, but to catch, not the burglar but the person who said he'd shot them.

Different stories can have similar structures

If you compare *Round Like a Shot* with a fairytale such as *Cinderella* you find a similar structure.

First the **scene is set**. We learn when and where the story takes place and who the main characters are. Cinderella lives with her cruel step-mother and step-sisters.

Then comes the **action** – a series of events. Cinderella is treated badly and has nothing to wear to a ball which is to be held. She gets help to make a dress, goes to the ball and meets the prince. She has to be back by midnight and runs away from the prince but in her haste loses one of her shoes.

Now the **problem** is introduced – finding the person who owns the shoe. After a long search Cinderella is eventually found and in the end marries the prince. The **problem is solved**.

TO SUM UP

- The purpose of a narrative is to entertain and, in some cases, to teach you something.
- At first you're given information about who, when and where.
- Then the action – a series of events take place.
- A problem is introduced.
- The problem is solved.
- Words indicating time are usually part of a story: *then, five minutes ago, a long time ago…*
- The story is usually written in the past tense: *It happened a long time ago, when I was a child, the other night.* etc.
- Dialogue can be used to help bring the characters and the action to life.

How to write a summary of or a commentary on a story

A summary

In writing a summary you pick out the most important points in a text but do not include any opinions of your own. Let's use the text *Round Like a Shot* as an example. Start by giving the title of the story and setting the scene, then go on to state the problem, and finally how it's solved. Here's a suggested summary:

Summary of *Round Like a Shot*

Round Like a Shot is a about a man who discovers that his shed is being robbed. He calls the police but they're not in the area and say they can't come. He calls the police again and tells them that he's taken care of the whole thing himself by shooting the men. Shortly afterwards the police arrive.

A commentary

In a commentary you give your thoughts on the story. In this example two statements are made about the main message of a short story. When reflecting on a longer story or a whole book, it's useful to quote parts of the story and write your reflections in connection with them.

I think the person in the text was very smart when he called the police again. And I also think that it's a pity that you have to act that way to attract the attention of the police.

How to write a review

When you write a review of a book or a film you may mix information about it and your opinions on it. You're expected to give information as well as criticize, assess and evaluate it.

In short, you should summarize the plot (the main story), mention the main conflict or conflicts, the main characters, the theme (the main subject) and the message, if any.

Here follows an example of how you can go about writing a genre like this, but don't forget that a good writer can find his or her personal way of writing. Don't be afraid to use ideas of your own about what and how to write.

A Slam for Sam

In the title or heading you state what you intend to focus on in your review. In this case the review will focus on what happens to Sam after he meets Alicia. Try to find a catchy heading that will draw your reader's attention. Don't use the title of the book or the film as a heading. You're not writing another book with that title, but a review that is focusing on what you found especially interesting about the novel.

Introduce the author and the title

Start by introducing the writer and the title of the book or film. In this introduction the theme – Sam's slam – of the book is also mentioned. Another way of introducing this book could be: 'A novel worth reading is *Slam* by the contemporary English author Nick Hornby'. Contemporary means that Hornby is an author living and writing today.

Slam is the title of a book by the English author Nick Hornby. Slam could also be a description of skater Sam's future life.

Summarize the plot, describe the characters and introduce the setting

In this part the plot is summarized, the main character Sam is described and the setting is introduced – namely 21st century suburban London. The main conflict of the novel is also made clear; Sam is 16 years old, lives near London and gets a girl pregnant. The underlying question is; how is he going to cope with this?

The book is about a 16-year-old boy called Sam who lives with his mother in the suburbs of London in the 21st century. The story starts when Sam meets Alicia and they fall in love with each other, but what Sam doesn't know is that his life is about to change for ever. There will be a major slam! Everything goes well for Sam and Alicia for a while until one day Sam suddenly loses his feelings for Alicia and dumps her. Sam continues living his life as normal until he finds out that Alicia is pregnant with his child.

Introduce the theme

Introduce the theme or the question that you wish to dig deeper into. In this case how is Sam affected by what happens to him?

How does Sam react to this slam that suddenly happens in his life?

Answer your own question

It's important that you try to answer the question – How did Sam react to what happened? – and, if possible, add a quote to support your point of view. What's being shown is that Sam takes responsibility, he matures, changes the direction of his life, but the question remains whether he's really happy. If you wish you can comment on the use of language as well as linking your theme to the setting.

Sam's world suddenly turns upside down and he decides to escape from everything to another city. He initially chooses to run away from the problem by almost denying that it ever happened. But he only stays in this city for a couple of days until he realizes that he must face up to the consequences of his actions, even though he is not very happy about the baby.
Considering his background and way of life it is surprising that he recovers so quickly from what has happened.

Use a quote

"But if you're asking me to give my life marks out of ten, I'm afraid I couldn't go any higher than three. This isn't what I had in mind. How could it be?" (p.336)

Sam doesn't value his life very much only giving it three out of ten, but he seems to overcome the crisis and sort everything out, which is a sign of maturity. On the surface Sam is quite a normal "kid". He does "OK" in school, he hasn't got any real ambitions in life except to become a famous skater. But there is a change when the baby comes. He takes care of and nurses his child, he finds a new and "better" girlfriend and he attends college.
What is really fascinating about Sam is his way of thinking about life. He says as soon as someone in his family makes a mistake there will be another person to correct it (the coming generations). His mother became a parent at 16, he became a parent at 16 and now Roof (his child) is born and hopefully he won't become a parent at the age of 16.
Since the novel is set in suburban London, it emphasizes the situation that Sam has got himself into. In the suburbs, there are many people without a future.
The slam helps Sam mature, but is he happy? It's really hard to tell whether he's really happy. The theme can appeal to many teenagers because this can happen to anyone and the story is told in a language that will appeal to young people.

The conclusion

Find a way of ending the review. It could be a conclusion that links up with the theme you've chosen.

There are many funny parts in this book, but as I start laughing, I stop almost immediately as I realize the sadness of the situation. Sam is in a real slam and he will never be able to escape from it.

To sum up

- The purpose of a review is to inform and evaluate e.g. a novel or a film.
- The writer and the title of the book/the name of the film and the director should be mentioned.
- The plot is briefly summarized.
- Time and place are mentioned.
- The main characters are described and analysed.
- Language style is commented on.
- The theme of the book or film is evaluated.

Firstly, pick a book that you'd really like to read.

When you've made your choice plan how many pages per day you have to read in order to meet your deadline. As you read, make notes about what's happening in the novel, how the characters develop, the importance of the setting and the time. Write down quotes that you can comment on.

When you've finished reading, decide on the theme for your review.

But before writing, make a plan of your review. What would be a good heading? How can you introduce the writer and the novel? (or the film and the director)? How can you summarize the plot in 5 to 10 sentences? What is relevant to the theme of your review?

Finally, decide how to end your review.

How to write instructions

Here's a guide to writing instructions on how to make a Pavlova.

How to Make Pavlova

Pavlova is a tasty dessert that is believed to come from either New Zealand or Australia and is named after the Russian ballet dancer Anna Pavlova who toured in both countries in the 1920s. ❶

The ingredients ❷

Serves 4–6 people

4 large free-range eggs

200 g caster sugar

2 teaspoons corn flour

1 teaspoon white wine vinegar

Step-by-step instructions ❸

Start by taking out the eggs from the fridge an hour or two before you start making the Pavlova base. Allow them to reach room temperature.

Prepare your baking sheet. Draw a 22 cm circle on baking paper and attach it to the baking sheet. Use a smear of butter if it won't stay in place.

Separate the eggs and put the whites in a large clean bowl and the yolk into a jug or cup.

Whip the egg whites using an electric whisk until they're standing in soft peaks.

Tip in 1/3 of the sugar and whisk it thoroughly.

Add the rest in two parts. Whisk in between.

Finally, stir in the corn flour and vinegar, fold with a metal spoon.

Turn out the mixture onto the prepared tray and spread it out to fit the circle.

Bake for an hour at 140°C. Do not open the oven door!

Switch off the oven and leave meringue to cool.

When cool, peel off the paper and put the base onto a presentation plate.

Serve with whipped cream and fruit of your choice.

1 The goal or end product is normally stated before the instructions are given. In this case your efforts will result in making a Pavlova. It's also common to have a picture or a drawing of what's to be achieved or made.

2 The second part of an instruction is information about what ingredients, items or pieces of equipment are needed – in this case the ingredients, namely eggs, caster sugar, corn flour and vinegar. If you were giving instructions on how to mend a puncture, the things you need would obviously be different.

3 Now give step-by-step instructions on how to do the task. These are usually divided into paragraphs or into numbered lists. Occasionally, illustrations may be included, for example when putting together something from IKEA.

The verbs in the text are always in the imperative form – add, tip, stir, serve, etc. And there's no irrelevant information. You only receive information about what you have to do next. Linking words such as first, second and finally are sometimes used.

Finally, in the case of making a Pavolva you get suggestions on how to serve it. In other types of instructions you might get information on how to use an item you have made, correctly or safely.

To sum up

How to write instructions

- Start by stating the goal.
- Introduce the ingredients or items needed.
- Give a list of step-by-step instructions. Use illustrations if required. The verbs are in the imperative form. Sometimes there are linking words such as first, second and finally.
- Finally, give some suggestions on what to do next.

How to write a formal letter

A letter written to a business, a college, or anyone not considered a friend or a family member should be written in a formal style. You need to keep to a strict and formal tone and to avoid informal language, for example short forms of verbs. Here is a letter written in answer to an advertisement for a flat to rent.

(1) 20 Chesterton Rd.
Chesterton Way
Leyfield
Tamworth B79 8DH
Tel: 074927718

Mrs B. Bridges (2)
18 Edward Road
Keresley
Coventry CV6 2GR

2 March 20XX (3)

Dear Mrs Bridges, (4)

Re: 2-bedroom flat to let in Vauxhall Road (5)

I am writing in answer to your advertisement for the above flat in Saturday's (6) Coventry Echo.
I have recently got a new job with HSBC bank in the centre of Coventry and need somewhere to live as it is too far to commute from Tamworth every day.
At present I am sharing a house with four other people, but there will be no problem leaving as someone else is already eager to move in.
I have lived at my present address for seven years and have always paid my rent on time. My landlord, Mr Garrett, is prepared to give me a reference. (Address supplied below.)
Would it be possible to view the flat as soon as possible as my job starts at the end of the month? (7)
I look forward to hearing from you in due course.

Yours sincerely, (8)

Charlotte Evans
Charlotte Evans (9)

This is my landlord's address:
David Garrett,
13 Leicester Road
Tamworth

1 Put your address on the right.

2 Put the address of the person you're writing to on the left.

3 Put the date under your address. You can write it in three ways:
March 2 2014 • 2 March 2014 • 2/3/14
NB in the US you write 3/2/14
Do not write 14-03-02.

4 Begin with a salutation:
Dear Sir, or Dear Madam
(if you don't know the name)
Dear Sir/Madam (if you don't know if it's a man or a woman)
Dear Mr/Mrs/Ms .... (if you know the surname of the person)

5 Where appropriate, you can use a heading to show what the letter is about. It often starts with the word Re: (which is short for regarding) and is usually underlined.

6/7 Set out a letter in brief paragraphs using formal English.
The first paragraph should be short and state the purpose of the letter.
The middle paragraph(s) should contain the relevant background information. Most letters in English aren't very long, so keep the information to the essentials and concentrate on organising it in a clear and logical manner rather than expanding too much.
Last sentence. If you're expecting a reply you can say:
I look forward to hearing from you in due course or I look forward to hearing from you soon.

8 End as follows:
Yours faithfully
(if you start with Dear Sir/Madam)
Yours sincerely
(if you start with Mr/Mrs)

9 Sign you name and type it underneath.

How to write a letter to the editor

When you're angry, upset or amused about something you've read in a newspaper or a magazine you can write a letter to the editor. You present your thesis (your opinion) and some arguments in support of it. Also try to make use of linking words!

Let's look at a letter written to the editor of the *National Post* complaining about the violence used in ice hockey in the NHL.

630 Eastern Avenue ❶
Toronto
Canada
M5M 1E4

5/21/18
The Editor ❷
National Post
150 Don Mills Road, Suite 300
Don Mills, Ontario
Canada
M6B 3R9

<u>Violence in NHL hockey</u> ❸

Dear Editor,
In answer to 'Tough Guys Still Hurt' (Friday September 8th)
I'm wondering when our NHL leaders will realize that fighting just doesn't have any place in hockey. Gary Bettman has always dreamed of raising the sport's profile in the U.S., but has consistently ignored the single largest segment of the population that could see him realize his goal – women. ❹

Firstly, we know fighting attracts a certain percentage of fans to the game. It's a sad fact, but it's reality. It seems, however, that nobody ever stops to think about the gains that could be made by making the game less violent. I could always get my former wife to watch Olympic hockey with me, but getting her to watch the NHL was impossible due to the violence. ❺

Secondly, sportsmen are supposed to be role models. Hockey players who encourage violence are hardly the role models we want for our children, so it's not surprising that many young people – especially young girls – are put off the sport. ❻

Finally, until the Neanderthal element of fighting is taken away from our beautiful game, hockey will be nothing but a minor sport – just a side show – in the minds of so many. ❼

Yours sincerely,

Marc Taillefer

Marc Taillefer ❽

1 Use the format of a formal letter. Start by putting your address on the right.
2 Next, put the newspaper's address on the left. Address it to The Editor. Also put the date on the left.
3 If you wish, you can think up a suitable heading to your letter. Start: Dear Editor.
4 Next there's an introduction with reference to a previous letter in the National Post on the issue of violence in NHL hockey. In this introductory paragraph, say what you think about NHL hockey.
5/6 In the body of your letter you present your arguments one by one. Try to make use of linking words! The first argument is about why violence in NHL hockey is excluding women.
The second argument is about role models and young people.
7 End your letter with a conclusion. You could perhaps make a recommendation or suggest some kind of action to be taken.
8 Finally, print your name under your signature.

To sum up

- Use the format of a formal letter.
- Start with a salutation.
- Make a reference to previous articles/articles if any.
- Present your thesis.
- Support your thesis with arguments. Use linking words!
- End your letter with a conclusion. Make a recommendation or a call for action.
- End the letter with Yours sincerely and your signature below.

How to write a project

Your task is to look closer at a subject area related to your education, to society, working life, cultural conditions, current issues or ethical issues.
Decide on a subject to investigate and what questions to answer. When using library books and encyclopedias or information from the Internet, use only sources in English.
Your project should consist of three parts: introduction, body and conclusion.
Use Times New Roman 12, spacing 1.5.

General outline

Title page

- The title of the project, your name and class.

Introduction

- State your subject and explain why you chose it.
- State the aim of your investigation. What you intend to do. What do you mean by this? What questions do you intend to answer?
- Keep this introduction short – maximum half a page.

Body

- What are your findings? No personal opinions in this part but only facts that you have found.
- The body of the project should be about 1½ pages.

Conclusion

- Discuss and draw some conclusions when summing up your project. Here you may comment and give your personal views on the result.
- Another half a page is sufficient.

References

- List the sources you have used.

Some advice when writing

Gather information

- Look for information from reliable sources. Use only sources in English.
- Look for useful information. Remember to list your sources for future reference. Be critical and compare different sources. (See p. 123.)
- Look up any words you don't understand.
- Write down keywords and/or draw a mindmap of your project.

Start writing

- Make a timetable showing when you'll have time to write and check your text. This will help you to meet your deadline.
- Use the general outline as you write your project.
- Don't 'copy paste'. Make sure you don't use or copy text from another writer. If you wish to quote another writer, show this by using quotation marks.
- Remember to structure your text using linking words! (See p. 142.)
- *Remember to hand in your project in good time.*

How to present your project

Follow these guidelines and the audience will enjoy your presentation.

- Use keywords or a mind map and practise giving your presentation until you can do it more or less by heart. In other words be prepared to practise a lot before your presentation.
- When speaking, make sure that you have eye contact most of the time with your audience.
- Try to be relaxed, use body language and facial expressions. Make eye contact with listeners, change your position in the room slightly, smile occasionally and so on.
- Use Powerpoint, pictures, music, maps, etc. to make your presentation more interesting.
- Keep you presentation to approximately 3-4 minutes.
- End your presentation by saying, *Thank you for listening.*

5 HOW TO USE LINKING WORDS

Linking words are essential for your writing to be natural and clear. They help you to connect ideas and sentences, so that people can follow your ideas. A piece of writing without linking words reads like a series of unrelated statements with no flow.

Linking words can be used to:

- link the flow of ideas in your writing.
- guide your reader towards the next stage of your argument.
- link paragraphs together.

Sample text

The words in **bold** in the following text are called linking words. When looking at the text you can see that the text would work without these linking words. Why use them? Well, the reason is that it helps the text to flow better, since one sentence naturally leads onto the next rather than having a text where sentences are simply piled one upon the other.

Paragraph one

Most families nowadays have a car **not only** for going back and forth to work **but also** for taking the children to and from various after school activities. **That is**, a car has become a necessity for most people **and** few can imagine life without one as it gives them freedom of movement.

This freedom of movement, **however**, has its negative side as more and more people spend increasing amounts of time being stuck in traffic jams and getting nowhere. **In other words**, this freedom has come at a great price and the situation is deteriorating year after year.

Paragraph two

So what can we do about it? **Firstly**, we need to make it less attractive for people to drive to work or into cities. **For example**, a congestion charge could be introduced, as in London, making people pay to enter the city centre between certain hours of the day. **In addition**, cars could be banned from entering city centres at peak times unless they have four people in them. This would have the effect of encouraging car sharing **rather than** having streams of cars with only one person in them.

Paragraph three

Another possibility is to encourage people to use public transport or to cycle to work. **For instance**, in London there are thousands of cycles to hire all over the city and it has been a resounding success.

To sum up, we cannot continue to use cars in the way we do now. Something has to change. **In reality**, it's unlikely that people will voluntarily give up their cars. **Furthermore**, there are very few politicians brave enough to pass such laws. **To put it simply**, the car and growing congestion are here to stay whether we like it or not.

Here's a selection of words used to link ideas, depending on the direction of your argument.

1 Adding more to a point already made

Also, Moreover, Furthermore, Again, What is more, In addition
Besides (that), Above all, As well as that,...
Not only... but, Similarly, In the same way, Likewise
In fact, In reality, It is found that...
As for, As to, With respect to, Regarding

Taking cannabis regularly can be addictive. *Furthermore/In addition/Moreover* it can lead to taking harder drugs such as heroin.

2 Writing in lists

Firstly, Second(ly), Third(ly)
Another, Yet another, In addition
To begin with, In the second place
Moreover, Additionally, In addition, Also
Next, Then, After that
And to conclude, Lastly, Finally

Too much caffeine is bad for your health. *Firstly/To begin* with, it is very addictive. *Secondly/In addition* it can lead to high blood-pressure.

3 Putting the same idea in a different way

In other words, Rather, In that case
To put it (more) simply...
In view of this, With this in mind
To look at this another way,...

Dogs are cuddly, loving, loyal and fun – *in other words* the perfect pet.

4 Introducing examples
That is (to say), In other words
For example, For instance, Namely, An example of this is...
As follows, As in the following examples, Such as, Including
Especially, Particularly, In particular, Specifically, Mainly, Mostly, Generally, Usually

> There are many different ways of getting rich – *for example/for instance*, you could win £1 million on the National Lottery.

5 Introducing an alternative viewpoint
By contrast, Another way of viewing this is..., Alternatively
One alternative is..., Another possibility is...
On the one hand..., On the other hand...
Conversely, In comparison, On the contrary, Though, Although

> 'Are you in favour of fox hunting?'
> 'No. *On the contrary*, I believe it's cruel, barbaric and should be banned.'
> *On the one hand*, people want a high standard of education and medical care, but *on the other hand* they aren't ready to pay for it through higher taxes.

6 Returning to emphasize your earlier viewpoint
However, Nonetheless, Nevertheless, Despite this fact, Although, Though, At the same time, On the other hand, All the same, Even if X is true,...

> A lot of money has already been spent on education. *However/Nevertheless*, a lot more will need to be spent in the future.
>
> New Zealand is a very small country. *Nonetheless/Despite this fact*, it has produced a large number of world class sportsmen and sportswomen.

7 Showing the results of something
Therefore, Accordingly, As a result
So, it can be seen that...
The result is..., The consequence is..., And that is way
Resulting from this, Consequently, As a consequence
We can see that..., It is evident that...
Because of this, Thus, For this/that reason, Owing/Due to X...
This suggests that ..., It follows that ...

He didn't work hard enough at university, and *consequently/as a result* failed his final exams.

The job meant moving to Canada for three years. *For that reason/Because of this,* she turned it down.

Our roads are getting increasingly congested. The government, *therefore/accordingly,* needs to do something to persuade more and more people to use public transport.

James was out fishing for the day on September 11, 2001. *Thus/Therefore* he didn't know about the terrorist attack on the World Trade Center in New York until he got home later that evening.

8 Summing up or concluding

Therefore, So, My conclusion is...
In short, In conclusion, To conclude, On the whole
To summarize, To sum up briefly, In brief, Thus, we can see that...

In conclusion, there can be no doubt that smoking causes lung cancer and other respiratory diseases.

6 INTERACT AND DISCUSS

I think...
In my opinion...
I believe that...
I feel that...
If you ask me...
Well, as I see it,...
The way I see things,...

How do you feel about...?
What's your feeling about...?
What do you think of/about...?
What's your opinion, (Jake)?
Would you agree that...?

Yes, I agree (with you).
Yes, you're right.
That's what I think too.
I agree with (Anna).
I couldn't agree more!
That's exactly how I feel.
Absolutely!/ Definitely!
Exactly!/ Precisely!

Yes, I agree but...
I agree in a way, but...
I see/get what you mean but...
I see/get what you're saying but...

I don't agree.
No, I disagree.
I'm sorry, I don't agree with you there.
I'm not sure about that.
No, I think you're wrong.

That's rubbish!
Come off it!
What a lot of crap! (very informal)

Can I just say something?
Can I (just) make a point here?
Can I get a word in, please!

I'm afraid I don't follow you.
I'm sorry, could you explain that again, please?

That's not quite what I meant.
I think you've misunderstood me.

7 PICK AND CHOOSE - EXERCISES FOR EXTRA READING

Discuss/Writing - general questions on fact and fiction

1 What's the title of the text?
2 Who wrote it?
3 Who's the main character? Describe him/her.
4 Are there any other people in the story/text? Describe them.
5 Where and when does the story take place?
6 What can you say about the type of language used?
7 Does the story/text have a message? If so, what is it?
8 Did you like the story/text? Give reasons.
9 What reflections did you make when reading the story/text?

Speaking/Acting

- Write down some key words and retell the text to a friend.
- Invite one of the characters to your "talk show". Prepare questions and interview him/her about his/her life.
- If the text has lots of dialogue, then try rewriting parts of it as a play. Then act it out with others.
- Make a presentation by using facts from a text you have read.

Writing

- One of the main characters is tweeting about something that has happened. What does he/she write?
- Write an email to one of the characters who perhaps has a problem, giving them advice on what to do.
- Continue writing the story. What happens after the end of it? Use your imagination!
- If you didn't like the end of the story, then try rewriting it with your own ending.
- Write a newspaper article based on facts from the text.
- Write an instruction on how to deal with a certain situation.
- Write a summary of the text.

Focus on language

- Look up any words you didn't understand.
- Write down useful phrases that would be good to know when speaking or writing.
- Were there any idioms or proverbs in the text? If so find out what they mean.
- Pick out 8–10 words and try to find synonyms or definitions for these words or try writing your own sentences using these words.

Find out more

- Find facts about the writer of the story.
- If you enjoyed the story, why not read a complete book by that author.
- Use *Suggested Links* to search the Internet for more information on a topic. Watch a film or a TV programme dealing with the topic you've studied.

1 GET DOWN TO IT

THE RIGHT LEVEL?

☐ Let's talk!
☐ Textwork
☐ Vocabulary: Definitions
☐ Interact
☐ Personal profile
☐ Check your English

WSM: NINE REASONS WHY ...

FOCUS ON GRAMMAR

LOSING MY VIRGINITY

☐ Starter
☐ Textwork
☐ Vocabulary: Right or wrong?
☐ Interact
☐ Speaking: A narrative
☐ Writing

PHENOMENAL WOMAN

☐ Interact

ROCK WHAT YOU'VE GOT

☐ Starter
☐ Interact
☐ Vocabulary: Words of similar meaning
☐ Idioms that describe people

LISTENING: FREEDOM WRITERS DIARY

☐ Starter
☐ Listen and recall
☐ Interact
☐ Looking at phrasal verbs 1
☐ Vocabulary Bank: Useful verbs 1

CHEAT!

☐ Starter
☐ Textwork
☐ Vocabulary: What does it mean?
☐ Activity

☐ Fun with vocabulary 1
☐ Sum up and comment
☐ Books to read and enjoy

THE RIGHT LEVEL? (page 10)

001 Let's talk!

Things we have in common

Work in groups of 3–4. How much do you have in common? Here's your chance to find out. Read and discuss the following and write down your answers.

Try to find:

1 a country or city you'd all like to visit one day. ____________
2 something you're all afraid of. ____________
3 some kind of exercise you all do at least twice a week. ____________
4 a "pet hate" you all share. ____________
5 a dish that's a favourite with everyone. ____________
6 the worst film you've all seen. ____________
7 a person you all admire and respect. ____________
8 something very expensive you'd all like to have. ____________

002 Textwork

Show that you've understood the text *The Right Level?* by completing the statements below with information from the text. Sometimes one or two words are enough.

1 The writer will be studying Italian for ________ hours a week.
2 She had got ready for her first day at the school the previous night by ________ .
3 Everyone on their first day has to take a test to make sure they are placed ________ .
4 The writer thinks being put in a Level One class would be ________ .
5 The test has both a written and an ________ part. She ends up in a ________ class.
6 She realized quite quickly that the level she had chosen ________ .
7 Compared to her, the rest of the people in the class seemed ________ in Italian.
8 Once the break comes she decides to ________ .

Practise the vocabulary in Wordmatch/Spelling

003 Vocabulary: Definitions

Here are definitions of eight words from the text. Can you work out what they are? To help you, the first and last letter of each missing word is given.

1 If an experience is ________ then it makes you feel ashamed or stupid and you may even lose the respect of others. h________g
2 To learn something so that you'll remember it exactly. m________e
3 One of the periods into which a year is divided at a college or university, especially in the USA. s________r

4 Another word for 'choose'. s________t

5 A person who's the same age as you or who has the the same type of job, social status, etc. p________r

6 Having a pleasantly soft rounded body or shape. It's a polite way of saying 'slightly fat'. p________p

7 When a person is ________ in a language, they can speak it really well. f________t

8 To run with quick, short steps. s________y

004 Interact

1 What do you think is a) the easiest thing b) the most difficult thing about learning English?

2 Which of the four language skills do you find most difficult in English – listening, speaking, reading or writing?

005 Personal profile

1 How old are you? How might your age affect both what you know and your attitude toward gaining knowledge?

2 What's your mother tongue? What other languages do you speak? How might your particular languages affect your knowledge e.g. about traditions, food, music?

3 What are your previous experiences of learning English? What strategies have you used when learning a language?

See Resource Section SLP p. 117 for advice on studying.

WSM: (WANT SOME MORE?)

Nine Reasons Why the English Language Is So Hard to Learn!

1 As she gave a slight **bow** of her head as a greeting, I noticed that she had a pink **bow** in her hair.

2 I think it's time to **polish** up my **Polish** before I go to Warsaw.

3 The French soldier decided to **desert** in the middle of the **desert**.

4 Although the **object** was very ugly, no one seemed to **object** to it.

5 They couldn't **close** the door because the bed was too **close** to it.

6 Amelia shed a **tear** after seeing a large **tear** in her favourite dress.

7 The committee have agreed to **present** their report to those **present** after lunch.

8 I'd love to **record** a **record**. The trouble is, I can't sing!

9 There was a **row** among the Oxford boat race team about how fast to **row**.

Try saying the above sentences out loud. How would you translate the words in **bold** type?

006 **Check your English**

The writer had to take a test to see how much Italian she already knew. This is a chance to see how much English you already know - especially English vocabulary. Work in groups of 3–4. Your teacher will give you more information.

FOCUS ON GRAMMAR

In this book you will work with grammar like this:

- In each chapter you will find *Focus on Grammar*.
- *Focus on Grammar* will tell you what to work with in each unit.
- Each grammar rule is explained in the Grammar section at the back of the textbook. References to these pages are given in each unit.
- In your e-book there are links to exercises to improve your grammar. These exercises are numbered and referred to in each unit.
- When writing a text don't forget to consult your grammar and also the *Checklist for writing* in the *Resource Section* p. 126.

FOCUS ON GRAMMAR

	Grammar	Interactive exercise
NOUNS		
Nouns in the plural	p. 313 ⧉	⧉
Countable/Uncountable nouns	p. 314 ⧉	
The Genitive	p. 315 ⧉	⧉
The Indefinite Article	p. 315 ⧉	
The Definite Article	p. 316 ⧉	

LOSING MY VIRGINITY (page 12 ⧉)

007 **Starter**

Work in small groups. What do you remember about your early schooldays? Think about:

The school you went to	A happy memory
The teachers	A school tradition
Your friends	A school outing

⧉ **Reading strategies p. 118. Try some new methods and become a better reader.**

008 **Textwork**

Read through the text *Losing My Virginity* and answer the following questions.

1 What two problems did Richard Branson have when he first went to school?

______

2 How were people with dyslexia regarded in those days?

______

3 What often happened to him at prep school?

______

4 What was he good at and how did that help him?

______

5 What happened in 1961 when he did the long jump?

______

6 What happened to him during a game of football?

______

7 What happened while they were operating on him in the hospital?

______

Say which of the following sentences which, according to the text, are true. (They're in no special order.)

a Sport is very important in British public schools. ______
b Richard Branson has now managed to overcome his dyslexia. ______
c Douglas Bader is someone who had lost both his legs. ______
d At school, Richard Branson was captain of the hockey team. ______
e His best friend at school was Victor Ludorum. ______
f Virgin originally sold records via mail order. ______
g *Losing My Virginity* was written by a journalist. ______
h At school, Richard Branson was very good at running. ______
i His mother felt sorry for him when he was recovering at home. ______

Practise the vocabulary in Wordmatch/Spelling

009 **Vocabulary: Right or wrong?**

Work in pairs. Check that you have understood some of the words used in *Losing My Virginity* by stating whether they are used correctly in the following sentences. Mark each sentence R (Right) or W (Wrong). If wrong, explain why and write a new sentence to show how the words should be used.

1 Our survey shows that one in four children is **bullied** at school. ______
2 Andrew Morton once wrote an **autobiography** of Princess Diana. ______
3 I have to hold the newspaper at arm's length when I read, as I'm terribly **short-sighted**. ______
4 His grandfather **founded** the company in 1882. ______

5 She fell off her horse and tore a **cartilage** in her back. ______
6 My grandmother has photographs of all her grandchildren on the **mantelpiece**. ______
7 The boat **soared** through the water. ______
8 It took her over six months to **recover** from her operation. ______
9 A woman was found at the side of the road by a cyclist. She was **unconscious** and could only speak very quietly. ______
10 Students learning English often **confuse** 'your' and 'you're'. ______
11 He's a **keen** sportsman and enjoys playing tennis, cricket and rugby. ______
12 They hired a large wooden **marquee** for the wedding party. ______

010 Interact

1 Richard Branson was bullied at school. How do you deal with bullying in your school? Come up with a 5-step program to stop bullying in schools.
2 What do you know about cyber bullying – especially on social network sites? What should be done about it, do you think?

011 Speaking: A narrative

The text about Branson is a narrative text. Work with a partner and take turns to retell parts of the text. Use keywords when retelling a story. This time you will be given some suggestions.

Branson – chairman – autobiography – trouble – dyslexic – stupid or lazy – good at sports – school hero – captain – long jump – hurt his knee – hospital – mother's advice

012 Writing

Richard Branson is a famous entrepreneur. Here are some others. Choose one and present a short biography of that person.

Warren Buffet (Investor)
Henry Ford (Ford Motor Company)
Howard Hughes (Aviation – TWA)
Estée Lauder (Cosmetics)
Pierre Omidyar (eBay)
Larry Page (Google, Inc)
Anita Roddick (The Body Shop)
Vera Wang (Fashion)
Oprah Winfrey (Harpo, Inc)

PHENOMENAL WOMAN (page 14)

First practise the vocabulary in Wordmatch/Spelling

013 Interact

1 What do you think the woman looks like?
2 How does she look at herself in the poem?
3 What do you think about the poem?

ROCK WHAT YOU'VE GOT (page 16)

014 Starter

Here are 25 adjectives to describe someone's personality. Working alone, write down five of the adjectives that **best** describe you.

affectionate, ambitious, cautious, cheerful, confident, determined, easy-going, efficient, forgetful, funny, hard-working, imaginative, impatient, impulsive, modest, outspoken, patient, punctual, reliable, sensible, sensitive, shy, stubborn, superstitious, talkative

Five adjectives that best describe me

Now find a partner. Compare and discuss what you have written. Are there any other words not in the list that you would have used?

015 Interact

Work in pairs. Take turns to ask and answer the following questions.

1 What did the mother do to support her daughter? Comment on her strategies to change her daughter´s way of thinking.
2 How important a role do parents or teachers have in making a child feel confident?
3 How can a person best build up his or her confidence and self-esteem?
4 How can you be more supportive to your classmates in school? Come up with five suggestions.

Practise the vocabulary in Wordmatch/Spelling

016 Vocabulary: Words of similar meaning

Complete the pairs of words below with another word that's similar in meaning. Choose from the following words, all taken from the text.

articulate	chubby	confident	flaw	sob
awkward	comfort	disgusting	implement	various

1 revolting, repellent, ____________
2 console, cheer someone up, ____________
3 weep, cry, ____________
4 say, enunciate, ____________
5 apply, carry out, ____________
6 assorted, diverse, ____________
7 positive, self-assured, ____________
8 difficult, troublesome, ____________
9 defect, fault, ____________
10 plump, tubby, ____________

017 Idioms that describe people

A Complete the definitions below with a suitable idiom. Choose from the following. Use a dictionary if necessary.

absent-minded	henpecked	light-fingered	thick-skinned
brainy	highly strung	long in the tooth	tight-fisted
down-at-heel	hot-blooded	pig-headed	two-faced
full of beans	laid back	stuck up	well-off

1 If you describe someone as ________, you mean that they're old.
2 Someone who's ________ is insensitive to criticism and isn't easily offended.
3 A ________ person is mean and doesn't like spending money.
4 A ________ person is very intelligent and is especially good at studying.
5 Someone who's ________ is very relaxed and doesn't seem to be worried about anything.
6 An ________ person tends to forget things because they're often thinking about something else.
7 If a man is described as ________, this means that he's always being told what to do by his wife and is afraid to disagree with her.
8 A ________ person is someone who thinks they're better or more important than other people.
9 A ________ person is very nervous and is easily upset.
10 If you describe someone as being ________, you mean that they've got a lot of money.
11 A child who is ________ is very lively.
12 If you describe someone as ________, you mean that they have a habit of stealing things.

13 Someone who's __________ is determined to do things their way and refuses to change their mind, even when there's a good reason for doing so. In other words, they're very stubborn.

14 A __________ person is someone dressed in old, worn-out clothes usually because they don't have much money.

15 A __________ person is very insincere and might agree with you to your face but will disagree with you behind your back.

16 Someone who's __________ is very emotional and passionate and tends to do things without thinking first.

B Now discuss the following in small groups.

1 Do you know anyone who's really **tight-fisted**? Why do you think some people are like this?
2 Do you think women are more **highly strung** than men? Give reasons.
3 How much money would a person in Sweden have to earn to be considered **well off**?
4 Think of some jobs where it might be useful (or even necessary) to be a bit **thick-skinned**.
5 Not only people but places can sometimes be **down-at-heel**. Can you think of any places you've visited that are beginning to look a bit down-at-heel?
6 Which would you prefer to be – popular or **brainy**? Give reasons.

LISTENING: FREEDOM WRITERS DIARY

018 **Starter**

1 What famous diaries do you know of?
2 What do people usually write about in their diaries?
3 A blog is another way of commenting on everyday life. What do you think about blogs? Do you read any? Which ones? Why? Why not?

019 **Listen and recall** To listen, follow this link

Listen to the following Diary entry and then answer the questions below by completing the sentences.

1 Why is Erin worried about her students thinking she's too young?
Because they __________________ .
2 Why are her friends worried about her going to teach in Long Beach?
Because __________________ .
3 Who called Long Beach California the 'gangsta-rap capital'?
It was __________________.
4 What kind of students attend the school?
According to Erin __________________.
5 What do students who live in what they call 'the hood' have to do every day?
They have to __________________

6 In what way has the Rodney King riots affected the school?
Since the Rodney King riots, ________________________.

7 The demographics of the school has changed. In what way?
The majority of students now ________________________.

8 What rumour did Erin hear about a student called Sharaud?
They say he had ________________________.

9 What seemed to be Sharaud's sole purpose in school?
He wanted to ________________________.

10 What sort of drawing did one of the students make of Sharaud?
It was a caricature where his lips ________________________,

11 Erin was very angry and compared this to what?
She compared it to the propaganda used by ________________________.

12 What really shocked Erin?
The fact that the students had never heard of ________________________.

13 What question did she ask which made almost every student put their hand up?
How many ________________________?

14 Erin decided to make tolerance the core of her curriculum and to bring history to life.
How was she going to do this?
By using ________________________, inviting ________________________ and going on ________________________.

020 **Interact**

1 What kind of person is Ms Gruwell?
2 Why did the picture of Sharaud trigger her to talk about the Holocast?
3 What do you think about her choice of teaching methods?
4 *The Freedom Writers Diary* has also been filmed? Have you seen it? What did you think of it?

Practise the vocabulary in Wordmatch/Spelling

021 **Looking at phrasal verbs 1**

Phrasal verbs with 'on' and 'off'

A Complete the definitions below with a suitable phrasal verb. Choose from the following and make any verb changes where necessary.

break off	count on	lay off	show off
bring on	drop off	pick on	tell off
catch on	go on	put off	try on

1 If you ______________ someone, you rely on them for their help and support.
2 If you ______________ a relationship, you end it.
3 If you ______________ someone ______________, you distract them in some way or discourage them from doing something.

4 If you __________ a piece of clothing, you put it on to see whether it fits and looks nice.
5 If something __________ an illness or physical discomfort, then it's the cause of it.
6 If an employer __________ workers, they lose their jobs, often temporarily, because there's no more work for them to do.
7 If you __________ someone __________, you scold or reprimand them for something they've done wrong.
8 If something __________, it becomes popular or fashionable.
9 To __________ means to fall asleep.
10 If you __________ doing something, you continue doing it.
11 People who __________ try to impress others with their skills or abilities.
12 If you __________ someone, you repeatedly and unfairly treat them badly, often by punishing them or giving them boring or unpleasant jobs to do.

B Now work in pairs or small groups and discuss the following.

1 Who do you think **show off** more – boys or girls? Give reasons.
2 Why is it wrong to **pick on** people? What makes some people do that?
3 Which fashions or websites have really **caught on** in the past year or so?
4 Name three things that would **put** you **off** eating a certain dish.

022 **Vocabulary Bank: Useful verbs 1**

There are a number of verbs, adjectives and nouns that are common both in speech and in writing which can be considered as 'essential' vocabulary which needs to be a part of your own vocabulary bank. In *Sold Gold 1* you'll get a chance to build on and revise some of the most useful ones. Let's start with verbs. Put the correct verb in each sentence. Change the verb form where necessary. Choose from:

admit bribe pretend punish waste

1 In some countries, it's quite normal to __________ government officials or police officers. *(muta)*
2 Don't __________ your money doing the National Lottery. You haven't got a hope of winning! *(slösa bort)*
3 James wanted to go home early, so he __________ to be ill. *(låtsas)*
4 'All right! I __________ it! I broke the vase!' Tom said to his mother. 'But it was an accident!' *(erkänna, medge)*
5 Do you think we should __________ criminals or try to cure them? *(straffa)*

Now turn to page 302 in Vocabulary Bank and do *Useful verbs 1*.

CHEAT! (page 19 ⧉)

023 **Starter**

1 How reliable is Wikipedia as a source?
2 What kind of sources would you recommend?
3 Read about critical reading and reviewing of sources in Resource Section p. 123.
4 Cut and paste is regarded as cheating. What other ways of cheating have you heard of?

024 **Textwork**

Read through the text *Cheat!* and decide which of the four alternatives (A, B, C or D) you think is correct. Sometimes two answers are correct.

1 Which new ways of cheating in exams are being used by some American students?
- A ☐ They use their cell phones to take a photo of the exam paper.
- B ☐ They text each other during the exam.
- C ☐ They get help from friends outside the classroom using their cell phones.
- D ☐ They photograph their answers using a special pen.

2 At the testing center of the University of Central Florida why aren't students allowed to chew gum?
- A ☐ Because it makes a mess.
- B ☐ Because they want to be able to see if a student is speaking to someone else outside the exam room.
- C ☐ Because they could pretend to speak to the person next to them.
- D ☐ Because they might choke during the exam.

3 Why is it impossible for the students to cheat using scratch paper?
- A ☐ Because they're not allowed to write on it.
- B ☐ Because the stamped date on it prevents them from handing in a different scratch sheet.
- C ☐ Because they're only allowed one sheet of paper altogether.
- D ☐ Because they're not allowed to take it out of the exam room.

4 What does a proctor do when he or she suspects a student of cheating?
- A ☐ He or she records her findings into a tape recorder as evidence.
- B ☐ He or she phones the police.
- C ☐ He or she takes photos of the student and stores them on her computer.
- D ☐ He or she films the student and copies the result onto a CD.

5 What do many students do?
- A ☐ Pass off work they've copied from the Internet as their own.
- B ☐ Try to cheat on assignments.
- C ☐ Download music from the Internet and pretend it's their own.
- D ☐ Share assignments by cutting and pasting from the Internet.

6 What do you learn about anti-plagiarism services?
   A ☐ They're being used by a third of all universities.
   B ☐ They're being used more and more.
   C ☐ They can tell if a student's work has been copied from the Internet.
   D ☐ They have prevented all cheating.

Practise the vocabulary in Wordmatch/Spelling

Another exercise on the vocabulary in the word list

025 Vocabulary: What does it mean?

You're now going to explain the meaning of some of the words used in the text *Cheat!* Complete the following sentences by giving English explanations of the words in **bold**. Make your explanations as exact as possible. Use a dictionary if necessary.

Example: Gum is a type of sweet that you ________ but don't usually swallow.
(*Answer*: chew)

1. If you describe something as **eternal** you mean that it lasts or goes on for ________ .
2. If a business is **booming**, then it's ________ .
3. An **accomplice** is a person who ________ .
4. To **cheat** in an exam is to behave ________ .
5. You use **scratch paper** for ________ .
6. In the USA, a **proctor** is someone who ________ .
7. In a **survey** people are usually asked ________ .
8. **Plagiarism** is when you ________ .
9. If you **snap** something (e.g. an exam paper), it means you ________ .
10. To **interpret** a dream means to try to ________ .

026 Activity

1. Search the Internet and pick two articles, one that you believe is telling the truth and one that you don't believe in. Give reasons.
2. What criteria would you use to tell the difference between a generally trustworthy website from an untrustworthy one?

027 Fun with vocabulary 1

Too many words

Work in pairs. Replace the words in **bold** type in the following sentences with a single word. To help you, the first letter of the missing word is given.

1 My sister is a **person who performs operations at a hospital.** s__________
2 She was a happy person who was always **expecting the best to happen**. o__________
3 James **said he was sorry** for arriving late. a__________
4 We've just booked a **holiday on a large ship** this summer – to the Mediterranean. c__________
5 Most of the **people who worked on the ship** were from Pakistan. c__________
6 This is my **brother's son**, Jack. n__________
7 Years after the accident, Julia still had **frightening dreams** about it. n__________
8 The **dead body of a person** was found by a man walking his dog in the woods. c__________
9 I've only seen my ex-wife once since the **legal ending of our marriage**. d__________
10 There was a large sign near the entrance saying '**people who steal from shops** will be prosecuted'. s__________
11 At the end of the war, Mata Hari was hanged as a **person who betrayed her country**. t__________
12 Be careful with that vase. It's **easily broken or damaged**! f__________
13 As I read my mother's letter, I began to feel more and more **unhappy because of being away from home and missing my family and friends**. h__________
14 My sister's **going to have a baby**, so she's stopped smoking. p__________
15 Jake has been **out of work** for over 6 months. u__________
16 Many people believe that a Third World War is **bound to happen**. i__________

028 Sum up and comment

1 What new strategies are you using when learning English?
2 What did you learn from reading *Rock What You've Got*?
3 What goals do you have with your studies in English?
4 What can you keep in mind when choosing a website from the Internet?

029 Books to read and enjoy

Branson, Richard: *Losing My Virginity*
Dahl, Roald: *Matilda**
Gilbert, Elizabeth: *Eat Pray Love*
Gruwell, Erin: *Freedom Writers Diary*
Hustvedt, Siri: *The Summer Without Men*
Kleinbaum, N.H: *Dead Poets Society**
Rhue, Morton: *The Wave**
Schwarzenegger, Katherine: *Rock What You've Got*

* teenage fiction or less advanced books.

2 MAKE IT HAPPEN

LISTENING: DOWN THE NIAGARA FALLS

- ☐ Starter
- ☐ Listen and recall
- ☐ Interact
- ☐ Writing/Speaking

WSM: MILLIONS WATCH ...

FOCUS ON GRAMMAR

FRY AND JOBS – STEPHEN MEETS STEVE

- ☐ Let's talk!
- ☐ Starter
- ☐ Textwork
- ☐ Vocabulary: Fill in the gaps
- ☐ Interact

WSM: STEVE JOBS – A MAN OF VISION

- ☐ Activity

ENCOUNTERS

- ☐ Starter
- ☐ Interact
- ☐ Vocabulary: Choose the meaning
- ☐ Focus on words to do with the environment
- ☐ Writing: Giving instructions

WSM: THE STORY OF GREYFRIARS BOBBY

LISTENING: ENCOUNTERS CONT.

- ☐ Listen and recall
- ☐ Vocabulary: Matching pairs
- ☐ Interact
- ☐ Speaking
- ☐ Looking at phrasal verbs 2

- ☐ Vocabulary Bank: Useful verbs 2
- ☐ Useful Expressions: Idioms 1
- ☐ Sum up and comment
- ☐ Books to read and enjoy

LISTENING: DOWN THE NIAGARA FALLS

030 **Starter**

How brave or daring are you?

Work alone. How brave are you? Which of the following would you do? Mark each one 1-5.
1 = *Yes, definitely* **2** = *Yes, maybe* **3** = *I'm not sure* **4** = *No, probably not*
5 = *No, definitely not*

I would...

hold a python or large spider. ______
get up and sing on my own in a karaoke bar. ______
go on a really scary rollercoaster ride. ______
lean over the side of a high building to admire the view. ______
make a speech in public. ______
dive off a high cliff into the sea. ______
go and help somebody who was being attacked. ______
get on a bus or train alone, wearing a silly fancy-dress costume. ______
jump into a river to save someone who was drowning. ______
give someone the kiss of life. ______

Now form groups of 4–5. Compare and discuss your answers.
What's the bravest thing you've ever done?

Become a better listener by trying some new methods.
Have a look at *Listening strategies* in Resource Section p. 119.

---

031 **Listen and recall** To listen, follow this link

Listen to the interview between a journalist for the *Bay City Times Press* and Annie Edson Taylor, a 63-year-old woman who, the day before – on October 24, 1901 – became the first person to go over the Niagara Falls in a barrel and survive. As you listen, say whether the sentences are true (T) or false (F). Before you start, read through the sentences and check the words in the word list.

1 She was completely unhurt after going over the Falls. ________
2 She believed she would survive the attempt. ________
3 There was plenty of room in the barrel. ________
4 The barrel had a small air hole to enable her to breathe. ________
5 The barrel had an animal inside it for the trial run. ________
6 She did it because she wanted to be rich and famous. ________
7 She was born in the 18th century in New York State. ________
8 She got married to David Taylor but quickly divorced him. ________
9 She lived for a time in Mexico City. ________
10 Her first thought was to walk across the Niagara Falls on a tightrope. ________
11 She floated down the Niagara River for about 20 minutes before the barrel went over the Falls. ________
12 She was quite rich when she died. ________
13 You're not allowed to do any Niagara Falls stunts nowadays. ________

032 **Interact**

Work in pairs. Take turns to ask and answer the following questions.

1 Annie Taylor wanted to be rich and famous. Do you think this is a common desire in most people? How easy is it to be rich and famous nowadays?
2 She finally decided that to get the world's attention she'd try to go over the Niagara Falls in a barrel. She called herself a 'daredevil'. How would you describe a 'daredevil'?
3 What was the most amazing thing about her feat?
4 Do you know of any similar daredevils and their feats?

Practise the vocabulary in Wordmatch/Spelling

033 **Writing/Speaking**

Here are the opening words of four dialogues. Working in pairs (one is A and one is B), choose one of the dialogues and see if you can continue it by writing at least another 10–12 lines. When you have finished, find another pair. Read out your dialogue to them and listen to theirs.

1

A: I wish I hadn't done it.
B: Sorry?
A: I said I wish I hadn't done it.
B: Done what?

2

A: Excuse me, but don't I know you?
B: No, I don't think so.
A: Yes, I'm sure we've met before.
B: Have we?
A: Yes, it was three years ago in ...

3

A: *(answering the phone)* 894320.
B: Oh, good morning. I'm phoning about the item you have for sale.
A: The pet crocodile, you mean?
A: Yes, that's right.

4

A: Stop doing that!
B: What?
A: You heard me. I saw you! Stop doing that!
B: I don't know what you're talking about!

WSM:
MILLIONS WATCH AS FELIX BAUMGARTNER BREAKS SOUND BARRIER WITH 24-MILE LEAP

FOCUS ON GRAMMAR

	Grammar	Interactive exercise
PRONOUNS		
The Possessive Pronoun	p. 317	
The Reflexive Pronoun	p. 317	
The Relative Pronoun	p. 317	
Some and Any	p. 318	
There is (There's) / There are	p. 318	
There is/are... / It is (It's)...	p. 318	

FRY AND JOBS – STEPHEN MEETS STEVE (page 22)

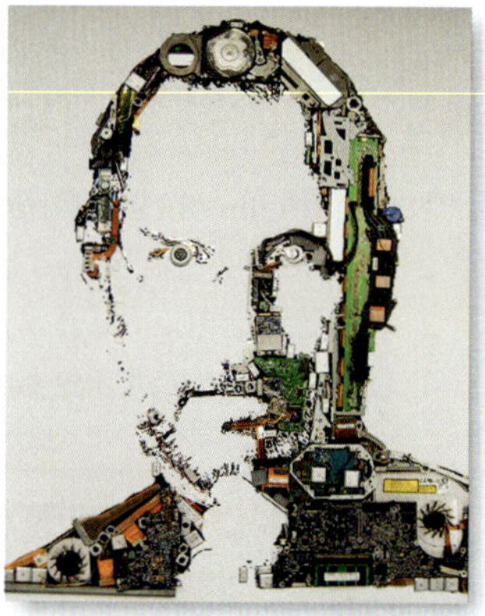

034 Let's talk!

Twenty Questions

Work in two groups – A and B (2–3 people per group). Group A looks at this page. Group B turns to page 297.
Below are ten questions to ask group B. They also have ten questions to ask you. But you yourselves decide which question to answer each time by choosing a number between 1–10. Say to Group B: *Ask us question (3).* Then cross the number out so you don't get the same question again!

Take turns to ask and answer. When you answer, one person can start and the rest of the group can join in. *You start by choosing a number.*

1	2	3	4	5	6	7	8	9	10

1 Who's the most boring person you've ever met? What made him or her so boring?
2 What things from Sweden would you miss if you ever emigrated to another country?
3 Who's the most important person in the history of your country and why?
4 Which person from history would you most like to have met and why?
5 What three pieces of advice would you give to a foreigner wishing to live and work in Sweden?
6 What do you consider to be the most important thing in the upbringing of children?
7 Which film or book has made the greatest impression on you and why?

8 Who, in your opinion, is the greatest writer ever (living or dead) and what makes him or her so special?
9 If you were applying for a job, what three things would you mention as being your strengths?
10 If you could change one event in history, what would that be and why?

035 **Starter**

Make a list of five inventions that you personally couldn't live without.

1 ______________________________.
2 ______________________________.
3 ______________________________.
4 ______________________________.
5 ______________________________.

Now work in small groups. Compare and discuss your answers.

036 **Textwork**

Work in pairs. Read through the text *Fry and Jobs – Stephen meets Steve*. Take turns to ask and answer the following questions.

1 How was Stephen Fry feeling before meeting Steve Jobs?
2 What did he consider Steve Jobs to be?
3 Which six nouns does Fry use to describe Steve Jobs? Which one do you think is the most flattering?
4 According to Fry, Apple's success is due to six factors. Name four of them. Which, in your opinion, is the most important one?
5 What did Steve Jobs nearly always wear?
6 Why has Steve Jobs lost weight?
7 What had Stephen Fry forgotten to do when he started interviewing Jobs?
8 What had Steve Jobs stood in front of during the launch of the iPad? Why?
9 Which adjective does Steve Job use to describe the iPad and the experience of using it?
10 How many health scares has Steve Jobs had in the past five years?
11 When Fry finally gets his hands on the iPad, what happens after he has been using it for ten minutes?

Practise the vocabulary in Wordmatch/Spelling

037 **Vocabulary: Fill in the gaps**

Fill in the missing words in the sentences below. Choose from the following words, taken from the text. Then make up your own sentences for the four words that are left over.

amusement	grin	launch	profound
delicacy	impostor	obituaries	recently
encounter	insistence	opportunists	reliability
finish	intersection	patient	slide show

1 The President had a telephone conversation with an ______________ claiming to be Uganda's president.
2 Rolls-Royce cars are famous for their quality and ______________ .
3 A chance ______________ in a restaurant in New York with Stephen Spielberg led to her first movie role.
4 A product ______________ at Apple is always an exciting occasion.
5 No one was convinced by her ______________ that she was not to blame.
6 Their new kitchen top had a beautiful granite ______________ .
7 My father's death had a ______________ effect on us all. In fact, I don't think my mother ever got over it.
8 They were singing and dancing in the street, much to the ______________ of passers-by.
9 Some crimes are committed by ______________ who wander into student rooms to steal cash or credit cards.
10 We waited at the ______________ of Lone Road and Castle Street for the lights to change.
11 Because of their great ______________ , the books can't be moved.
12 My grandfather always reads the ______________ in *The Times* every morning, just to make sure he's still alive!

038 **Interact**

1 Have you ever bought an Apple product yourself? Which one or ones? Why did you buy them?
2 Apple gave us the iPod, iPhone and iPad. What other products would you like to see in the future?
3 How important is design when you buy a computer, a tablet or a phone?
4 How important is it to have the latest gadget? Is there status in that?
5 Do you think technological progress is too slow, too fast or just right for you?

WSM: STEVE JOBS - A MAN OF VISION

Without Steve Jobs and his incredible vision we wouldn't enjoy the range of user-friendly and powerful products we use today. But who was he – the man who gave us the Mac, the iPod, the iPhone, the iPad and iTunes?

He was born on February 24, 1955 in San Francisco, California. His parents – Joanne Simpson and Abdulfattah Jandali – were unmarried university students and decided to have him adopted. So he grew up with Clara and Paul Jobs near Silicon Valley.

When he was only 13 years old he met 18-year-old Stephen Wozniak, who was an electronics wiz kid. Years later – in 1976 – they started their own company which they called Apple Computer. In the early days they worked from the Jobs' family garage where they sold the Apple I and Apple II computers. Then in 1984 they introduced the Macintosh, the first user-friendly computer.

However, Steve Jobs sold his shares and resigned from the company in 1985 after a controversy with the board of directors. One of his next projects was Pixar, the company that made the computer-animated movie *Toy Story*, a huge success all over the world.

In 1997, Steve Jobs was back at Apple and began developing new products. A year later Apple launched the iMac followed by the iBook and – in 2001 – the iPod. It was one of Apple's greatest successes and completely revolutionized the music industry. Then in 2007, Jobs launched the iPhone – the first 'smartphone' which, just as the iPod had revolutionized music listening, completely changed the mobile phone industry and launched the idea of phone apps. Finally, in 2010, Jobs introduced the iPad which again became a hit worldwide.

Sadly, Steve Jobs was diagnosed with cancer in 2003, went through surgery but was not totally cured. He died on October 5, 2011 – the day following the launch of the iPhone 4S which he watched from his deathbed.

President Barack Obama said of Steve Jobs: "Steve was among the greatest of American innovators – brave enough to think differently, bold enough to believe he could change the world, and talented enough to do it."

039 **Activity**

1 How would you define science?
2 Would you regard the following as sciences? Give reasons.

Acupuncture - the belief that inserting needles into the body can relieve and cure various disorders.
Astrology - the belief that our characters are determined at the time of our birth.
Crystology - the belief that crystals have healing powers.
Graphology - the belief that by analysing a person's handwriting you can learn about that person's character.

ENCOUNTERS (page 25 ↗)

040 Starter

The top 10 animal horrors

People have a fear of certain animals and a list has been compiled by the Animal Planet website of what they consider to be 'The top 10 animal horrors'. Working in pairs or groups of three, look at the following list of fifteen animals and mark 1–10 the animals you think came top in the list (1= the greatest animal horror).

bats ____________

bees ____________

crocodiles ____________

dogs ____________

great white sharks ____________

grizzly bears ____________

lizards ____________

mice ____________

mosquitoes ____________

parasitic worms ____________

piranhas ____________

rats ____________

snakes ____________

spiders ____________

wolves ____________

bat fladdermus
grizzly bear gråbjörn
lizard ödla
parasitic worm parasitmask
piranha piraya

To check your answers, turn to page 298 ↗. Were you surprised by any of the results?
What about you? Which five animals do you fear most?
Are there any other animals that you think should be in the list?

041 Interact

Work in pairs. Take turns to ask and answer the following questions.

1 Why do you think she says she would feel sorry for the animals she sees and then leave?
2 Why did she think her visit was going to be a complete waste of time?
3 She says she was 'shocked' after going through the entrance. In what way?
4 What was her impression of the reptile enclosures?
5 Why do you think she described the crocodiles she saw as 'modern day dinosaurs'?
6 What were her first impressions of Steve Irwin?
7 What particularly impressed her about him?
8 She says 'I recognized the passion'. What does she mean by this?
9 She calls him a 'kindred spirit'. What does this mean?

Practise the vocabulary in Wordmatch/Spelling

Another exercise on the words in the word list

042 Vocabulary: Choose the meaning

The following words and expressions in **bold** are all found in the text. Mark the alternative (A, B, C or D) that best corresponds to the meaning of the words and expressions as they are used in the text.

1 ... on an unlikely **quest** to find homes for rescued American cougars.
a) *adventure* b) *examination* c) *search* d) *journey*
2 I **headed** ... toward the park.
a) *made my way* b) *walked quickly* c) *took a shortcut* d) *walked slowly*
3 I found on the other side: the most beautiful, **immaculately kept** gardens.
a) *well-designed* b) *very clean and tidy* c) *very original* d) *exquisite*
4 Peacocks **strutted** around.
a) *wandered* b) *walked slowly* c) *roamed freely* d) *walked proudly*
5 ... the snakes **glistened**.
a) *sparkled* b) *made hissing noises* c) *shone and looked wet*
d) *curled up into a tight ball*
6 Then I saw the man, a tall, **solid** twenty something.
a) *strongly built* b) *fat* c) *heavy* d) *rather stupid*
7 He knelt beside the croc that had just tried to **nail** him.
a) *hurt* b) *hit* c) *eat* d) *catch*
8 Every inch of this man **exuded** his passion for crocodiles.
a) *proved* b) *showed clearly* c) *explained* d) *hinted at*

043 **Focus on words to do with the environment**

Here are 16 words to do with the environment. Fill in the missing words in the sentences below.

acid rain	consumerism	extinct	pollution
climate change	contamination	greenhouse effect	preservation
congestion fee	erosion	ozone layer	toxin
conservation	exhaust fumes	pesticides	waste disposal

1. When we talk about the ______________ we mean an increase in the amount of carbon dioxide and other gases in the atmosphere, which is believed to be the cause of a gradual warming of the surface of the Earth.
2. There are many animals in danger of becoming ______________ , including the Black rhino and the Sumatran tiger.
3. As more and more people move into cities, the problem of ______________ – of getting rid of all the rubbish generated – is becoming increasingly difficult.
4. A lot of the recent freak storms, floods, etc. are, in many people's eyes, due to ______________ .
5. A nuclear power station may be regarded as 'clean', but when there's an accident, there can be serious radioactive ______________ in the surrounding area.
6. To cut down the number of cars entering city centres, many cities – London, for example – have started introducing a ______________ .
7. The ______________ from cars, motorbikes, etc. are one of the main causes of ______________ in cities such as Bangkok and Jakarta.
8. Sulphur, falling as ______________ is killing fish in the Great Lakes.
9. When we talk about ______________ we mean the process by which rock or soil is gradually destroyed by wind, rain or the sea.
10. The ______________ that farmers spray on their crops kill pests but they can also damage people's health.
11. ______________ is the protection of natural things such as animals, plants, forests, etc. to prevent them from being spoiled or destroyed.
12. There is great public concern about some of the chemicals used in food ______________ .
13. During the past 25 years there has been a marked increase in ______________ – of people wanting to buy, buy, buy!
14. A ______________ is a poisonous substance, especially one that's produced in plants and animals.
15. The ______________ prevents harmful ultraviolet light from the sun from reaching the Earth. So it's important we don't damage it.

044 **Writing: Giving instructions**

Write instructions on either how to save energy or how to lead a healthy life style. Use a numbered list of 6-8 bullets. For information and layout on how to write instructions see Resource Section p. 134.

LISTENING: ENCOUNTERS CONT.

045 **Listen and recall** To listen, follow this link

Listen to another extract from *Encounters* and then answer the questions below by completing the sentences.

1 When crocodiles court, the male nudges up and down alongside the female. Why is he doing this?
To see if ___

2 According to Steve, crocodiles develop what for each other?
They ___

3 What happened when Steve fed the crocodile with some meat?
The crocodile almost ___

4 What did the crocodile's jaws closing sound like?
They sounded like ___

5 As she watched this, she could hardly breathe. Why not, do you think?
Because she ___

6 According to Steve, crocodiles are no threat as long as you follow what?
As long as you follow ___

7 Why does Steve try to catch a 'naughty' croc that's bothering people?
To stop it from ___

8 How would Steve catch a crocodile that was shorter than six feet?
He'd ___

9 Why did he shine a spotlight across the water?
In order to ___

10 How would he grab the crocodile?
He'd grab the crocodile ___

11 What would he do next?
He'd ___

12 What would the crocodile be trying to do when Steve was hanging on?
The crocodile would be trying to ___

13 What did she think of Steve's story?
She thought it was ___

Practise the vocabulary in Wordmatch/Spelling

046 **Vocabulary: Matching pairs**

On the left are twelve words found in the extract you listened to. Check that you understand them by finding a sentence on the right that can be 'paired off' in some way.

____	1 a piece of cake	a) Are you sure it won't sink?
____	2 accomplish	b) Another word for 'show'.
____	3 affection	c) A volcano might do this.
____	4 dinghy	d) He's badly behaved.
____	5 dislodge	e) It's so easy!
____	6 erupt	f) It's so dark and muddy!
____	7 incredible	g) Remove something from its normal position.
____	8 murky	h) To push against gently.
____	9 naughty	i) Another word for 'achieve'.
____	10 nudge	j) Today's is "Women in Politics".
____	11 reveal	k) I can't believe it!
____	12 topic	l) What you hope your boyfriend or girlfriend will show you.

047 **Interact**

1 Did you ever watch any TV programmes featuring Steve Irwin? If so, what do you remember about him? Can you remember how he died?
2 There are many endangered animals in the world. Which ones do you know of?
3 How can endangered species be protected? Is there anything *you* can do?
4 Why is it important to work for the preservation of animals?

048 **Speaking**

Write a short presentation of one of the following people.
Present it to a small group or the class.

Steve Irwin
Cesar Milan ("The dog whisperer")
Gerald Durrell
Dian Fossey
George Schaller
David Attenborough
Sylvia Earle
Jacques Cousteau
Jane Goodall
Joy Adamson
Alan Rabinowitz
Rachel Carson
Archibald Belaney ("Grey Owl")
Biruté Galdikas

049 **Looking at phrasal verbs 2**

Phrasal verbs with 'up' and 'down'

A Complete the definitions below with a suitable phrasal verb. Choose from the following and make any verb changes where necessary.

blow up	own up	cut down	pull down
hold up	pull up	get down	settle down
make up	put up	let down	turn down

1 If you ____________ someone ____________, you disappoint that person by failing to do what he or she has been relying on you to do.
2 When a vehicle ____________, it slows down then stops.
3 If you ____________ something ____________, such as a building, you destroy it by using explosives.
4 If you ____________ a request, an offer, an invitation, etc. you refuse or say no to it.
5 If you ____________ to something, you admit that you did it.
6 If you ____________, for example, the number of cigarettes you smoke, you smoke fewer than before.
7 If you ____________, this usually means that you get married, set up home and start leading a quiet, routine life.
8 If you ____________ someone ____________, you let them stay with you for one or more nights.
9 If people ____________ a bank, a post office, a security van, etc. they rob it, usually by threatening with weapons.
10 If something ____________ you ____________, it makes you feel depressed.
11 If two people ____________, this means they've become friends again after a quarrel.
12 If you ____________ a building, you demolish or destroy it.

B Now work in pairs or small groups and discuss the following.

1 When was the last time you read about someone **holding up** a bank? Have you ever seen any films with this theme?
2 What things would you hope to do before you **settle down**? What's the best age to settle down?
3 When was the last time someone **let** you **down**? Describe the occasion.
4 What sort of things **get** you **down**?
5 Would you **turn down** an offer to go and live and work in another country for a charity organisation? What if that country was Afghanistan?

050 Vocabulary Bank: Useful verbs 2

In Unit 1, you learnt some useful verbs. Here are some more.
Put the correct verb into each sentence. Make any necessary changes. Choose from:

apply for   boast   celebrate   expire   explore

1 'How do you usually ______ Midsummer in England?' (*fira*)
'We don't!'
2 My son has ______ a job with the BBC. (*söka*)
3 Would you like to ______ the jungles of South America with me? (*utforska*)
4 Some people love to ______ about their achievements, don't they? (*skryta*)
5 I must renew my passport soon. It ______ at the end of the month. (*gå ut, förfalla*)

Now turn to page 303 in Vocabulary Bank and do *Useful verbs 2.*

051 Useful expressions: Idioms 1

An idiom is a group of words that has a special meaning different from the ordinary meaning of each separate word. For example, to be **under the weather** is an idiom meaning 'to be ill' while to **smell a rat** means 'to become suspicious'.

To be really fluent in English you need to both understand and know how and when to use idioms. In this book you're going to meet a lot of useful ones.

A Complete the definitions below with a suitable idiom. Choose from these. To help you, a Swedish translation is given in brackets.

be on the dole
fly off the handle
get into hot water
get the sack
give someone the cold shoulder
let the cat out of the bag
make a mountain out of a molehill
make ends meet
pull someone's leg
pull your socks up

1 To ______ is to tell someone something that's not true – usually as a joke. (*driva/skoja med någon*)
2 To ______ is to suddenly get very angry. (*mista självkontrollen, bli topp tunnor rasande*)
3 To ______ is to completely ignore someone. (*ignorera någon, visa sig avvisande mot någon*)
4 To ______ is to make a slight difficulty seem like a serious problem. (*göra en höna av en fjäder, förstora upp allting*)
5 To ______ is to be in or get into trouble because you've done something wrong. (*få problem, få det hett om öronen*)
6 To ______ is to try to improve your work or behaviour because it isn't good enough. (*skärpa sig, ta sig i kragen*)

7 To __________________ is to be unemployed or out of work (and usually receiving money from the government). *(vara arbetslös, gå och stämpla)*
8 To __________________ is to tell someone a secret, usually by mistake. *(avslöja en hemlighet)*
9 To __________________ is to be dismissed from your job, usually because you've done something wrong. *(få sparken)*
10 To __________________ is to have only just enough money to buy the things you need. *(få det att gå ihop ekonomiskt)*

B Now complete the sentences using seven of the idioms from A.
Make any necessary changes.

1 If you hope to pass the exam next summer, then you're going to have to ______________ .
2 The teacher really __________________ when the students wouldn't stop talking during the test.
3 I honestly don't know what all the fuss is about. If you ask me, the government are __________________ .
4 You didn't believe him when he told you he was a famous photographer, did you? Didn't you realise he was only __________________ !
5 We're going to have a surprise birthday party for Sarah on Friday, so don't __________________ !
6 Now that there's a recession, many families are finding it hard to __________________ .
7 He __________________ for using the office phone for private calls.

C Now write your own sentences for the three idioms left over.

____

____

____

052 Sum up and comment

1 What new strategies are you using when listening?
2 Do you have any role models in life? Who are they and why are they important to you?
3 What have you learnt about Steve Jobs that you did not know before? Has he become an icon? Give reasons.

053 Books to read and enjoy

Burgess, Melvin: *Billy Elliot**
Downham, Jenny: *Before I Die**
Irwin, Terri: *Steve & Me*
Isaacson, Walter: *Steve Jobs*
Krakauer, Jon: *Into the Wild*
McDougall, Christopher: *Born to Run*
Townsend, Sue: *The Woman Who Went to Bed For a Year*
Witi, Ihimaera: *The Whale Rider**

*teenage fiction or less advanced books

3 CROSSING LINES

SO WHERE YOU FROM?

- ☐ Starter
- ☐ Interact
- ☐ Vocabulary: Definitions
- ☐ Interact
- ☐ Activity
- ☐ Role play: Small talk

WSM: HOW TO READ A PERSON LIKE A BOOK

FOCUS ON GRAMMAR

WSM: WORLDWIDE ENGLISH

- ☐ Interact
- ☐ Speaking
- ☐ Focus on words to do with communication

WSM: AMUSING SIGNS FROM AROUND THE WORLD

LISTENING: WHERE ARE THEY?

- ☐ Listen and recall
- ☐ Vocabulary Bank: Useful verbs 3

WATCH YOUR STEP

- ☐ Starter
- ☐ Textwork
- ☐ Interact
- ☐ Looking at phrasal verbs 3

WSM: THE POSSIBLE ORIGIN OF A POPULAR SUPERSTITION

OCD

- ☐ Textwork
- ☐ Vocabulary: Fill in the gaps
- ☐ Interact
- ☐ Speaking: Making a summary
- ☐ Focus on adjectives to do with moods and feelings

SEXY

- ☐ Starter
- ☐ Interact
- ☐ Vocabulary: What does it mean?
- ☐ Writing: Formal and informal English

- ☐ Fun with vocabulary 2
- ☐ Sum up and comment
- ☐ Books to read and enjoy

SO WHERE YOU FROM? (page 28)

054 **Starter**

Read through the following statements and mark with a cross any that you agree with.

1 People usually shake hands each time they meet each other. ☐
2 A woman shouldn't look a man in the eyes when he's talking directly to her. ☐
3 Asking someone how much they earn is okay. ☐
4 Asking someone about their religious beliefs is okay. ☐
5 When invited to a party, bringing a friend is okay. ☐
6 When eating dinner at a friend's house, asking for a second helping is okay. ☐
7 A woman's primary role in life is to serve her husband and raise his children. ☐
8 It's common for students to call teachers by their first names in secondary schools. ☐
9 Parents decide who their children will marry. ☐
10 It's OK for teenagers to go out on dates. ☐

Now work in groups of 3–4 and compare your answers.

Which statements, if any, would you say should be true for all cultures?

055 **Interact**

Work in pairs. Take turns to ask and answer the following questions.

1 What seems to be her feelings towards 'small talk'?
2 What do you think she means when she says 'There are few things more insufferable than ungrateful immigrants'?
3 How did she feel in Europe compared to America?
4 Why do you think she dreaded going in lifts?
5 How did people know she was an immigrant?
6 When someone compliments her on her English, she is pleased but she also thinks something else? What?
7 What information has she told complete strangers?
8 What's the reaction when she refuses to tell a young woman her address?
9 What do you think she means when she says 'Why do nice people have to ruin everything'?

Practise the vocabulary in Wordmatch/Spelling

056 Vocabulary: Definitions

Here are definitions of ten words from the text. Can you work out what they are? To help you, the first and last letter of each missing word is given.

1 If you're ________, you don't show or express thanks for something somebody has done for you. u________l
2 To make known something that was previously secret or unknown. r________l
3 The opposite of 'polite'. r________e
4 Someone whose job is to receive or pay out money in a shop. c________r
5 If a feeling or action is ________ (e.g. laughter), then other people are quickly affected by it and start doing it too. c________s
6 A more formal word for 'job'. o________n
7 To ________ something is to feel anxious or worried or about something that's going to happen or may happen. d________d
8 To spoil or destroy something completely. r________n
9 If something is ________, it is extremely annoying or unpleasant. i________e
10 To ________ someone is to make them angry or upset by doing or saying something that they think is rude, unkind, etc. o________d

057 Interact

1 It can be difficult to ask strangers questions about themselves. What questions would you be prepared to answer about yourself, for example when chatting on a train?
2 When you meet someone for the first time what things do you choose to talk about? Are there any subjects you'd try to avoid talking about?

058 Activity

1 What stereotypes, if any, do you think exist in your culture concerning the following groups?
Americans - Italians - Chinese - Arabs - lawyers - traffic wardens - computer hackers - feminists - hairdressers - journalists - politicians
2 What other common stereotypes exist in your culture? Why is that?

Become a better speaker by practising. Have a look at Speaking Strategies in the Resource Section page 120.

059 Role play: Small talk

'Small talk' is polite friendly conversation about ordinary or unimportant subjects, often between people who do not know each other well and especially at social occasions, for example, at a party. Here's your chance to see how good you are at 'small talk'. You're to imagine you're at an international conference in London. It's the first evening and you've been invited to a welcome party where you'll get a chance to meet other people attending the conference.

Before you start, make up a totally fictional background for yourself. Consider the following:

Your name
Your age
Where you're from (country, city)
What your job is
If you're married or single
How many children you have
Where you're staying in London. If it's your first visit. What you're hoping to see or do in London.
What your hobbies are.
etc.

When everyone is ready, you can begin. Walk around the class, talking to complete 'strangers' and trying to indulge in small talk with each person you meet.

Useful phrases – talking to people for the first time

Introducing yourself
Hello/Hi! My name's...

When having a conversation (to show interest)
How/That's interesting!
Really?

When you don't hear or understand
Sorry? What did you say?

When you want to leave
It's been nice talking to you.
It was nice meeting you.
See you again.
See you later.
Goodbye.
Bye!/Bye for now!

WSM: HOW TO READ A PERSON LIKE A BOOK

FOCUS ON GRAMMAR

	Grammar	Interactive exercise
Adjectives		
The Adjective	p. 310	
Adverbs		
Adverbs	p. 311	
Adjectives or Adverbs	p. 311	
Adverbs of manner	p. 311	
Adverbs of frequency	p. 311	

WSM: WORLDWIDE ENGLISH

Read about English around the world

060 Interact

1 Why do you think English has become a worldwide language?
2 In what situations have you used English apart from school?
3 Have you found English useful in any non-English-speaking countries? Which?

061 Speaking

Use the Internet and find some facts about various aspects of the English language.

1 What are the following – RP, Queen's English and Estuary English?
2 What's typical of Cockney? Find some examples of rhyming slang.
3 Find some examples of the differences between English and American English vocabulary and grammar.
4 What's typical for Australian English, Indian English or any other variant of English?
5 In which countries is English an official language?
6 What do we mean by the term 'lingua franca'?
7 What are Pidgin English and Creole?
8 What is Globish? Do you think it's a good idea?

062 Focus on words to do with communication

Write down the Swedish words for the words in **bold type**.

When people (1) **communicate**, they naturally use (2) **language**, but would it surprise you to learn that according to some people, nearly 80% of communication is (3) **non-verbal** – commonly known as (4) **body language –** and some people claim that mastering this is a big advantage as various (5) **gestures** and (6) **facial expressions** are often clues as to what the person you're talking to is really thinking. But not all people can communicate (7) **orally**. Deaf people, for example, either learn to (8) **lip read** or they use (9) **sign language** which, some people say is far more (10) **communicative** than 'normal' language.

(11) **Native speakers** usually have a much wider (12) **vocabulary** than (13) **non-native** speakers. They tend to use more (14) **colloquialisms**, (15) **idioms**, (16) **phrasal verbs** and (17) **slang** when they (18) **interact** with others. Although there are more people in the world who are (19) **fluent** in Chinese than any other language, it's English that's become the (20) **lingua franca** - especially when it comes to international conferences and business. This is very useful and it certainly reduces the cost of hiring hundreds of (21) **interpreters**. (22) **Pronunciation** and (23) **intonation** are also important when it comes to speaking. Most people who don't have English as their (24) **mother tongue** speak with a certain (25) **accent** which is easily recognizable. But whereas Scandinavians and Dutch people can pick up a 'passable' English accent, Chinese people, French people, Italians and Spaniards are often **(26) misunderstood** simply because of the way they pronounce certain words. Or is the above merely an example of (27) **stereotyping** people?

But to communicate successfully in English you have to be prepared to make mistakes. No one is born fluent. Language is a skill, just as driving or learning to play a musical instrument is, and becoming more (28) **proficient** can be summed up in three words - practise, practise, practise!

WSM: AMUSING SIGNS FROM AROUND THE WORLD

People's English is not always that good, so when they try to help tourists by writing signs in English, the results can often be very amusing or ambiguous. Here are some examples.

Sign in bargain basement shop in Istanbul
DON'T GO INTO ANOTHER SHOP TO BE CHEATED - COME IN HERE

Hong Kong tailor shop
LADIES MAY HAVE A FIT UPSTAIRS

Rome doctor
SPECIALIST IN WOMEN AND OTHER DISEASES

Bangkok dry cleaners
DROP YOUR TROUSERS HERE FOR BEST RESULTS

Paris hotel
A SPORTS JACKET MAY BE WORN TO DINNER, BUT NOT TROUSERS

Zanzibar barber shop
GENTLEMEN'S THROATS CUT WITH NICE SHARP RAZORS

Paris hotel
PLEASE LEAVE YOUR VALUES AT THE RECEPTION DESK

Istanbul hotel
TO CALL ROOM SERVICE, PLEASE OPEN DOOR AND CALL ROOM SERVICE

LISTENING: WHERE ARE THEY?

063 **Listen and recall** To listen, follow this link

You're going to listen to ten short dialogues. Try to work out where the people are in each one. Fill in the letter of the place or situation you choose in the appropriate box below. You'll only hear the dialogues **once**. Before you start, look at the list of possible situations.

A buying a laptop
B taking a photo
C at a restaurant
D at the police station
E buying clothes
F at a job interview
G at the chemist's
H at a wedding reception
I visiting the dentist
J having a driving lesson
K on a sightseeing bus
L visiting the vet
M at the garage
N at the travel agent's
O making wedding plans
P visiting the doctor
Q buying a car
R a parking incident

Write your answers here:

1	2	3	4	5	6	7	8	9	10

Practise the vocabulary in Wordmatch/Spelling

064 **Vocabulary Bank: Useful verbs 3**

Put the correct verb into each sentence. Make any necessary changes. Choose from:

hesitate obey recognize remind sneeze

1 Sorry Paula, I didn't ______________ you with short hair.' (*känna igen*)
2 If you have hay fever, your eyes run and you tend to ______________ a lot. (*nysa*)
3 'You ______________ me of the sea.' (*påminna*)
'What – wild and exciting?'
'No. You make me sick!'
4 Her mobile phone rang. Kathy ______________ for a minute before answering it. (*tveka*)
5 Do you think small children should ______________ their parents without question? (*lyda*)

Now turn to page 304 in Vocabulary Bank and do *Useful verbs 3*.

WATCH YOUR STEP (page 31)

065 **Starter**

Superstitions

Work in groups of 4–5. Talk about and then write down 5–6 common superstitions in your culture.

1 ______________________________
2 ______________________________
3 ______________________________
4 ______________________________
5 ______________________________
6 ______________________________

066 **Textwork**

Without looking back at *Watch Your Step*, see if you can remember which superstitions *Sisi*Blandina warned about. Match the openings 1–6 with the endings a–f.

1 You should never cut your hair outdoors because
2 Boys and girls mustn't spy on each other while they dress because
3 If you walk over a person's legs, you must
4 You shouldn't play outside in the rain if you're wearing something red because
5 You mustn't walk over a person's legs because
6 You mustn't sit on the road because

a walk back the other way to reverse the action.
b you'll grow festering boils on your bottom.
c you'll get struck by lightning which will burn you from inside out.
d *varoyi* will put a spell on you.
e you'll stop them from growing.
f they'll get styes in their eyes.

067 Interact

The text deals with various superstitions. Do you have any?

- Do you have a lucky number? If so, what is it?
- Do you do anything special before an exam, test, etc. to bring you good luck? If so, what?
- Do you wear or have with you anything that's supposed to be lucky?

Practise the vocabulary in Wordmatch/Spelling

068 Looking at phrasal verbs 3

A Complete the definitions below with a suitable phrasal verb. Choose from the following and make any verb changes where necessary.

break into	fall out	look into	put out
come across	get over	pass away	run out of
do away with	go in for	pick up	take to

1 To ______________ a fire is to make it stop burning.
2 To ______________ something is to examine the facts about a problem or situation.
3 To ______________ something, for example a new language, is to learn it by practising it rather than studying it.
4 To ______________ something is to begin to feel better after a very upsetting experience.
5 To ______________ something, for example playing golf, is to start liking it.
6 To ______________ something is to find or discover it by chance.
7 To ______________ is to argue with someone and stop being friendly with them.
8 To ______________ is to enter a building by force or illegally, usually in order to steal.
9 To ______________ something, a competition for example, is to enrol for it.
10 To ______________ is another way of saying to die.
11 To ______________ something is to remove something or to stop using it.
12 To ______________ something is to use it all so that there's none left.

B Now work in pairs or small groups and discuss the following.

1 If there was a fire in your kitchen, what would you do to try to **put** it **out**?
2 What precautions can you take to stop thieves **breaking into** your house or flat?
3 Name something in your life that you've really **taken to**? Is there anything you've tried to but didn't really take to it?
4 Do you think Sweden should **do away with** the monarchy and have a president instead?
5 Name three things that couples often **fall out** about.

WSM: THE POSSIBLE ORIGIN OF A POPULAR SUPERSTITION

"The number 13 is unlucky."

Fear of the number 13 has its origins in Norse mythology. In a well-known tale, 12 gods were invited to dine at Valhalla, a magnificent banquet hall in Asgard, the city of the gods. Loki, the god of strife and evil, gatecrashed the party, raising the number to 13. The other gods tried to kick Loki out, and in the struggle that ensued, Balder, the favourite god among them, was killed.

This dislike of the number 13 spread south to the rest of Europe. It was reinforced in the Christian era by the story of the Last Supper, at which Judas, the disciple who betrayed Jesus, was the thirteenth guest at the table.

In the modern era, the number 13 is still considered unlucky. President Franklin D. Roosevelt was really afraid of the number 13, and took great pains to avoid hosting a meal for a group of that size. They say that if he had a cancellation and it looked as if there might be 13 people to lunch, he invited his secretary to join them so that there wouldn't be 13.

The fear of the number 13 is so widespread, if fact, that it even has a phobia named after it – triskaidekaphobia. Based on this phobia, airlines don't usually have a 13th row, and most tall buildings don't have a 13th floor.

But despite all these fears, there is no statistical evidence that the number 13 is unlucky.

OCD (page 32)

069 Textwork

Here are the answers to ten questions. Read the text *OCD* and try to find suitable questions to the answers.

1 ____?
It's short for Obsessive Compulsive Disorder.

2 ____?
David Beckham.

3 ____?
20.

4 ____?
They're called compulsions.

5 ____?
They're mental thoughts rather than physical actions.

6 ____?
They're rituals acted out as the result of disturbing thoughts.

7 ____?
To avoid touching germs.
8 ____?
No, we can't yet identify a definite cause.
9 ____?
It's a chemical in the brain which controls either a person's feeling of well-being or anxiety.
10 ____?
Some of the effects are that people can't go to school or keep a job.
11 ____?
It's a support organization for OCD sufferers.
12 ____?
They're given anti-depressants

Practise the vocabulary in Wordmatch/Spelling

070 Vocabulary: Fill in the gaps

Fill in the missing words in the sentences below. Choose from the following words, taken from the text. Then make up your own sentences for the four words that are left over.

anxiety	crippling	incapable	psychiatrist
behaviour	disorders	irrational	severe
compelled	germs	label	unbearable
covert	hoard	paranoid	weird

1 Two common eating ______________ are bulimia and anorexia.
2 My brother's very fashion conscious and will only wear clothes with a designer ______________ .
3 A ______________ was called as an expert witness to give her opinion on the mental state of the defendant.
4 The defence minister felt ______________ to resign because of the scandal.
5 I had a really ______________ dream last night. I dreamt I got married to a horse!
6 The CIA was accused of ______________ military operations against the regime.
7 My uncle's ______________ of walking past a betting shop without going in and placing a bet on something.
8 The kitchen staff at restaurants should wash their hands often to make sure they don't get ______________ on the food.
9 When I first visited Singapore I found the heat and humidity totally ______________ , so I spent most of the time inside my air-conditioned hotel room.
10 Children normally feel a lot of ______________ about their first day at school.
11 Harry started feeling ______________ and was convinced his boss was going to fire him.
12 Alzheimer's disease is one of the most ______________ and distressing diseases of the elderly.

071 Interact

1 Some athletes have to tie their shoe laces three times before a match. Do you recognize this type of "obsessive" behaviour?
2 Comment on Beckham's behaviour. Do you think it's common to act this way?
3 When does OCD become a real problem?
4 What kind of help can you get?

072 Speaking: Making a summary

The text about OCD is a newspaper article. Work with a partner and take turns to make a summary of the text using your own words. Read through the text and write down some key words before you start. Also, see Resource Section p. 285.

073 Focus on adjectives to do with moods and feelings

In the text *OCD*, one of the adjectives used was the word 'paranoid'. This is an adjective to describe a mood or a feeling. Here are some other useful adjectives to describe moods or feelings.

A Complete the definitions below with a suitable adjective.
Choose from the following: Use a dictionary if necessary.

amazed	delighted	fed up	irritable
apprehensive	disillusioned	furious	paranoid
baffled	edgy	homesick	terrified

1 If you're feeling ____________, then you're feeling unhappy and dissatisfied.
2 A person who's ____________ is easily annoyed and tends to get angry at small things, often because they already feel bad-tempered about something.
3 If you're feeling ____________, then you're very surprised – especially by something good or by something that seems hard to believe.
4 To be ____________ is to be very frightened.
5 If you're feeling ____________ with something then you're really pleased and happy about it.
6 If you're feeling ____________, then you're feeling nervous and can't seem to relax or behave in a calm way.
7 If you're feeling ____________, then you're worried and nervous about the future or something you're going to do.
8 If you're feeling ____________, then you're unhappy because you're away from home and missing your family, friends, etc.
9 If you're feeling ____________, then you're extremely angry about something.
10 To feel ____________ is to feel bitter and disappointed because you've lost your belief that someone is good or that an idea or plan is right.

11 If you're feeling ______________, then you're completely unable to explain or understand something, or find a solution to it. In other words, you're very confused.

12 If you're feeling ______________, then you're constantly convinced that people hate you or that bad things will happen, even though this isn't true.

B Now work in pairs or small groups and discuss the following.

1 Have you ever felt **apprehensive** about something? Tell the others about it.

2 Many young people feel **disillusioned** with politicians and politics. What about you? How do you feel?

3 Describe an occasion when you (or someone you know) was **furious**.

4 What sort of things can make you **irritable**?

5 Talk about something that left you feeling **amazed**.

6 Do you ever get **fed up**? Why? What do you do to try to overcome the feeling?

SEXY (page 35)

074 Starter

Work in groups of 3–4.

1 Do you judge people by the way they look? Give reasons.

2 Think of some ways in which people dress and behave in order to look and be different.

3 Do you believe it when people say 'I only dress to please myself.'? Give reasons.

075 Interact

Work in pairs. Take turns to ask and answer the following questions.

1 'Soon as he turned sixteen, put on weight and began to get attention for his looks, things began to turn weird.' In which ways do you think things began to turn weird?

2 Why do you think he tried to make himself ugly when older girls and women in their twenties looked at him?

3 'Darren was a guy's guy'. How would you describe a guy's guy?

4 What effect did Darren have on women? Do you think he was aware of this? Give reasons.

5 What was it really that made him walk away after talking to a girl?

6 Why were Darren's parents so against him and his brother using swear words?

Practise the vocabulary in Wordmatch/Spelling

076 Vocabulary: What does it mean?

You're now going to explain the meaning of some of the words used in the text *Sexy*. Complete the following sentences by giving English explanations of the words in **bold**. Make your explanations as exact as possible. Use a dictionary if necessary.

Example: **Trailer trash** is an offensive expression for ______________ .
(*Answer*: poor white people from a low social class)

1. If a character is **fictional**, this means he or she ______________ .
2. An **adult** is a fully-grown person who ______________ .
3. When you **blush** you usually go red in the face because ______________ .
4. To **glower** at someone is to look at them ______________ .
5. A **moth** is an insect which is similar to a butterfly but which usually ______________ .
6. **Hives** is a disease in which a person's skin ______________ .
7. If a person **mumbles** then it's difficult to ______________ .
8. In the USA, a **sophomore** is a student who ______________ .
9. When a person is **startled** by something, they are ______________ .
10. If a sweatshirt is **frayed at the cuffs** it means that ______________ .

077 Writing: Formal and informal English

Here's a letter to a newspaper explaining why teenagers should be allowed to vote in the election. The ideas are good, but the writing is too informal. Rewrite the letter using more formal language. Also see Resource Section p. 138 on how to write a letter to the editor.

Hi guys!

This is about voting in elections, OK? I think us teenagers have a right to vote too, just as much as the old people. It's our country and it's gonna be us running it soon. We're the future of the country, not them, right? My parents say we haven't got our heads screwed on straight so we shouldn't be allowed to vote. I say it's them that should have their heads looked at! Getting old doesn't mean you understand everything best. Anyway, young people have good ideas and should have a chance to prove it.

All for now

Jeannie

Find the hidden novel

Choose the correct missing words in the following sentences. Each correct answer has a letter after it. Put the letters into the numbered boxes below to find the name of a famous novel by Charles Dickens.

1 The police _____ him for burglary.
a) accused [**E**] b) charged [**K**] c) arrested [**A**] d) convicted [**O**]

2 She had a three-roomed flat in a new residential area on the _____ of London.
a) border [**L**] b) suburbs [**S**] c) near [**M**] d) outskirts [**P**]

3 According to statistics, drivers over 50 have _____ accidents than drivers under 25.
a) fewer [**R**] b) less [**M**] c) smaller [**P**] d) lower [**Y**]

4 Was it Bell or Edison who _____ the telephone?
a) devised [**B**] b) invented [**L**] c) discovered [**P**] d) created [**R**]

5 Take an umbrella with you _____ it rains.
a) because [**O**] b) in case [**I**] c) even though [**E**] d) despite [**A**]

6 I wonder if you could give me _____ with the washing up?
a) a help [**A**] b) the assistance [**I**] c) support [**O**] d) a hand [**E**]

7 In _____, women live longer than men in most countries.
a) the whole [**R**] b) reality [**I**] c) general [**E**] d) average [**S**]

8 They have just started _____ for oil off the west coast of Ireland.
a) piping [**H**] b) exploring [**W**] c) boring [**T**] d) drilling [**D**]

9 The earthquake has caused _____ damage.
a) extensive [**I**] b) broad [**O**] c) thorough [**C**] d) important [**R**]

10 It was a long meeting and by 10 o'clock they still had several items left on the _____ .
a) programme [**F**] b) schedule [**B**] c) agenda [**D**] d) timetable [**G**]

11 Who else went with you to the cinema _____ David and Jean?
a) apart [**G**] b) besides [**D**] c) except [**W**] d) beside [**S**]

12 The train was _____ for several hours because of floods.
a) delayed [**O**] b) prevented [**E**] c) detained [**A**] d) cancelled [**U**]

13 Even years after his death, Michael Jackson's music continues to bring joy to _____ millions all over the world.
a) endless [**T**] b) overwhelming [**H**] c) widespread [**L**] d) countless [**P**]

14 How much does Sweden spend on foreign _____?
a) help [**T**] b) aid [**V**] c) assistance [**U**] d) support [**N**]

15 The accident was caused by a car _____ uncontrollably across the icy road.
a) skidding [**F**] b) slipping [**B**] c) skating [**B**] d) gliding [**B**]

16 If you spell the word with a 'z' here, you must spell it with a 'z' everywhere. You must be _____ .
a) consequent [**J**] b) similar [**D**] c) consistent [**C**] d) reliable [**P**]

11	1	14	5	8

16	12	2	13	6	3	15	9	7	4	10

079 **Sum up and comment**

1 What new strategies are you using when speaking?
2 In what ways are you more aware of stereotypes? How are they created?
3 Time to assess your level of English! Turn to the Resource Section p. 122 and evaluate how you're progressing.

080 **Books to read and enjoy**

Boyne, John: *The Boy in the Striped Pyjamas**
Chbosky, Stephen: *The Perks of Being a Wallflower**
Gappah, Petina: *An Elegy for Easterly*
Hornby, Nick: *About a Boy, Slam**
Hosseini, Khaled: *The Kite Runner, A Thousand Splendid Suns*
Oates, Joyce Carol: *Sexy*; Big Mouth and Ugly Girl**
Winterson, Jeanette: *Why Be Happy When You Could Be Normal?*

*teenage fiction or less advanced books

4 MOVING ON

LEAVING HOME

- [ ] Let's talk!
- [ ] Interact
- [ ] Focus on travel words
- [ ] Writing: A formal letter

FOCUS ON GRAMMAR

BEIJING TO LONDON

- [ ] Starter
- [ ] Textwork
- [ ] Writing
- [ ] Vocabulary Bank: Useful adjectives 1

WSM: THE SAYINGS OF CONFUCIUS

LISTENING: TAPAS AND TEARS

- [ ] Starter
- [ ] Listen and recall
- [ ] Interact
- [ ] Vocabulary: Right or wrong?
- [ ] Writing/Speaking

SINGAPORE AND BACK

- [ ] Starter
- [ ] Textwork
- [ ] Vocabulary: Matching pairs
- [ ] Interact
- [ ] Speaking
- [ ] Looking at collocations 1

WSM: SINGAPORE – "THE LION CITY"

- [ ] Useful expressions: Idioms 2
- [ ] Sum up and comment
- [ ] Books to read and enjoy

LEAVING HOME (page 40)

081 Let's talk!

Just a minute!

Work in two groups - A and B (2-3 people per group). Group A looks at this page. Group B turns to page 299.

You're going to be asked in turn to talk about a subject for one minute. Below are the subjects for group B. They also have subjects for you to talk about, but you yourselves decide on a subject by choosing a number between 1-10. The person who's going to talk says to Group B: *I'd like to talk about subject (2).* Then cross the number out so you don't get the same subject again!

One person in Group B will now read out the subject you asked for. Try and talk for one minute. (Someone in Group B will tell you when to stop!) If you manage to do it, your team scores 1 point. *Your group starts by choosing a number.*

1	2	3	4	5	6	7	8	9	10

Subjects for group B

1 A job I would like to have.
2 Things that annoy me.
3 My ideal partner.
4 Weddings.
5 How to bring up children.
6 Modern fashions and trends.
7 Things that make me happy.
8 My family.
9 How to make...*(choose a food dish)*
10 My hobby or pastime.

082 Interact

1 Who are the two people in the text?
2 Where do you think they're from?
3 What is her reason for leaving?
4 Why do people decide to break up and leave their homes?

First practise the vocabulary in Wordmatch/Spelling

083 **Focus on travel words**

A Fill in the missing words in the sentences below. Then write your own sentences for the four words left over.

cruise	excursion	itinerary	traveller
departure lounge	fare	off the beaten track	trek
destination	globetrotter	stopover	voyage
embark	gridlock	tailback	youth hostel

1 On our way to Australia, we had a two-day ______________ in Singapore.
2 Included in the tour was an ______________ to the Grand Canyon.
3 In the days before air travel and the Suez Canal, the ______________ from England to India could take up to six months.
4 Due to the strike by baggage handlers, the ______________ was full of stranded and angry passengers.
5 There was a five-mile ______________ on the M25 motorway due to a serious accident.
6 Last summer we went on a Mediterranean ______________ . I loved it but my mother didn't as she was seasick half the time.
7 Last summer I took my backpack and joined some friends on a ______________ across the mountains of central China.
8 My uncle's a real ______________ . I don't think there are many countries he hasn't visited.
9 When you travel by ferry, passengers with cars usually ______________ first.
10 We deliberately hired a cottage ______________ as we wanted total peace and quiet.
11 It's usually cheaper to stay at a ______________ than a hotel.
12 The traffic in Bangkok is really something. Most of the time there is total ______________ there.

B Now work in pairs or small groups and discuss the following.
1 Would you like to go on a **cruise**? If so, where to? If not, why not?
2 What's the best and the worst **youth hostel** you've ever stayed at? What's the standard like in Sweden compared to other countries?
3 If you could be a **globetrotter**, which five countries (that you've never been to) would you visit first and why?
4 When you plan a holiday on your own, do you always make up an **itinerary** or do you prefer to 'play things by ear' and not plan things too carefully?
5 What's the most interesting **excursion** you've ever been on? Why was it so interesting?
6 Have you ever visited a city where there's been total **gridlock**? As cities get bigger and bigger, what can be done to ease this?
7 What are the advantages and disadvantages of having a holiday cottage **off the beaten track**?
8 What advice would you give to **travellers** visiting Sweden for the first time?

084 **Writing: A formal letter**

You've been accepted to study at the University of Sussex, in Brighton.
You need somewhere to live and have seen the following advertisement on the Internet.
Write a letter in answer to it.

Need help? See Formal letter in Resource Section p. 136.

STUDIO APARTMENT TO RENT

Suitable for one student only
No animals and non-smoker

Please apply by letter to:
Mary Truman PhD
30 Western Road
Brighton BN2 5AP
England

When you've written your letter, find a partner.
Change letters and take turns to comment on it.

Make use of Peer response – writing in Resource Section on p. 127.

FOCUS ON GRAMMAR

	Grammar	Interactive exercise
VERBS		
The Present Simple	p. 312	
The Present Continuous	p. 313	
The Past Simple	p. 313	
The Past Continuous	p. 305	

BEIJING TO LONDON (page 42)

085 Starter

Work in pairs. Write down five things you think you know about China.

Now find another pair and compare your answers.

086 Textwork

We learn quite a few things about Zhuang Xiao Qiao from the text. What do we know about the following?

1 Her name and date of birth.

2 The place she was born.

3 Why she is going to London.

4 What her parents do for a living.

5 Which person from the West she has met.

6 What happens to American TV series in China.

7 How she's feeling.

Practise the vocabulary in Wordmatch/Spelling

087 Writing

Her command of English isn't very good. Look at the following paragraph and try to rewrite it so that it flows better and is grammatically correct.

As I far away from China, I asking me why I coming to West. Why I must to study English like parents wish? Why I must to get diploma from West? I not knowing what I needing. Sometimes I not even caring what I needing. I not caring if I speaking English or not. Mother only speaking in village dialect and even not speaking official Mandarin, but she becoming rich with my father, from making shoes in our little town. Life OK. Why they want changing my life?

088 Vocabulary Bank: Useful adjectives 1

In Units 1–3 we looked at useful verbs. Now it's time to look at useful adjectives – in this case adjectives to describe people's character and personality. Put the correct adjective into each sentence. Choose from:

efficient emotional hostile sensitive witty

1 Mary was very __________ about her hair. She thought it was too curly! *(känslig)*
2 He makes us laugh a lot. He's very __________ . *(kvick, vitsig)*
3 Pamela was a very __________ secretary. *(effektiv)*
4 They say that women are more __________ than men. Do you think that's true? *(känslomässiga)*
5 For some reason, the man was very __________ towards us. *(fientlig)*

Now turn to page 305 in Vocabulary Bank and do *Useful adjectives 1.*

WSM: THE SAYINGS OF CONFUCIUS

Confucius, whose name literally means "Master Kong", was China's most famous philosopher. He lived in Ancient China during the Zhou Dynasty. He was a government official, and during his lifetime (he lived from 551 to 479 B.C.) saw growing disorder and chaos in the system. Perhaps due to the turmoil and injustices he saw, he set himself to develop a new moral code based on respect, honesty, education, kindness and strong family bonds. His teachings later became the basis for religious and moral life throughout China.

Confucius' sayings were recorded after his death by his followers in a book called *The Analects*. Many of these sayings are universal and timeless and are as valid today as on the day they left Confucius' mouth. Here are ten of this famous Chinese philosopher's quotes:

Confucius says...

"A man who has committed a mistake and doesn't correct it, is committing another mistake."

"Everything has its beauty but not everyone sees it."

"He who learns but does not think, is lost. He who thinks but does not learn is in great danger."

"I hear and I forget. I see and I remember. I do and I understand."

"Ignorance is the night of the mind, but a night without moon and stars."

"It does not matter how slowly you go, so long as you do not stop."

"Our greatest glory is not in never falling, but in getting up every time we do."

"Real knowledge is to know the extent of one's ignorance."

"Respect yourself and others will respect you."

"When anger rises, think of the consequences."

"Wheresoever you go, go with all your heart."

Which of the above is your favourite saying? Explain why.

But because Confucius is so famous, he's also been the inspiration for many other sayings – intended to be humorous. Here are three of them.

"A man with one chopstick goes hungry."

"War does not determine who's right, war determines who's left."

"It is better to keep silent and be thought a fool, than to speak and remove all doubt."

Can you think up your own humorous Confucius saying?

LISTENING: TAPAS AND TEARS

089 **Starter**

1 What do you know about language courses?
2 Have you heard of or experienced exchange programmes between two schools? What do you think about them?
3 Is it important to go abroad to learn a language? Give reasons.
4 How would you feel about going abroad and staying with a host family for three weeks?

090 **Listen and recall** To listen, follow this link

Listen to an extract from *Tapas and Tears*. As you listen, fill in the missing information or choose the correct answer (a, b or c).

1 The exchange visit in Spain is for ____________ weeks.
2 The students can only go on it if *a) it's cheap enough b) they're good at Spanish c) their parents agree to it.*
3 How will the accommodation be arranged in Spain? Who will the pupils stay with?
____
4 Describe their class teacher, Miss Martinez.
She's young and ____________ with ____________ hair and a very good ____________ .
5 What impression do you get of her?
a) She's a pushover. b) She knows how to control a class. c) She won't take any stick from bitchy boys.
6 What's happened in the past when some students have misbehaved in class? The whole class has ended up in ____________ .
7 We get the impression that Jaime *a) often b) never c) sometimes* misbehaves in class.
8 They get a lot of supply teachers at the school because a lot of the regular staff are often ____________ .
9 What was Jaime's reaction to the exchange visit?
a) She was looking forward to it. b) There was no way she'd do it. c) She would only go if they had lots of excursions.

Practise the vocabulary in Wordmatch/Spelling

091 **Interact**

1 Jamie isn't very keen on staying with a host family. What are her reasons? What do you think about this?
2 Why do you think Miss Martinez wants to go with her class on this trip?

092 Vocabulary: Right or wrong?

Work in pairs. Check that you have understood some of the words used in the text *Tapas and Tears* by stating whether they are used correctly in the following sentences. Mark each sentence R (Right) or W (Wrong). If wrong, explain why and write a new sentence to show how the words should be used.

1. As the pupils had behaved so badly, their teacher put them in **detention**. ____
2. After the final performance of *Les Miserables*, the director threw a party for all the actors in the **staff**. ____
3. Pupils - especially boys - will usually **try it on** with a new teacher. ____
4. My wife was driving and asked me to **keep an eye on** signposts for Llangollen. ____
5. Alice often says unkind and unpleasant things about others. She's so **bitchy**. ____
6. Only people with **universal** qualifications need apply for this job. In other words, we're looking for graduates. ____
7. Included in the tour to Las Vegas is an **excursion** to the Grand Canyon. ____
8. Because so many people are ill at the moment, the meeting has been **put up** for a week. ____
9. 'We cannot ignore the **misery** of the people in this country who are forced to live on the streets,' said the Prime Minister. ____
10. For many people, marriage is a long-term **commitment**. ____

093 Writing/Speaking

Work in pairs. Type "educational student tours" into your favourite search engine. Decide on where you want to go on a language course for two or three weeks. Find information about the following:

Destination (Europe, South America, Africa, Asia, Australia)
Which country?
Itinerary (things to do and see; sport activities, cultural activities, excursions)
Type of lodging (host family, hostel, boarding school)
Length or tour
Costs
Language classes per week
Number of students per class

When you're ready, present your information to another pair.

SINGAPORE AND BACK (page 44)

094 **Starter**

Write down five or six very important moments from your life so far, e.g. *moving to a new town, your first day at school, your first holiday abroad, etc.*

Now find a partner. Show each other what you have written and talk about the various events.

095 **Textwork**

Show that you have understood the text *Singapore and Back* by completing the statements below with information from the text. Sometimes one or two words are enough.

1 Although he was born in __________, his early years were spent in __________.
2 He would have been Australian had his father __________ he was offered there.
3 His start in life was different __________.
4 His memories of Singapore aren't __________.
5 His first words were in __________ which he'd picked up at __________.
6 From watching television he __________.
7 His early years abroad resulted in him __________.
8 The trouble with travelling as a professional footballer is that you don't __________ __________.
9 He was only __________ old when his father took a job in Singapore to do with __________.
10 His father's first job was working as a __________. It was while he was in Cheshire that he __________.

11 West Middlesex Colts were ______________________________.

12 One of the worst times Peter remembers in his football career was when __________________ ______________________________ .

13 Both his parents have ______________________________.

14 Sometimes people want to know his sister because ______________________________.

15 His parents didn't ______________________________ before they moved to Singapore.

16 In Singapore, they lived ______________________________ , not with expats.

17 In Singapore he was considered unusual by the local people because ____________________ .

18 When he went missing as a child, he was eventually found ______________________________ .

Practise the vocabulary in Wordmatch/Spelling

096 Vocabulary: Matching pairs

On the left are ten words found in the extract you have read. Check that you understand them by finding a phrase or sentence on the right that can be 'paired off' in some way.

______	1 advertising agency	a) a new planet, America, etc.
______	2 average	b) "I don't have any money!"
______	3 discover	c) It's hard to believe that TV was once a ______ !
______	4 in earnest	d) Another word for 'salary'.
______	5 novelty	e) "My job is to write commercials."
______	6 originally	f) The soldier wore his medals with ______ .
______	7 plush	g) in the beginning, before things changed
______	8 skint	h) The ______ income is £30,000 a year.
______	9 pride	i) very comfortable, expensive, of good quality
______	10 wages	j) The election is approaching and campaigning has begun ______ .

097 Interact

1 The world has become a global village with more and more people travelling and migrating to other countries. What are the benefits of migration?

2 In what ways does learning English contribute to and expand your knowledge of the world?

3 Peter Crouch became a famous football player in England's national team. Many sports people live and work abroad. Give examples.

4 What other professions give you the opportunity to live and work abroad?

5 Are you interested in an international career? Give reasons.

098 Speaking

Using the Internet, prepare a short speech on a famous footballer or other sportsman or sportswoman. Present it to a small group or the class.

099 Looking at collocations 1

For the next three units we're going to look at common collocations. But what are collocations? A collocation is a word or phrase which is often used along with another word or phrase, in a way that sounds correct to native speakers, e.g. *a strong wind, a tall building, a high mountain, a hard frost, a crying shame, commit a crime, make a cup of tea, do your homework,* etc. To be really fluent in a language, you need to know as many common collocations as possible.

Adjective + noun collocations

A Complete the definitions of collocations below by adding a suitable adjective to each noun. Choose from the following. The nouns are in **bold** type.

active	deadly	fatal	naked	rough	vivid
confirmed	delicious	infectious	narrow	unwritten	worthy

1 When you make a ___________ **guess** about something, e.g. how many people were at a football match, then the guess isn't accurate, it's just an approximate guess.
2 A ___________ **meal** is a meal that tastes really nice.
3 If you support or give money to a ___________ **cause**, this is because you think the cause is worth supporting or fighting for.
4 An ___________ **volcano** is one which might erupt at any time, e.g. Mount Etna in Italy.
5 If something can be seen with the ___________ **eye**, this means it can be seen without using a telescope, a pair of binoculars or any other instrument.
6 If someone has an ___________ **laugh**, this means that the person's laugh spreads to other people. In other words, they can't help laughing too when they hear it.
7 If you have a ___________ **escape**, this means that you only just avoid danger.
8 Someone who's a ___________ **bachelor** is a man who has decided never to marry and seems quite happy with the way of life he's chosen.
9 A person with a ___________ **imagination** is someone who has the ability to imagine unlikely situations very clearly.
10 A ___________ **weapon** is one that will kill, e.g. a gun.
11 An ___________ **law** is a law which doesn't exist officially but which people generally accept and obey.
12 A ___________ **accident** is an accident which results in someone's death.

B Now work in pairs or small groups and discuss the following.
1 Do you think some men choose to be **confirmed bachelors** or is it just something that they have no control over?
2 Have you or anybody you know ever had a **narrow escape**? If so, tell the others about it.
3 What's the most **delicious meal** you've ever eaten? What made it so delicious?
4 Name a **worthy cause** that you think is worth supporting.
5 A writer has to have a **vivid imagination**. Can you think of any other professions where a vivid imagination would be useful?
6 Name an **unwritten law** that applies in most schools.

WSM: SINGAPORE – "THE LION CITY"

How is it that a small city-state located in Southeast Asia with a total land area measuring only 710 square kilometres has become one of the most successful countries in the world? A country with a free-trade economy, a highly efficient workforce and a per capita income higher than many western countries. The answer lies in its geography and history.

The history of Singapore

According to legend, Singapore was founded centuries ago when a prince from Sumatra landed on the island and saw a lion. He took it as a good omen and founded a city called Singapura, which means "Lion City". The legend is probably not true as the nearest lions to Singapore (apart from those in the zoo) are 2,500 miles away! But it makes a nice story and the lion head symbol is to be seen everywhere in Singapore.

More about Singapore

100 Useful expressions: Idioms 2

A Complete the definitions below with a suitable idiom. Choose from these. To help you, a Swedish translation is given in brackets.

be in stitches
be like a cat on hot bricks
get hold of the wrong end of the stick
get something for a song
have a bone to pick with someone
keep your hair on
money for old rope
pull the wool over someone's eyes
put your foot in it
turn a blind eye to something

1 To ______________ is to try to trick someone or to hide your real actions or intentions from someone. *(slå blå dunster i ögonen på någon)*
2 To ______________ is to be very nervous. *(sitta som på nålar)*
3 To ______________ is to buy something very cheaply. *(köpa något för en spottstyver)*
4 To ______________ is to completely misunderstand something. *(få det hela om bakfoten)*
5 To ______________ is to be angry with someone about something and want to discuss it with them. *(ha en gås oplockad med någon)*
6 To ______________ is to pretend not to notice something bad that's happening, so that you don't have to do anything about it. *(blunda för)*
7 To ______________ is to laugh a lot (usually because you've heard or seen something really funny). *(hålla på att spricka av skratt)*
8 The phrase "______________" is used to tell someone to keep calm and not get annoyed. *(behålla lugnet)*
9 To ______________ is to make a stupid, embarrassing mistake. *(trampa i klaveret)*

10 If something is ____________________, it's money you get for doing something very easily. *(vara lättförtjänta pengar)*

B Now complete the sentences using seven of the idioms from A. Make any necessary changes.

1 'What's the matter with you, Dave? You're ____________________.'
'Yes, I know. I'm waiting for my exam results.'
2 Since the owner was moving into a smaller flat I got this sofa and two armchairs ____________________. I only paid £40 for them.
3 Trust you to ____________________! How could you offer her a meat sandwich when you knew she was a vegetarian?
4 Although we weren't really allowed to chew gum in class, most of the teachers ____________________ it.
5 'Hurry up or we'll be late!'
'All right! All right! ____________________! I'm coming!'
6 That's not what I meant at all! As usual, James, you've got ____________________!
7 The film had us all ____________________. It was so funny!

C Now write your own sentences for the three idioms left over.

____

____

____

101 Sum up and comment

1 What did you learn by using Peer response – writing? How did it improve your letter?
2 Do you think it's important to be open to international contacts and influences? Why?
3 How can you benefit from international contacts?

102 Books to read and enjoy

Cleave, Chris: *Little Bee*
Crouch, Peter: *Walking Tall: My Story*
Guo, Xiaolu: *A Concise Chinese-English Dictionary for Lovers**
Higgins, Chris: *Tapas and Tears**
Joyce, Rachel: *The Unlikely Pilgrimage of Harold Fry*
Nicholls, David: *One Day*
Treman, Rose: *The Road Home*

*teenage fiction or less advanced books

SOME NAMES WORTH KNOWING

Find an interesting project

Some Names Worth Knowing in your textbook pp. 48–50 and *Changes in the 20th Century* will give you a platform for further research into a subject area of interest to you. Start by reading those texts to give you some ideas for what to work with.

When you've written your project, make sure to use *Checklist for writing* p. 126. Also use *Peer response – writing* p. 127 and *Peer response – speaking* p. 127.

SOCIAL SCIENCE, ARTS AND HUMANITIES PROGRAMMES

1 There are many people of interest in politics, film, art, literature, drama and the media. Choose a person of interest for your presentation.
Focus on:
- the person's background
- what he/she is famous for
- any awards he/she has got
- any other items of interest

2 The 20th century is a period of many changes. Choose an important historical event.
Focus on:
- what happened
- who was/were involved
- why the event happened
- what the consequences were

3 Present an English-speaking country.
Focus on:
- its history
- population
- places of interest
- anything else of interest

4 Cultural differences in another country.
Focus on:
- what good manners are
- common customs and traditions in this culture
- national holidays
- anything else of interest

5 Find facts on the political system in the US, in the UK, in Hong Kong – or any other English-speaking country in the world.
Focus on:
- what political parties there are
- who the leaders of the different parties are and what they stand for
- how the voting process is conducted

NATURAL SCIENCE AND TECHNOLOGY PROGRAMMES

1 Many scientists have an interesting life story. Choose a person to present.
Focus on:
- his/her life and background
- the importance of his/her work
- anything else of interest

2 Inventions have an effect on people's lives. Choose and present one.
Focus on:
- what is so special about it
- what impact it has on our daily lives
- anything else of interest

3 Climate change and endangered species are important issues. Pick one that's important to you.
Focus on:
- what the situation is like
- what is being done about it
- hopes for the future

4 There are a number of fascinating constructions around the world, e.g. Burj Khalifa in Dubai, The International Commerce Centre in Hong Kong, the Golden Gate Bridge in San Francisco. Pick a building to present.
Focus on:
- the architect
- the construction itself; material, costs, etc.
- anything else of interest

BUSINESS MANAGEMENT AND ECONOMICS PROGRAMME

1 Entrepreneurs have contributed to society in various ways.
Focus on:
- an entrepreneur
- the business idea/ideas this person has
- how successful he/she has been
- any future plans for the enterprise
- anything else of interest

2 Micro loans are a way to start enterprises in some countries.
Focus on:
- what micro loans are
- what they are used for
- if they are effective
- anything else of interest

3 The Nobel Prize in Economics is awarded every year.
Focus on:
- a winner of the prize
- the economic concept
- the importance of his/her research
- anything else of interest

5 IN REAL LIFE?

MOVIE REVIEW – THE HUNGER GAMES

- [ ] Starter
- [ ] Textwork
- [ ] Interact
- [ ] Vocabulary: Definitions
- [ ] Writing: A review
- [ ] Speaking

WSM: A–Z OF FILM GENRES

FOCUS ON GRAMMAR

LISTENING: THE REAPING

- [ ] Starter
- [ ] Listen and recall
- [ ] Interact
- [ ] Vocabulary: Fill in the gaps
- [ ] Vocabulary Bank: Useful adjectives 2

WSM: JAPAN'S CHILDREN PLAY SAFE

BOLLYWOOD PEOPLE AND PLOTS

- [ ] Starter
- [ ] Textwork
- [ ] Interact
- [ ] Vocabulary: Words of similar meaning

WSM: SOME BOLLYWOOD FACTS

INSTANT MILLIONAIRE

- [ ] Starter
- [ ] Textwork
- [ ] Interact
- [ ] Let's talk!
- [ ] Looking at collocations 2
- [ ] Trivia quiz

PUBLIC, PRIVATE

- [ ] Starter
- [ ] Textwork
- [ ] Interact
- [ ] Focus on media words
- [ ] Role-play: Newspaper interviews

- [ ] Fun with vocabulary 3
- [ ] Sum up and comment
- [ ] Books to read and enjoy

MOVIE REVIEW – THE HUNGER GAMES (page 52)

103 Starter

Work in groups of 3- 4 and discuss the following questions.

1. Which is your favourite film right now? Why?
2. Which TV series are you watching at the moment? What do you think makes a TV series so interesting?

104 Textwork

Work in pairs. Read through the text *Movie Review – The Hunger Games*. Take turns to ask and answer the following questions.

1. How many books are there in "The Hunger Games" series?
2. Which word does the reviewer use to describe the presentation of the film?
3. What sort of society is depicted in the film and where do most of the population live?
4. What are "the hunger games"?
5. Who takes part in the show?
6. Who are Katniss and Peeta?
7. What does the reviewer say is 'intense' in this film?
8. The reviewer describes "The Hunger Games" as a movie without what?
9. What does the reviewer think is the most brilliant part of the movie?
10. Which adjectives does the reviewer use to describe a) Josh Hutcherson b) Liam Hemsworth and c) Wes Bentley and Toby Jones?
11. Which roles in the film do Woody Harrelson and Lenny Kravitz have?

105 Interact

1. Have you seen any of the films or read any of the books? If so, what did you think of it/them?
2. Do you think the subject matter – children killing children – is suitable entertainment, especially for young people? Give reasons.
3. Katniss and Peeta, the two main characters in *The Hunger Games*, make up a famous movie couple. What other film couples do you know of? Any favourites?

Practise the vocabulary in Wordmatch/Spelling

106 Vocabulary: Definitions

Here are definitions of ten words from the text. Can you work out what they are? To help you, the first and last letter of each missing word is given.

1 A ____ is a swear word or a religious word used in such a way that it shows you don't respect God or holy things. p__________y

2 Another word for 'disappointment'. l________n
3 A series of three books or plays written about the same situation or characters, forming a continuous story. t________y
4 If something is ____ , then it's made weaker in some way. d________d
5 An ____ person is considered by others to be strange or unusual. e________c
6 The ____ is the main story (or plot) in a book, film, etc. s________e
7 To ____ is to offer to do something without being forced to do it or without getting paid for it. v________r
8 Someone's ____ is how well or badly someone does an activity, e.g. acting. p________e
9 Another word for 'choose'. s________t
10 If something is off ____ , then it's forbidden or not allowed. l________s

Now write your own definition for <u>two</u> of the following words, again found in the text.

cast *(v)*   contestant   facilitate   off-putting

107 Writing: A review

Write a review of a film you've seen or a book you've read.
Need help? See the Resource Section p. 130.

108 Speaking

Work in pairs. Use your review as the basis for an oral presentation. You can choose to show a few scenes from the film or pictures of the author of the book.

Before you give your presentation let your friend give you some feedback by using *Peer response – speaking* **in Resource Section on p. 127.**

WSM: A-Z OF FILM GENRES

FOCUS ON GRAMMAR

	Grammar	Interactive exercise
The Perfect Simple	p. 323	
The Past Perfect	p. 323	
The Future	p. 323	
Be going to	p. 323	
Will	p. 323	

LISTENING: THE REAPING

109 **Starter**

Work in groups of 3–4. Think about some dramatic scenes you've seen from various films. Which scenes can you remember and what made them so memorable? Describe your favourite one to the others in the group.

110 **Listen and recall** To listen, follow this link

Listen to the extract *The Reaping* from *The Hunger Games* and choose the best answer (a, b or c). You're going to listen to it in two parts. In Part 1 answer questions 1–5, then listen to Part 2 and answer questions 6–12. Before you start, read through the sentences and check the words in the word list.

Part 1

1 The Reaping takes place in the square. You have to attend it unless you're *a) very young b) almost dying c) an official.*
2 The square today feels *a) bright b) pleasant c) grim.*
3 *a) 12–18 year olds b) Family members c) Racketeers* line up around the perimeter.
4 Some people bet on *a) which two children will be chosen b) who will be shot c) which merchant will cry.*
5 On the stage are *a) two b) three c) four* glass balls containing paper slips with names on them.

Part 2

6 Panem is a country that used to be called *a) Europe b) South America c) North America.*
7 One disaster the mayor talks about is *a) the sea covering much of the land b) a big earthquake c) the war against another country.*
8 The Hunger Games is a reminder that the dark days must never be repeated and happens *a) every other year b) annually c) every Leap year.*
9 The winner of the Hunger Games is the person who *a) kills the most people b) fights the best c) is the only person alive at the end.*
10 It's the Capitol's way of showing the population that *a) they're going to be destroyed b) trying to rebel would be useless c) they need to sacrifice their children.*
11 There are *a) forty-two b) hundreds c) thousands* of slips with names on in the glass ball.
12 The first name to be drawn out of the ball is *a) a boy b) a girl c) Effie Trinket.*

Practise the vocabulary in Wordmatch/Spelling

111 Interact

1 What does 'the reaping' mean?
2 Why are the hunger games repeated every year?
3 What are the rules of the hunger games and what do you think about them?
4 What role does the Capitol play?
5 Why do you think some people watch movies that they know beforehand will terrify them or make them cry?
6 Do you think watching violent movies makes people more or less likely to be violent?

112 Vocabulary: Fill in the gaps

Fill in the missing words in the sentences below. Choose from the following words, taken from the text. Then make up your own sentences for the four words that are left over.

banners	drought	participate	surround
claustrophobic	imprisoned	prosperity	temporary
concern	keep tabs on	rebellion	vast
defeated	mandatory	spotted	wasteland

1 We encourage all students to ____________ fully in the running of the college.
2 During the past twenty years ____________ areas of the Amazon rainforest have been destroyed.
3 There is growing ____________ about violence in films and on TV.
4 In 1991, the British government made it ____________ to wear rear seat belts in cars.
5 The demonstrators walked along the street, waving ____________ and shouting angrily.
6 Marks & Spencer always take on ____________ staff during the Christmas period.
7 News is just coming in of an armed ____________ against the military regime.
8 In East Africa, three years of ____________ have left 10 million people in urgent need of food and water.
9 My sister's ____________, so she hates being in lifts or crowded trains or buses.
10 A girl answering the description of the missing teenager has been ____________ in Liverpool.
11 I like Internet banking because it means I can easily ____________ all my bank accounts.
12 The North ____________ the South in the American Civil War.

113 Vocabulary Bank: Useful adjectives 2

Put the correct adjective into each sentence. They're all adjectives to describe moods, states and feelings. Choose from:

annoyed broke giddy homesick relieved

1 'Coming with us to the pictures tonight?'
'I can't. I'm ____________!' *(pank)*
2 Mary felt very ____________ when she first moved to London. She really missed her family and friends. *(hade hemlängtan)*
3 My father got very ____________ when another driver stole his parking space. *(irriterad)*
4 She was very ____________ when her doctor told her she was not seriously ill. *(lättad)*
5 I could never climb a mountain. I get ____________ just standing on a thick carpet! *(yr)*

Now go to page 306 in Vocabulary Bank and do *Useful adjectives 2.*

WSM: JAPAN'S CHILDREN PLAY SAFE

BOLLYWOOD PEOPLE AND PLOTS (page 54)

114 Starter

What do you think of when you hear the word 'Bollywood'?
Are any of these people familiar to you?

Men	**Women**
Shah Rukh Khan	Aishwarya Rai
Amitabh Bachchan	Mallika Sherawat
Salman Khan	Katrina Kaif
Anil Kapoor	Shilpa Shetty
Aamir Khan	Kareena Kapor

Try looking some of them up on the Internet. Were you surprised at what you found out?

If you had to compile a list of the top five male and female actors/actresses in Sweden, who would you choose?

115 Textwork

Read *Bollywood People and Plots* and then fill in the missing information or choose the correct answer (a, b or c). The sentences are in no special order.

1 To be a hero in a Hindi film you have to *a) speak many great lines b) defeat the villain in a fight c) become a partner with the villain.*
2 Most Hindi films are about *a) greed b) ambition c) love.*

3 In older films, lovers were often kept apart due to differences in ____________ .
4 A well-established pattern in Hindi films is to pair a hero against ____________ .
5 Unless the villain is badly beaten in the fight, the audience feel *a) dissatisfied b) contented c) cheerful.*
6 Nowadays a common theme in Hindi films is the difference in *a) caste b) family income c) jobs* between the boy and girl.
7 There are *a) only a few b) many c) just six* ways that the villain can keep the lovers apart.
8 A wealthy family whose daughter has fallen in love with a penniless boy might even try to *a) have him killed b) offer him a job with a good salary c) buy him off.*
9 The fight in Hindi movies is the ____________ to the movie.

116 Interact

1 What kind of pattern do the Indian love stories follow? Is it a pattern you recognize? Give examples.
2 How has the plot been influenced by changes in society? Is the same thing happening in western films? Give examples.
3 What, in your opinion, are the main ingredients that make a good film?

Practise the vocabulary in Wordmatch/Spelling

117 Vocabulary: Words of similar meaning

Complete the pairs of words below with another word that is similar in meaning. Choose from the following words, all taken from the text.

considerable	essential	opponent
courage	myriad	punch-up
devious	narrative	thwart
envious	obstacle	villain

1 adversary, antagonist, ____________
2 baddie, scoundrel, ____________
3 block, foil, ____________
4 bravery, valour, ____________
5 countless, infinite, ____________
6 fight, brawl, ____________
7 jealous, covetous, ____________
8 large, substantial, ____________
9 setback, hurdle, ____________
10 sneaky, underhand, ____________
11 story, tale, ____________
12 vital, crucial, ____________

WSM: SOME BOLLYWOOD FACTS

Bollywood is often referred to as India's equivalent to Hollywood. It began in Bombay (renamed Mumbai) in the 1930s and developed into an enormous film empire. The term "Bollywood" was adapted from a combination of the words **Bo**mbay and Ho**llywood**. The term is often incorrectly used to refer to the whole of Indian cinema. However, it's only a part of the total Indian film industry, which includes other production centres producing films in multiple languages.

Roughly defined, Bollywood is a film genre that incorporates many aspects of India's cultural wealth. It's often formally referred to as Hindi cinema. The typical Bollywood film is characterized by bright colours, song and dance sequences, and a host of other conventions. The sets and costumes are very ornate and there's a great emphasis on movement and expression through dance.

On average, a Bollywood film lasts for about three to four hours. The films are so long because the film plays out the entire story to completion. Not much is left out as far as content goes. Thus, by the end of a Bollywood film, the viewer has been taken on a roller coaster of different sensations: love, sorrow, suspense, adventure, anger, and the like.

Bollywood was originally considered a movement, but has now grown into a full-fledged genre because of its overwhelming popularity within India and with international audiences.

Bollywood exports films to more than 95 countries around the world and actually produces more films annually than Hollywood does.

Some fun facts:

- Bollywood is the largest film producer in India with over 1,000 films produced each year (approximately 3 films a day), with annual ticket sales of $3.6 billion.
- India is home to the largest film studio in the world – Ramoji Film City.
- Many Bollywood screenplays are adaptations of popular western scripts.
- 14 million Indians watch Bollywood movies on a daily basis and pay the equivalent of the average Indian's day's wages ($1–3) to see a film.
- The vast majority of Hindi films are still dubbed. Playback singers record the songs, which the actors and actresses lip-synch to in the films.

INSTANT MILLIONAIRE (page 56)

118 **Starter**

Make a list of your five favourite TV quiz programmes – past or present.

1 ______
2 ______
3 ______
4 ______
5 ______

Work in groups of 3–4 and compare your answers.
Why do you think quiz programmes are so popular?

119 **Textwork**

Show that you have understood the text *Instant Millionaire* by completing the statements below with information from the text. Sometimes one or two words are enough.

1 The film *Slumdog Millionaire* was based on an Indian ______ .
2 The large screen in the studio is for ______.
3 Contestants can win ______ rupees.
4 The audience begin clapping when they see ______.
5 The contestants have been chosen ______.
6 The contestant who appears to be the most well-educated is ______ from ______.
7 Prem Kumar scowls at Ram Mohammad Thomas because ______.
8 When asked 'And what will you do if you win today?' one answer he might have given is, ' ______.'
9 You can quit at any time as long as ______ .
10 'A Friendly Tip' and 'Half and Half' are known as ______ .
11 The first question is about ______ .
12 While Prem is thinking of his answer you can hear music and ______ .

120 **Interact**

1 The programme *Who Wants to Be a Millionaire?* has been popular all over the world. Are there any other TV programmes (not only quizzes) that have been popular in lots of countries?
2 Are there many reality shows in Sweden, e.g. *Big Brother*? Can you explain why they seem to be so popular?
3 What effect do you think these series have on people's lives?

Practise the vocabulary in Wordmatch/Spelling

Another exercise on the words in the word list

121 Let's talk!

What if...?

Work in groups of 3- 4 people and discuss the following statements.

1 If you could be the son or daughter of one famous person who is still alive, who would you want it to be and why?
2 If you could have one special talent what would that be and why?
3 If you had the chance being either rich, famous, happy or very intelligent, which would you choose and why?
4 If you believed the world was going to end in a week's time, how would you spend that week?
5 If you had to eat the same food every day for a whole month (and nothing else) what would you choose and why?
6 If there was the equivalent of an Oscar for the performance (live speeches, etc.) of politicians, who would win the award in your country?
7 If you could have chosen your own first name and surname, what would you have chosen instead of your present name?
8 If you had to be without something you like for a week, what would you least like to be without and why?
9 If you had to emigrate to another country to find work, which country would you choose and why?
10 If you could travel back in time and change one event in history, what would that be and why?

122 Looking at collocations 2

Verb + noun collocations

A Complete the definitions of collocations below by adding a suitable verb to each noun. Choose from the following. The nouns are in **bold** type.

abandon	commit	foot	hold	make	run
catch	do	foretell	lose	play	take

1 When you ______________ someone **a favour**, you do something for them in order to help them or to be kind to them.
2 When you ask someone who's phoning you to ______________ **the line**, you want them to wait.
3 When you ______________ **precautions**, you do something in order to prevent something dangerous or unpleasant from happening.
4 To ______________ **a cold** is to become ill with a cold.

5 To ______________ **a fuss** is to complain or become angry about something, especially when it's not really necessary.
6 If you can ______________ **the future**, then you're able to say what's going to happen.
7 If the captain gives the order to ______________ **ship** then he wants the crew and passengers to leave it because it's sinking.
8 To ______________ **truant** is to stay away from school without permission.
9 To ______________ **face** is to do something which makes other people stop respecting you.
10 To ______________ **a crime** is to break the law by doing something illegal.
11 To ______________ **the bill** is to be responsible for paying something - especially something expensive that you may not want to pay for.
12 To ______________ **a bath** is to fill it up with water.

B Now work in pairs or small groups and discuss the following.

1 If you could **foretell the future**, would you put your talent to good use or would you use it for personal gain?
2 When was the last time you **did a favour** for someone? Tell the others about it. When was the last time someone did you a favour? Again, tell the others about it.
3 Are there any ways you know to prevent you from **catching a cold**? If you've already caught a cold, what's the best treatment for it?
4 Do people in Sweden realize that they are **committing a crime** when they take a bar of chocolate or something else small from a shop without paying for it? What are some of the reasons why people commit crimes?
5 Have you ever **played truant**? Why? What excuse did you give for not being at school?
6 Who usually **foots the bill** for a wedding in Sweden? Does it depend on your nationality or religion?

123 Trivia quiz

Work in teams of 3–4 per team. Now's your chance to see how good you are at quizzes. Your teacher will give you more information.

PUBLIC, PRIVATE (page 59)

124 Starter

Work in pairs. Write down five advantages and five disadvantages of being a 'celebrity'.

Advantages	Disadvantages
______________	______________
______________	______________
______________	______________
______________	______________
______________	______________

Now find another pair. Compare and discuss your answers.

125 **Textwork**

Read through the text *Public, Private!* and decide which of the four alternatives (A, B, C or D) you think is correct. Sometimes two answers are correct.

1 What do we learn about Dannii Minogue's day at the beginning of the extract?
- A ☐ She's been competing on the *X Factor.*
- B ☐ She's going to make a vegetarian dish for two friends of hers.
- C ☐ She's driving a Jaguar through London.
- D ☐ She's late.

2 Why does Nathan phone her?
- A ☐ He wants to tell her a joke.
- B ☐ To tell her that a national newspaper has found out that she's expecting a baby.
- C ☐ To force her to deny the story.
- D ☐ To give her the results of a scan she had recently.

3 What's the main reason why she doesn't have a glass of wine when she gets home?
- A ☐ Because she's pregnant.
- B ☐ Because she's too tired.
- C ☐ Because she has to make a phone call.
- D ☐ Because she has to prepare the meal.

4 Why is Dannii so upset about the newspaper wanting to publish the story?
- A ☐ Because her parents know nothing about her pregnancy.
- B ☐ Because she hasn't told her boyfriend, Simon, yet.
- C ☐ Because she's only six weeks pregnant.
- D ☐ Because she won't get paid for the story.

5 How can they prevent the newspaper from publishing the story?
- A ☐ By trying to bribe the editor.
- B ☐ By telling the newspaper that she's less than three months pregnant.
- C ☐ By issuing a denial.
- D ☐ By standing up for her rights.

6 Which of the following is/are true?
- A ☐ She sends an email to Kris telling him about everything.
- B ☐ She tries texting her parents.
- C ☐ She ends up having to make a decision on her own.
- D ☐ Before today, her PR company had no idea that she was pregnant.

126 Interact

1 The media is often blamed for not showing respect for celebrities' private lives. Why is that so?
2 Why are their private lives so interesting to people in general?
3 Would you like to read about your own private life in the papers? How important is it to keep your private life private? Give reasons.
4 Do you agree with the saying 'There is no such thing as bad publicity'? In other words 'Any publicity is good publicity'.

Practise the vocabulary in Wordmatch/Spelling

Another exercise on the words in the word list

127 Focus on media words

Here are 34 words to do with various media. Put the words under the correct headings.

article, avatar, blockbuster, blog, browser, captions, circulation, colour supplement, credits, director, editor, extras, follower, forum, headline, journalist, on location, plot, podcast, producer, profile, scoop, screenplay, soundtrack, special effects, subscription, subtitles, tabloid, trailer, tweet, unfriend, upload, website, widget

Newspapers & Magazines (10 words)

____________	____________
____________	____________
____________	____________
____________	____________
____________	____________

Films & Television (12 words)

____________	____________
____________	____________
____________	____________
____________	____________
____________	____________
____________	____________

Social Media & The Internet (12 words)

____________	____________
____________	____________
____________	____________
____________	____________
____________	____________
____________	____________

128 **Role-Play: Newspaper interviews**

Work in pairs - A and B. A is a newspaper reporter while B is someone who's going to be interviewed. Decide your roles. When you've done it once, you can change roles and do it again. Your teacher will give you more information.

129 **Fun with vocabulary 3**

Newspaper misprints

Newspapers don't always print the truth and sometimes what you read is not exactly what the newspaper intended. A letter in the wrong place or left out can completely alter the meaning of a sentence.

Work in pairs or groups of three. Look at the following extracts from newspapers and magazines. Each contains a misprint. Underline the word which is wrong and suggest which word should have been used instead.

Example:
Student (female) wanted to share <u>fat</u> with two others.
(Correct word: **flat**)

1 Artist Pablo Cassels, lost his pants on the London Underground last week and he has offered £200 to the person who returns them. ____________
2 At dawn a small group of fishermen gathered outside government offices to protest against the plans to restrict fishing in the North Sea. The crowd began to smell and by noon had brought traffic in the area to a standstill. ____________
3 Celebrate Christmas in the heat of Scotland at the Lochmuir Inn. ____________
4 CLOTHES BRUSH: The genuine pigskin back opens with a zip and inside are tweezers, scissors, nail file and a bomb. ____________
5 Competitors from all over the world are arriving in Ottowa, Canada, for the World Ice-Dancing Championships. Many people think the British will win because they have the strongest tea. ____________
6 Fun-loving male, 23, tall and slimy, looking for female 20–25 for companionship, possibly romance. ____________
7 Ice cream sellers in London say they have ordered huge socks because of the unusual hot weather spell. ____________
8 The elderly couple in the top flat found the stars too much for them and they sold it. ____________
9 Win a free weekend for two! You'll get free fights, hotel rooms and spending money. ____________
10 Police are looking for a man who attacked a young girl in the city zoo. The police now have a photofit picture of the man. He is in his 30s, tall, with blond hair and a brown bear. ____________
11 The price of the holiday includes all food, plus wind, coffee and cakes. ____________

12 Very young children will pick up insects and they will even try to eat them. It is important that parents teach their children about the different kinds of insects. For example, it is important that they know that bees sing when they are touched. ______________

130 Sum up and comment

1 What did you learn by using *Peer response – speaking*? How did it improve your presentation?
2 Why is it necessary to be critical to what's broadcast on TV or what's written in the newspapers?
3 Has working with this unit influenced your attitude towards media in any ways? Give reasons.

131 Books to read and enjoy

Adiga, Aravind: *Last Man in Tower*
Collins, Suzanne: *The Hunger Games**; *Catching Fire**; *Mockingjay**
Dirie, Waris: *Desert Flower, Desert Dawn*
Kabir, Nasreen Munni: *Bollywood: The Indian Cinema Story*
Minogue, Dannii: *My Story*
Pearl, Mariane: *A Mighty Heart*
Swarup, Vikas: *Slumdog Millionaire**

*teenage fiction or less advanced books

6 CITY LIFE

THE BIG APPLE
☐ Textwork ☐ Interact ☐ Speaking

WSM: ABOUT NEW YORK CITY

FOCUS ON GRAMMAR

LISTENING: WHICH CITY?
☐ Starter
☐ Listen and recall
☐ Vocabulary: Definitions
☐ Writing

VERTICAL LIVING
☐ Starter
☐ Textwork
☐ Interact
☐ Focus on types of accommodation
☐ Activity
☐ Vocabulary Bank: Useful adjectives 3
☐ Role play: Holiday home to let

IF MY DAD WERE STILL HERE
☐ Starter ☐ Vocabulary: What does it mean?
☐ Textwork

THE BALLAD OF SONNY PAYNE
☐ Starter
☐ Textwork
☐ Vocabulary: Fill in the gaps
☐ Interact
☐ Looking at collocations 3
☐ Speaking/Writing

WSM: CENTREPOINT – THE LEADING CHARITY

NEW YORK, NEW YORK
☐ Interact

☐ Useful expressions: Idioms 3
☐ Sum up and comment
☐ Books to read and enjoy

THE BIG APPLE (page 64)

132 Textwork

Without looking back at the text *The Big Apple,* match the opening sentences (1–18) with the correct endings (a–r). They're in no special order.

_____	1	The Statue of Liberty was a gift
_____	2	The Grand Central Station
_____	3	In Downtown, you'll find
_____	4	Brooklyn Bridge spans
_____	5	Broadway
_____	6	Strawberry Fields is connected with
_____	7	New York got its nickname "The Big Apple"
_____	8	The Empire State Building
_____	9	Macy's
_____	10	The Twin Towers used to be
_____	11	There are five boroughs
_____	12	Wall Street houses
_____	13	You can get to the Statue of Liberty
_____	14	The United Nations building
_____	15	'Ground Zero' is where
_____	16	Central Park
_____	17	People in Harlem
_____	18	Annually, 50 million tourists

a) the East River.
b) is in Uptown.
c) in the 1920s.
d) in Downtown.
e) from France.
f) visit the city.
g) is at the end of 42nd Street.
h) the New York Stock Exchange.
i) is a popular meeting place.
j) is in Midtown.
k) are mostly African-American.
l) the Twin Towers used to be.
m) is the theatre district.
n) is a large department store.
o) by ferry from Manhattan.
p) Chinatown and Little Italy.
q) in New York City.
r) John Lennon.

Now check your answers by reading *The Big Apple* again.

133 Interact

1. What do you think it would be like to live in a city with more than 8 million people?
2. If you ever visited New York City, what would you like to do?
3. What movies have you seen that take place in New York City? What impression do you get of the city?
4. Most people in the world nowadays live in cities – often mega cities of 15 million or more. This trend will probably increase in the future as the world's population grows. What are the dangers or problems of such a trend?

Practise the vocabulary in Wordmatch/Spelling

134 Speaking

Find out more about people connected to New York City. What are they famous for? Present your information to a group. Here are some suggestions:

Andy Warhol	Helen Keller	Lady Gaga
Dag Hammarskjöld	Jacqueline Onassis Kennedy	Peter Minuit
Gertrude Stein	Jonas Bronck	Woody Allen
Greta Garbo	Keith Haring	Yoko Ono

WSM: ABOUT NEW YORK CITY

FOCUS ON GRAMMAR

	Grammar
Asking questions	p. 324
Verb + to / Verb + -ing	p. 325

LISTENING: WHICH CITY?

135 Starter

Work in pairs. Make a list of the 10 top cities to visit. If you can agree, put them in order 1–10.

1 ______	6 ______
2 ______	7 ______
3 ______	8 ______
4 ______	9 ______
5 ______	10 ______

Now find another pair and compare your answers.
Were they very similar or very different?

136 **Listen and recall** To listen, follow this link

You're going to listen to ten short dialogues. Try to identify in which city the people are. Fill in the letter of the place you choose in the appropriate box below. You'll only hear the dialogues **once**. Before you start, look at the list of cities.

A Dublin	**F** San Francisco	**K** Gibraltar	**P** Kolkata (Calcutta)
B Toronto	**G** Washington	**L** Singapore	**Q** Kingston
C Sydney	**H** Manchester	**M** Ottawa	**R** Paris
D Hong Kong	**I** Auckland	**N** Manila	
E Cape Town	**J** Edinburgh	**O** New York	

Write your answers here:

1	2	3	4	5	6	7	8	9	10

Practise the vocabulary in Wordmatch/Spelling

137 **Vocabulary: Definitions**

Here are definitions of ten words found in the listening exercise. Can you work out what they are? To help you, the first and last letter of each missing word is given.

1 To walk or travel around an area without any definite aim or direction. r________m
2 A type of thick skirt made of tartan that's traditionally worn by Scottish men and boys. k________t
3 Someone who's _____ is rude in an amusing or annoying way. c________y
4 A violent storm with very strong winds, especially in the western Atlantic Ocean. h________e
5 You might easily feel _____ if you were looking down from a high building. d________y
6 To look at something or someone for a long time with your eyes wide open. s________e
7 The area of Australia that's far away from the coast and towns, especially the desert areas in central Australia. o________k
8 An area of water on the coast, protected from the open sea by strong walls, where ships can shelter. h________r
9 Something that's _____ is connected with God or a god and/or considered to be holy. s________d
10 A current of unpleasantly cold air blowing through a room. d________t

Now write your own definitions for <u>two</u> of the following words, again found in the listening exercise.

fabulous handsome moan subway

138 **Writing**

Using the text *The Big Apple* as a guide, write your own text about one of the cities (except New York City) in the listening exercise *Which City*?

VERTICAL LIVING (page 68)

139 **Starter**

As more and more people move into cities, the problem arises of where to house them all. The only logical solution is to go 'up' – in other words to house people in high-rise buildings.

Work in groups of 3–4.

1. How do you feel about living in high-rise buildings?
2. Should there be a limit on how many storeys a building has? Give reasons.

140 **Textwork**

Show that you have understood the text *Vertical Living* by completing the statements below with information from the text.
Sometimes one or two words are enough.

1. The first high-rise buildings were made possible by ______________________ .
2. Taller skyscrapers were possible by 2000 because of ______________________ .
3. A skyscraper has to be strong enough to cope with natural forces such as ______________ and ______________ .
4. The ______________ carry the weight of the building.
5. The frame of a skyscraper is usually made of ______________ or ______________ .
6. In many modern skyscrapers, ______________ bear the load.
7. The two categories of skyscraper frames are ______________ and ______________ .
8. The main support in a cable-hung skyscraper is from a ______________ . This acts as both ______________ and as ______________ .

141 **Interact**

1. What famous skyscrapers in the world do you know of?
2. Which building is the highest today?
3. What does it take to work as a construction worker on a skyscraper? Picture yourself 800 meters up in the air!
4. What would be your ideal home? *(flat, house, centre of town, by the coast, in the countryside, with a garden,* etc.). Describe it.

Practise the vocabulary in Wordmatch/Spelling

142 Focus on types of accommodation

A Work in pairs or groups of three. Here are 30 different types of accommodation. How many are you familiar with? Which ones have you never heard of? Test yourself on some of them by matching ten of them to the definitions below.

barracks	flat/apartment	lighthouse	semi-detached house
bedsit	gated community	listed building	shack
block of flats	guesthouse	lodge	tent
bungalow	hostel	log cabin	terraced house
caravan	hotel	maisonette	villa
condominium	houseboat	mansion	youth hostel
cottage	hut	penthouse flat	
detached house	igloo	ranch	

1 A ______________ is joined to another house by a wall on one side that is shared.
2 A ______________ is an apartment building in which each apartment is owned separately by the people living in it, but the shared areas are owned by everyone together.
3 A ______________ is a house usually in the countryside or near the sea, especially in southern Europe, and often one which people can rent for a holiday.
4 A ______________ is a rented room which has a bed, table, chairs and somewhere to cook in it.
5 A ______________ is a flat or apartment with rooms on two floors that's part of a larger house, but usually with its own entrance.
6 A ______________ is a house built all on one level, without stairs.
7 A ______________ is a group of houses surrounded by a wall or fence, with an entrance that's guarded.
8 A ______________ is one of a row of houses that are joined together on each side.
9 A ______________ is a small house, usually in the countryside. Some of them might even have a thatched roof.
10 A ______________ is a building of great historical or artistic value which is officially protected to prevent it from being changed or destroyed.

B Which of the above are these?

1 vandrarhem ______________
2 husvagn ______________
3 hyreshus ______________
4 fyr ______________
5 timmerstuga ______________

C If you had to live in one of the above, which would you choose and why? Which would you definitely not like to live in?

143 **Activity**

Work in small groups. Professionals like artists, designers and architects all have creative jobs. But what is actually art?

1 How would you explain to a group of Martians what art is?
2 How would you convince them of the value of art?
3 Does it matter what pictures, sculptures, designer goods and buildings look like?

144 **Vocabulary Bank: Useful adjectives 3**

Put the correct adjective into each sentence. Choose from:

essential fortunate poisonous rural thorough

1 It's a lot harder to get to a hospital if you live in a ________ area. *(lantligt)*
2 If you're going walking in the mountains this weekend, it's ________ that you have a good pair of walking boots. *(väsentligt)*
3 After a ________ examination by Norwegian typewriting experts, they have come to the conclusion that the Viking Diary found just over a year ago is, in fact, a forgery. *(grundlig)*
4 He crashed into a tree and was very ________ not to have been killed. *(lyckosam)*
5 Many ordinary plants in the garden are, in fact, ________ . *(giftiga)*

Now turn to page 307 in Vocabulary Bank and do *Useful adjectives 3.*

145 **Role play: Holiday home to let**

Work in pairs – A and B. Your teacher will give you more information.

IF MY DAD WERE STILL HERE (page 71)

146 **Starter**

On September 11, 2001, the Twin Towers in New York were destroyed when two planes that had been hijacked flew directly into each tower. Nearly 3,000 people were killed.

1 How much do you know about the 9/11 terrorist attack?
2 Are there any other terrorist attacks you can remember?
3 Have there ever been any in Sweden?

147 Textwork

Work in pairs. Read through the text *If My Dad Were Still Here*. Take turns to ask and answer the following questions.

1. How old was Max when he heard the news of his father's death and where was he when he heard it?
2. He was taken to see his mother. What does he remember about that meeting?
3. What had happened by the time they got home that day?
4. What is Max's last memory of his father?
5. What activity that he'd shared with his father helped him cope with his grief?
6. What other of his father's passions did he take up?
7. What is the significance of the tattoo on his forearm?
8. What memories does he have of his dad on Sundays?
9. Why wasn't his graduation day as special as it might have been?
10. What's difficult about his birthday this year?
11. What did he learn at a very young age?
12. What did the death of Osama bin Laden mean for him and his mother?

Practise the vocabulary in Wordmatch/Spelling

Another exercise on the words in the word list

148 Vocabulary: What does it mean?

You're now going to explain the meaning of some of the words used in the text *If My Dad Were Still Here*. Complete the following sentences by giving English explanations of the words in **bold**. Make your explanations as exact as possible.

*Example***:** To **chase** someone is to ________________ .
(*Answer*: quickly follow them in order to catch them / run after them and try to catch them)

1. A **memorial service** is usually held to remember people who ________________.
2. Max had a photo of his father holding him as an **infant**. This means the photo was taken when Max was ________________ .
3. When you **hug** someone, you ________________ .
4. When you **coach** a baseball team, you ________________ .
5. The army is **plotting** to overthrow the government. This means the army is ________________ to overthrow the government.
6. Max is a **sophomore** at the University of New Haven. This means he's ________________ .
7. To **graduate** from high school means you ________________ .
8. He realized how **valuable** life could be. This means he realized that life was ________________ .
9. When you **hang up** when someone phones you, this means you ________________ .
10. To **quote** something is to ________________ .

THE BALLAD OF SONNY PAYNE (page 74)

149 Starter

Read the following text about *The Big Issue* and write **ONE** word in each gap. The word you write must make sense in the text and be grammatically correct.

The Big Issue was launched in 1991 by Gordon Roddick and John Bird (1)__________ response to the growing number of rough sleepers on the streets of London. The two set out to address the (2)__________ of homelessness by offering homeless people the (3)__________ to earn a legitimate income; to 'help them to help themselves'.

(4)__________ than twenty years on, the organisation has helped thousands of vulnerable people to take control (5)__________ their lives, and currently works with (6)__________ 2,000 homeless and vulnerably housed people across the UK.

In order to become a *Big Issue* vendor an individual must (7)__________ that they are homeless or at risk of homelessness, and must undergo an induction process and sign (8)__________ to the code of conduct. Once they have done so they are allocated a fixed pitch and issued with a number of free (9)__________ of the magazine. Once they have (10)__________ these magazines they can purchase further copies, which they buy for £1.25 and sell for £2.50, thereby making a (11)__________ of £1.25 per copy.

Source: http://www.bigissue.com/about-us

Have you ever heard of *The Big Issue*? Do you think it's a good idea? Would you buy it?

150 Textwork

Read *The Ballad of Sonny Payne.* Then fill in the missing information or choose the correct answer (a, b or c). The sentences are in no special order.

1 Sonny always aims to make $ __________ a day.
2 Sonny never drinks __________ because it doesn't agree with him
3 Twenty-three years ago, Sonny *a) quit his job b) was sacked from his job c) was made redundant.*
4 When Sonny is given money, he usually *a) counts it b) puts it into one of his pockets c) weighs it.*
5 The writer has known Sonny for __________ years.
6 When he has enough coins, Sonny changes them into __________ .
7 Sonny used to __________ when he lived with his mother in Queens.
8 Seeing Sonny always *a) made the writer feel happy b) made the writer sad c) cost the writer a lot of money.*

9 Sonny prefers to stay in *a) city-run shelters b) small churches c) disused apartments.*
10 Sonny says he finds being homeless very *a) relaxing b) exciting c) stressful.*
11 Sonny came to America from ____________ .
12 Which of these is true about Sonny?
a) He prefers living on the street. b) He's afraid of responsibility
c) He'd like to live in an apartment again.
13 'Leashes' is Sonny's word for ____________ .

Practise the vocabulary in Wordmatch/Spelling

151 Vocabulary: Fill in the gaps

Fill in the missing words in the sentences below. Choose from the following words, taken from the text. Then make up your own sentences for the four words that are left over.

access	gang up on	respond	shakes
adequate	laid off	responsibility	shelter
dime	leash	review	sigh
exchange	on average	rough	tease

1 There was a sign in the park saying, "All dogs must be kept on a ____________ ."
2 They opened a ____________ to provide temporary housing for the city's homeless.
3 His salary wasn't that high, but it was ____________ for his needs.
4 The new Hobbit film got a very good ____________ in most newspapers. The critics seemed to like it.
5 Nearly 500 workers have been ____________ at the Tata Steelworks in South Wales.
6 I asked her what her name was, but she didn't ____________ .
7 You can ____________ your currency for dollars at the hotel.
8 Don't ____________ him about his big ears – that's very cruel!
9 The only ____________ to the island was by boat.
10 Prices have risen ____________ by about 5% this year.
11 If I drink too much coffee, I always get the ____________ .
12 It must be really ____________ to have two children and nowhere to live.

152 Interact

1 What's your opinion of the life Sonny Payne leads?
2 What makes school children tease homeless people?
3 What do you think about his explanation as to why people remain homeless?
4 Why is there an increasing number of homeless people in Sweden?
5 Suggest some causes for people becoming homeless.
6 What can be done to help homeless people?

153 Looking at collocations 3

More verb + noun collocations

A Complete the definitions of collocations below by adding a suitable verb to each noun. Choose from the following. The nouns are in **bold** type.

bear	cut	fill	have	recite	serve
change	drop	forge	quench	resist	use

1 To ____________ **a poem** is to say it out loud or from memory, especially for other people to listen to.
2 When you ____________ someone **a line**, you write a short letter to them.
3 To ____________ **a fit** is to be very angry, shocked or upset.
4 To ____________ **time** is to spend a period of time in prison.
5 To ____________ **a grudge** is to have a feeling of anger or dislike towards someone because of something bad they've done to you in the past.
6 To ____________ **a signature** is to make an illegal copy of it in order to cheat people.
7 To ____________ **your thirst** is to stop yourself feeling thirsty by drinking something.
8 To ____________ **your losses** is to stop doing something that isn't successful before the situation becomes even worse.
9 If you say, "____________ **your head**!" to someone, you're telling them in a slightly angry way that they should think more carefully about what they're doing.
10 To ____________ **your mind** is to form a new opinion or make a new decision about something which is different from your old one.
11 To ____________ **a vacancy** is to find or be a new person for a job.
12 To ____________ **the temptation** is not to give in to a strong desire to have or do something – especially something that you know is bad or wrong.

B Now work in pairs or small groups and discuss the following.

1 Is there anyone famous in Sweden who has **served time**? What was it for?
2 What sort of things make people **bear a grudge** towards others?
3 Have you ever had to **recite a poem**? If so, which poem was it and how did you feel? If not, which poem would you choose if you were ever asked to recite one?
4 Is it difficult to **resist the temptation** to do certain things? What, for example?
5 What can you drink, apart form water, to **quench your thirst**?
6 Describe an occasion when you **changed your mind** about something.

154 Speaking/Writing

Work in groups. Use the library or the Internet to find a charity devoted to helping the homeless. Gather facts, photos, etc. then design a poster drawing attention to the plight of homeless people. Bring your poster to class to show to the other groups. Discuss the posters. Which one made the biggest impression?

WSM:
CENTREPOINT – THE LEADING CHARITY FOR HOMELESS YOUNG PEOPLE IN THE UK

In the UK, 80,000 young people experience homelessness every year. Centrepoint's mission is to end youth homelessness and to give homeless young people a future.

Our Mission

We work to give homeless young people a future. To realise this future we work directly with over 1,000 young people aged 16-25 every year. We also collaborate with other organisations across the UK, conduct research and influence government policy which affects homeless young people. Crucially, we also give homeless young people a voice through the Centrepoint Parliament.

Supporting young people

- Centrepoint supports over 1,000 young people a year.
- Since 1969, Centrepoint has helped more than 75,000 young people.
- Centrepoint works with young people with a diverse range of needs and personal histories.
- Centrepoint provides a range of housing and support so young people can start tackling the issues that lead to them becoming homeless.

More than just housing

We believe in an integrated solution starting with a safe home and building on this to create firm foundations for the future. So we provide more than just accommodation for homeless young people. Our award winning Support and Development approach helps young people expand their social and life skills, gain education and training and move on to independent living.

Tackling the causes of youth homelessness

Through policy and research work, we try to increase public understanding of the causes and effects of youth homelessness. We push for practical changes in policies which would reduce homelessness and enhance the life chances of the young people who use our services.

Collaborating

We partner with smaller organisations across the country to share best practice, experience and resources, helping to build capacity and improve outcomes.

Our patron

Prince William became Centrepoint's patron in 2005.

http://www.centrepoint.org.uk/home

Q: Are there any similar charities in Sweden?

NEW YORK, NEW YORK (page 76)

155 Interact

Work in pairs. Take turns to ask and answer the following questions about the lyrics to *New York, New York*.

1 How is New York City described in the song?
2 What other songs about famous cities do you know?
3 Compare *New York, New York* to the song *Streets of London*.

156 Useful expressions: Idioms 3

A Complete the definitions below with a suitable idiom. Choose from these. To help you, a Swedish translation is given in brackets.

(be) a piece of cake
(be) at a loose end
have a chip on your shoulder
have a finger in every pie
live beyond your means
pass the buck
pull strings
put your foot down
speak your mind
talk shop

1 To ____________ is to spend more money than you receive as income. *(leva över sina tillgångar)*
2 To ____________ is to say firmly that someone must do something or must stop doing something. *(säga ifrån, sätta ner foten)*
3 To ____________ is to be involved in and have influence over many different activities, often in a way that people don't approve of. *(ha ett finger med i spelet)*
4 To ____________ is to blame someone or make them responsible for a problem that you should deal with. *(vältra över ansvaret på)*
5 To ____________ is to use your influence with important people in order to get what you want or to help someone else. *(använda sitt inflytande, utnyttja kontakter)*
6 If you find yourself ____________, this means you have nothing to do. *(sysslolös, utan något att göra)*
7 To ____________ is to tell people exactly what you think – even if it offends them. *(säga sin åsikt)*
8 To ____________ is to talk about work with colleagues, when you're not at work – for example at a party. *(prata jobb)*
9 If you say that something was ____________, you mean that it was very easy. *(lätt som en plätt; hur enkel som helst)*
10 To ____________ is to seem angry all the time because you think you've been treated unfairly or feel you're not as good as other people. *(vara lättstött; vara snarstucken; tro sig förfördelad)*

B Now complete the sentences using seven of the idioms from A. Make any necessary changes.

1 My daughter wanted to stay out until 4 o'clock in the morning, but I soon __________________ and made her come home at 11.30.
2 I hate going to a party with groups of doctors or nurses as they always seem to want to __________________ .
3 My father always told me to be careful with money - to save rather than borrow and, above all, never to __________________ .
4 You usually have to wait at least two years to be a member of this club, unless of course you know someone who can __________________ for you.
5 'What was the exam like, Carol?'
'Really easy! It was __________________ .'
6 Whenever Charles gets the blame for something, he always tries to __________________ .
7 If you're __________________ on Friday evening, why not come round to my place? We can have a meal and a chat.

C Now write your own sentences for the three idioms left over.

____

____

____

157 Sum up and comment

1 Sum up and comment on your opinions about big city life.
2 Why is it difficult for young people to find somewhere to live in big cities?
3 Time to assess your level of English! Turn to the Resource Section p. 122 and evaluate how you're progressing.

158 Books to read and enjoy

Auster, Paul: *True Tales of American Life*
Cabot, Meg: *The Princess Diaries**
Cohn Rachel & Levithan David: *Dash & Lily's Book of Dares**
Doyle, Roddy: *Oh, Play That Thing*
Ellis, Bret Easton: *American Psycho*
King, Stephen: *The Stand*
Kraus, Nicole: *The History of Love*
Safran Foer, Jonathan: *Extremely Loud & Incredibly Close*

*teenage fiction or less advanced books

7 GET (DIS)CONNECTED

CHILDHOOD MEMORIES

- [ ] Starter
- [ ] Textwork
- [ ] Interact
- [ ] Vocabulary: Choose the meaning
- [ ] Let's talk!

- [ ] **FOCUS ON GRAMMAR**

LISTENING: THE STORY OF THE MAKGABE

- [ ] Starter
- [ ] Listen and recall
- [ ] Interact
- [ ] Writing: Mini sagas

CAN YOU SEE ME?

- [ ] Starter
- [ ] Interact
- [ ] One word only
- [ ] Vocabulary Bank: Useful nouns 1

PLAYING THE ENEMY

- [ ] Starter
- [ ] Textwork
- [ ] Vocabulary: Definitions
- [ ] Interact
- [ ] Looking at word-building 1

LISTENING: AFTER THE GAME

- [ ] Listen and recall
- [ ] Interact

WSM: FOCUS ON APARTHEID

- [ ] Fun with vocabulary 4
- [ ] Sum up and comment
- [ ] Books to read and enjoy

CHILDHOOD MEMORIES (page 78)

159 **Starter**

What do you think of these three quotations?
Is there any truth in them?

"We may not be able to prepare the future for our children, but we can at least prepare our children for the future." *Franklin D. Roosevelt*

"There is always one moment in childhood when the door opens and lets the future in." *Graham Greene*

"All of us are products of our childhood." *Michael Jackson*

160 **Textwork**

Read *Childhood Memories* and then fill in the missing information or choose the correct answer (a, b or c). The sentences are in no special order.

1 It didn't rain while they were out flying their kites. *a) True b) False*
2 They were told to go to sleep at about *a) half past nine b) half past ten c) half past eleven.*
3 They both like playing with ______________ .
4 Grainne is from *a) Wicklow b) Belfast c) Dublin.*
5 She smelt of ______________ and ______________ .
6 The writer's father only called him 'son' when he was *a) angry b) drunk c) tired.*
7 Grainne left the following morning without ______________ .
8 The band the adults were listening to was called ______________ .
9 He wanted Grainne to see his *a) collection of videos b) CD collection c) favourite books* when he took her to his room.
10 The writer's *a) father b) mother c) stepmother* came into their room and told them it was time to go to bed.
11 The writer had never kissed a girl before. *a) True b) False*
12 Grainne always laughed when ______________ .

161 **Interact**

Work in pairs. Take turns to ask and answer the following questions.

1 Who is the narrator in this story?
2 Where does the story take place? What do you know about the setting?
3 The story takes place during a relatively short period of time? How short?
4 How would you describe Grainne?
5 Did playing with the kite feel different in some way when Grainne was there? In what way, do you think?

6 How does the narrator and Grainne's relationship develop?
7 Why do you think she doesn't wake him up before leaving?

Practise the vocabulary in Wordmatch/Spelling

Another exercise on the words in the word list

162 Vocabulary: Choose the meaning

The following words and expressions in **bold** are all found in the text. Mark the alternative (a, b, c or d) that best corresponds to the meaning of the words and expressions as they are used in the text.

1 His story 'Grainne' **features** in *Born in the 1980s.*
a) *is the main story in* b) *is based on* c) *is found in* d) *is reviewed in*
2 We spent the afternoon **messing around** by the stream.
a) *doing nothing special* b) *being naughty* c) *catching fish* d) *getting dirty*
3 We got back to the house and the rain **poured**.
a) *started* b) *came down heavily* c) *was very light* d) *lasted all day*
4 There were two beds... Grainne would sleep in the **spare** one.
a) *cleanest* b) *bigger* c) *extra* d) *smaller*
5 I had never kissed a girl but I **could sense** it was coming.
a) *was clever enough to know* b) *was afraid* c) *hoped* d) *could feel*
6 I was a **naïve** child of divorce on holiday in Wicklow.
a) *an unhappy* b) *an innocent* c) *an unfortunate* d) *a very young*
7 ...before I was pushed on to one of my **nanas**...
a) *nannies* b) *crazy aunts* c) *cousins* d) *grandmothers*

163 Let's talk!

Ask the right question
Work in two groups – A and B (2–3 people per group). Your teacher will give you more information.

FOCUS ON GRAMMAR

	Grammar	Interactive exercise
MODAL VERBS		
Can, can't, could, couldn't,	p. 326	
Would, wouldn't	p. 326	
Must, mustn't, have to needn't,	p. 327	
Don't have to, should, shouldn't	p. 327	

LISTENING: THE STORY OF THE MAKGABE

164 Starter

Work in pairs. Here's a list of authors who have written books or stories for young adults. Match up 1–10 with a–j.

______	1 J. M. Barrie	a) The Butterfly Tattoo
______	2 Roald Dahl	b) Alice's Adventures in Wonderland
______	3 Beatrix Potter	c) Witch Crag
______	4 Enid Blyton	d) The Chronicles of Narnia
______	5 Philip Pullman	e) The Princess Diaries
______	6 J. K. Rowling	f) Charlie and the Chocolate Factory
______	7 C. S. Lewis	g) The Famous Five
______	8 Lewis Carroll	h) Peter Pan
______	9 Kate Cann	i) Harry Potter and the Sorcerer's Stone
______	10 Meg Cabot	j) The Tale of Peter Rabbit

165 Listen and recall To listen, follow this link

Listen to *The Story of the Makgabe* and choose the best answer (a, b or c). Before you start, read through the sentences and check the words in the word list.

1 Alexander McCall Smith's book series about a detective agency is set in *a) Zimbabwe b) Botswana c) Edinburgh.*
2 A makgabe is *a) a dress b) a scarf c) an apron* that young girls wear.
3 The makgabe was made by her *a) grandmother b) mother c) eldest sister.*
4 The other girls wanted to get rid of the girl's makgabe because they thought *a) it brought bad luck b) it was nicer than theirs c) it would make clever people jealous.*
5 They went swimming *a) in the nude b) in the lake c) wearing just their makgabes.*
6 The girl's makgabe was thrown into the river near a place where a very big *a) crocodile b) hippo c) snake* lived.
7 The snake *a) swallowed b) attacked c) slithered over* the girl and her makgabe.
8 The snake spat the girl and her makgabe out because she *a) was too big b) didn't smell nice c) didn't taste nice.*
9 The slime from the snake caused the girl to *a) cry b) smell bad c) sing.*
10 The girl's mother refused to let her *a) sing any more b) wear her makgabe c) enter the house.*
11 The only person who would let her into her house was *a) her uncle b) her aunt c) her grandmother.*
12 Her parents wanted her back again when they heard *a) she was no longer smelly b) she was going to get married c) she was living with a rich chief.*

166 Interact

1 Why do you think the girls treated her so badly?
2 Would parents act like hers in real life? Give reasons.
3 What's the moral of the story?
4 What do you think of the ending of the story?
5 Do you like reading stories like this one? Have you ever read anything similar?

Practise the vocabulary in Wordmatch/Spelling

Another exercise on the words in the word list

167 Writing: Mini sagas

Since 1988 *The Daily Telegraph* newspaper has organized a 'mini saga' competition. A mini saga is a very short story which was invented by the science fiction writer Brian Aldiss. He was working on a very long novel at the time (three volumes) and he suddenly had the idea that it might be fun, as a complete contrast, to try to tell a whole story in just 50 words. The rules of the competition are simple. The text must be 50 words exactly and it must tell a story. The best stories are published each year in book form. Here are two examples:

Generation Gap
He was worried. Unfortunately, since his wife's death his teenage daughter had become increasingly difficult.
They had agreed 2.00 a.m. as the latest to return home from nightclubs.
It was now 3.30. He prepared himself for confrontation as the door opened.
"Dad!" she shouted angrily. "I've been frantic. You're late again!"

A Disastrous Holiday
The vampire snarled, and folded his black silk cloak around him before slamming the coffin lid shut. "Just my luck", he hissed.
It had seemed a good idea to leave his castle for Greenland and lots of healthy unsuspecting Eskimos.
Nobody at Transylvanian Tours Ltd. had mentioned the midnight sun.

Now try writing your own mini saga. It must be 50 words **exactly** (not including the title). Hyphenated words can be counted as one word or two. In addition, the title can't be more than 15 words. The story must be a narrative text, but you can include direct speech. Something must happen, preferably something which will keep the reader thinking.

1 Think of a plot (and of a final twist!)
2 Write a first draft without worrying about the number of words.
3 Now count the words and try to cut or add words until the story has exactly 50 words.
4 Write your final story and bring it to class! Get into small groups. Take turns to read out your mini sagas. Decide which one was best.

Exchange mini sagas with a friend and make use of Peer response – writing in Resource Section on p. 127 or on the web.

CAN YOU SEE ME? (page 81)

168 Starter

Look at the photograph. What thoughts spring to mind as you look at it? What can you guess about this old man? How do you think he feels? How do you think he spends his day? Make up your own 'life story' about him.

169 Interact

Work in pairs.

1. The text ends with the words "All I want is not to die on a day when I went unseen." Find examples from the text where he tries to make sure that people see him.
2. What does the text tell you about the old man?
3. How much contact do you have with old people? Should we do more to try and engage with them?
4. Is Sweden a good country to grow old in? Give reasons.
5. Is it a child's duty to look after his or her parents when they grow old?

Practise the vocabulary in Wordmatch/Spelling

Another exercise on the words in the word list

170 One word only

Read the following text about an old nurse remembering her past and write **ONE** word in each gap. The word you write must make sense in the text and be grammatically correct.

An Old Nurse Remembers

The old nurse (1)__________ in a rocking chair on the veranda. I slowly walked up to her and introduced (2)__________ . I'm a journalist and was there to interview her (3)__________ the local hospital. I wanted to talk to elderly patients and staff to (4)__________ out what life was like at the hospital 50 years ago.

She (5)__________ me a glass of iced tea, asked me to sit down and we started talking. I listened and took notes. She was a good storyteller and had an excellent memory. We talked for hours and there was one story she told me that I will always (6)__________ .

She was quite young at the time and was sitting on the bus on her (7)__________ home in the morning (8)__________ working a long night at the hospital. She was feeling hot and tired. Opposite her was an elderly man with a beautiful (9)__________ of flowers on his lap. She couldn't help looking at the flowers and silently wishing they were for her.

The man (10)__________ at her and said that he was happy that she liked the flowers. She felt very embarrassed, but the man (11)__________ on talking. Finally, he offered her the bouquet of flowers, but she said that she couldn't possibly accept (12)__________ a generous gift.

"What would the lady you bought the flowers for say?" she asked him. "She wouldn't be very (13)__________ ."

"Oh, my wife will understand if I don't come with flowers today," he answered. "I'll just tell her who I gave them to and - believe me - she'll be (14)__________ happy as I am to give them to you."

As the man got ready to get off the bus, he held out the flowers to her. "Please (15)__________ them!" he said. "Please!"

She felt (16)__________ for the old man and took them from him. "Thank you," she said with a smile. "They're really beautiful."

The next minute, the bus came to a stop and the man got off. As the bus (17)__________ away again, she looked out through the bus window and saw the man slowly (18)__________ into the cemetery.

171 Vocabulary Bank: Useful nouns 1

In Units 4–6 we looked at adjectives. Now it's time to look at various nouns. Put the correct noun into each sentence. Choose from:

athletics disaster equipment permission prescription

1 'Excuse me. Have you got __________ to be in here?' the security guard asked. *(tillåtelse)*
2 Britain has always been quite good at __________ . *(friidrott)*
3 What __________ do you need to go scuba diving? *(utrustning)*
4 The doctor gave her a __________ for some medicine. *(recept)*
5 It was the second air __________ in the country since Christmas. *(katastrof)*

Now turn to page 308 in Vocabulary Bank and do *Useful nouns 1.*

PLAYING THE ENEMY (page 82 ⧉)

172 Starter

Work in pairs or small groups. How much do you know about the following?

Nelson Mandela	South Africa	apartheid
rugby	the film *Invictus*	

173 Textwork

Work in pairs. Read through the text *Playing the Enemy*. Take turns to ask and answer the following questions.

1 Who or what are the Springboks and what was happening in South Africa in 1995?
2 What was Nelson Mandela hoping that the Springboks could do?
3 Which team were South Africa about to play and who were the favourites?
4 What was Mandela wearing and what did the crowd chant?
5 François Pienaar was unable to do something. What was that and why do you think he couldn't do it?
6 What had happened in the Springboks' dressing room earlier?
7 Why was Pienaar so amazed and filled with emotion when he saw Mandela wearing a Springboks jersey?
8 What sort of people usually wear the jersey of their team?

⧉ Practise the vocabulary in Wordmatch/Spelling

174 Vocabulary: Definitions ⧉

Here are definitions of ten words found in the text. Can you work out what they are? To help you, the first and last letter of each missing word is given.

1 The opposite of 'friend'. e__________y
2 To practise a play, a piece of music, etc. in order to prepare it for public performance. r__________e
3 The former political system in South Africa in which people of different races were separated. a__________d
4 An area of ground for playing particular sports, especially football. p__________h
5 A shirt worn by players of sports such as football and rugby. j__________y
6 To repeat or sing a word again and again. c__________t
7 To _____ the World Cup is to provide the necessary space, equipment, venues etc. for it. h__________t
8 A nervous worried feeling that makes it impossible for you to relax. t__________n

9 Another word for 'remember'. r__________l
10 To become _____ is to show strong feelings about something. e__________l

Now write your own definitions for <u>two</u> of the following words, again found in the text.

(national) anthem   dressing room   fiancée   supporter

175 Interact

1. Pienaar says. "There are no words to describe the emotions that ran through my body." What emotions do you think they were?
2. What effect do you think Nelson Mandela's visit to their dressing room had on the team?
3. Did you see the film *Invictus* starring Morgan Freeman and Matt Damon, directed by Clint Eastwood? If so, what did you think of it? Which other films about sport have you seen and enjoyed?
4. Why do you think so many people are passionate about watching their team or country play?

176 Looking at word-building 1

Words come in many forms - nouns, adjectives, verbs and adverbs. They're often built from one basic form. For example, from the verb 'believe' we could have disbelieve *(verb)*, belief, believer *(nouns)*, believable, unbelievable *(adjectives)* and unbelievably *(adverb)*. In this and the following two units we're going to be looking at word-building.

Changing nouns and verbs into adjectives

The word in bold type at the end of each of the following sentences can be used to form a word that fits suitably in the blank space. Fill each blank in this way. Change nouns into adjectives for 1-10 and verbs into adjectives for 11-20.

1. I can't sleep on this bed. It's too __________! **comfort**
2. Mary's flat in the city is rather small but it's very __________, so she can easily walk to work. **centre**
3. I understand your problem, Miss Brown, and don't think I'm not __________, but we really can't allow you to phone up your boyfriend in America using the office phone. **sympathy**
4. Although he'd lived in Britain for over 20 years, he was still very __________ of the fact that he was born in Russia. **pride**
5. She was very __________ and aimed to be Prime Minister one day. **ambition**
6. You have to be careful when picking mushrooms as so many of them are __________. **poison**
7. Amanda's farewell party before she emigrated to New Zealand was a very __________ occasion. **emotion**
8. *The Times* is perhaps the most famous __________ newspaper in Britain. **day**
9. The tennis player was so __________ with himself at losing the match, that he smashed his racket into the net and stormed off the court. **anger**
10. Be careful with that microscope - it's a very __________ instrument! **sense**

Now change the verbs into adjectives.

11 After years of fighting, the country finally became ____________ in 1982. **depend**

12 This knife is ____________ – it won't cut! **use**

13 The weather in this country is so ____________ ! You never know what to expect. **predict**

14 There was ice on the pavement which made it very difficult to walk as it was so ____________ . **slip**

15 He's such a ____________ driver! It's a miracle he hasn't had an accident yet. **care**

16 To survive today, a company needs to be very ____________ . **compete**

17 He was very ____________ with the way he'd played. Both he and his coach knew he should have played a lot better. **satisfy**

18 I've been ____________ since June. I must find work soon. **employ**

19 He works for an ____________ agency. **advertise**

20 The trouble with Mr Brown is that he's so ____________ . One minute he goes mad when you come late; the next he says nothing. You never know where you are! **consist**

LISTENING: AFTER THE GAME

177 **Listen and recall** To listen, follow this link

The final between South Africa and New Zealand was won by South Africa 15-12. Listen to the following extract which takes place after the match and then answer the questions below by completing the sentences.

1 What was the slogan that Edward Griffiths had invented? The slogan was "________________________________"

2 What did Nelson Mandela hand over to François Pienaar?
He handed over to him ________________________________.

3 What was one of the Boers saying with tears in his eyes?
He was saying "________________________________."

4 What was Pienaar's reply in answer to the question "What did it feel like to have 62,000 fans supporting you here in the stadium?"
He replied, "We didn't have 62,000 fans behind us, we had ________________ ________________________________."

5 What flags were showing at the end of the game?
The new ________________________________ .

6 Which adjective best describes how many people felt about Nelson Mandela?
They felt ________________________________ of him.

7 How did François Pienaar reply to Nelson Mandela thanking him?
He replied, "Thank you for ________________________________."

Read the following short text about apartheid. A number of words have been left out. Below you will find four alternatives for each gap. Choose the **best** alternative and write your choice, A, B, C or D in the appropriate box below.

WSM: FOCUS ON APARTHEID

Apartheid consisted of ___**1**___ laws that allowed the ruling white minority in South Africa to segregate, exploit and terrorize the vast majority – Africans, mostly, but ___**2**___ Asians and Coloureds (people of mixed race). In white-ruled South Africa, black people were denied basic human rights and political rights. Their labour was exploited and their lives ___**3**___ .

Under apartheid, racist ___**4**___ were enshrined in law and any criticism of the law was suppressed. It was a system which dictated how and where the large black majority would live, work and die.

Ultimately, blacks demonstrated, held strikes and rioted over such discriminatory practices. As a result diplomatic ___**5**___ mounted abroad for change. In 1990, Nelson Mandela, who had devoted his life to democracy, equality and learning for all South Africans, was ___**6**___ from prison after serving 27 years for those beliefs. He was elected president of the African National Congress the following year, and in 1993 ___**7**___ the Nobel Peace Prize on behalf of all South Africans who suffered and sacrificed so much to bring peace to their country. On May 10, 1994, Nelson Mandela was elected South Africa's first black President, in that country's first ___**8**___ democratic election.

1	A numerous	B few	C lots	D varying
2	A additional	B possibly	C also	D furthermore
3	A separated	B divided	C changed	D segregated
4	A confidence	B beliefs	C vows	D trust
5	A force	B power	C pressure	D wishes
6	A broken out	B released	C let go	D delivered
7	A received	B awarded	C gained	D held
8	A incredibly	B legitimately	C eventually	D truly

1	2	3	4	5	6	7	8

178 Interact

1 What feeling is expressed in the story?
2 Sport seems to have united the whole of South Africa. Can you remember a sporting occasion when the whole nation was proud of being Swedish?
3 Sport can encourage teamwork in many ways. Give examples.

Practise the vocabulary in Wordmatch/Spelling

Another exercise on the words in the word list

179 Fun with vocabulary 4

Cross them out

Work in pairs. Read the instructions below carefully and cross out the words in the table. When you've followed all the instructions there should be **four** words left in the table. What are they and what connects them?

1 Cross out any verbs that are similar to 'hate' in column B.
2 Cross out any fish in row 10.
3 Cross out any crimes in column A.
4 Cross out any words to do with 'bravery' in row 6.
5 Cross out any sounds animals make in row 2.
6 Cross out any insects in column C.
7 Cross out any verbs to do with laughing in row 1.
8 Cross out any herbs in row 4.
9 Cross out any verbs to do with heating or burning in column A.
10 Cross out a word that means 'very big' in row 8.
11 Cross out a verb to do with stealing in row 10.
12 Cross out any birds in column D.
13 Cross out any natural disasters in column B.
14 Cross out any words to do with poverty or lack of money in column D.
15 Cross out a wild animal in row 9.
16 Cross out any diseases in column C.
17 Cross out any verbs to do with speaking in row 8.
18 Cross out any tools or gardening equipment in row 9.

You should now be left with four words. Write them down here.

__________ __________ __________ __________

How are they connected?

	A	B	C	D
1	giggle	loathe	snigger	stare
2	rape	bray	neigh	broke
3	gaze	drought	flea	magpie
4	simmer	sage	glance	thyme
5	arson	detest	mumps	cuckoo
6	scald	bold	peer	daring
7	perjury	avalanche	gout	vulture
8	stutter	huge	gnat	lisp
9	rake	hedgehog	pliers	destitute
10	pilfer	plaice	earwig	trout

180 **Sum up and comment**

1 In what ways are people in this unit connected or disconnected with each other or the world around them?

2 How important will a job be in your future life? Do you think you're likely to have more than one job and/or that you'll work in more than one country?

3 What did you learn by using *Peer response – writing*? How did it improve your mini saga?

181 **Books to read and enjoy**

Agassi, Andre: *Open: An Autobiography*
Carlin, John: *Playing the Enemy*
Coetzee, J.M: *Boyhood*
Diaz, Junot: *The Brief Wondrous Life of Oscar Wao*
Frost, Mark: *The Greatest Game Ever Played*
McKenzie, Sophie: *Girl, Missing**
Parkinson, Siobhán: *Sisters...No Way!*
Phelps; Michael (Cazenueve, Brian): *Beneath the Surface*
Sherwood, Ben: *The Death and Life of Charlie St. Cloud**
Yelland, David: *The Truth about Leo**

*teenage fiction or less advanced books

8 HOT ISSUES

CARS ARE DISGUSTING!

- ☐ Starter
- ☐ Textwork
- ☐ Interact
- ☐ Vocabulary: Right or wrong?
- ☐ Focus on British and American English
- ☐ Let's talk!
- ☐ Parts of a car
- ☐ Writing

WSM: SOME GENUINE INSURANCE CLAIMS

FOCUS ON GRAMMAR

CONVENIENCE FOOD

- ☐ Starter
- ☐ Textwork
- ☐ Interact
- ☐ Vocabulary: Fill in the gaps
- ☐ One word only
- ☐ Writing: My favourite recipe

WSM: MCDONALDS – A BRIEF HISTORY

SURRENDER TO PEACE

- ☐ Starter
- ☐ Textwork
- ☐ Interact
- ☐ Vocabulary: Words of similar meaning
- ☐ Vocabulary Bank: Useful nouns 2

IMAGINE

- ☐ Starter
- ☐ Textwork
- ☐ Focus on musical genres
- ☐ Project

WSM: MARK DAVID CHAPMAN – THE MAN WHO KILLED JOHN LENNON

LISTENING: THE FINAL CURTAIN

- ☐ Starter
- ☐ Listen and recall
- ☐ Vocabulary: Unscramble the letters
- ☐ Speaking
- ☐ Looking at word-building 2

WSM: THE EARLY LIFE OF MICHAEL JACKSON

WHO CAN YOU TRUST?

- ☐ Starter
- ☐ Textwork
- ☐ Interact
- ☐ Vocabulary: Choose the meaning
- ☐ Speaking/Writing: Ambiguous headlines

- ☐ Useful expressions: Idioms 4
- ☐ Sum up and comment
- ☐ Books to read and enjoy

CARS ARE DISGUSTING! (page 86)

182 Starter

Work in pairs. Write down five good things and five bad things about having a car.

For	Against

Now find another pair. Compare and discuss your answers. What's your true opinion?

183 Textwork

Work in pairs. Take turns to ask and reflect on the following questions based on the text *Cars Are Disgusting!*

1. Do you agree with the writer's statement "If action is not taken, all will be lost!"
2. The writer says "We must destroy all cars to break the mind-set that makes it impossible to see beyond our own most immediate and selfish needs." Does he have a point?
3. Do you think his comparison of starting your car in your garage and sitting beside it, reading the paper, while your garage fills up with exhaust is a valid one? Why? Why not?
4. Give two examples of how he's sick of cars. Do you agree with any of them?
5. Which three things does he denounce? Do you agree with any of them?
6. What impression do you get of James Hoff from the essay he wrote?

See Resource Section p. 148 for some phrases you can use when discussing things.

184 Interact

1. Is learning to drive and getting a driving licence too expensive? Should getting a licence be subsidized? Give reasons.
2. Explain to someone from another country what rules apply in Sweden when getting a driving licence.
3. Do you have a favourite make of car? Which make? Why do you like it?
4. What do you think about congestion charges in cities?
5. Do you think any kind of cars have a future? What kind(s)?

Practise the vocabulary in Wordmatch/Spelling

185 Vocabulary: Right or wrong?

Work in pairs. Check that you have understood some of the words used in the text *Cars Are Disgusting!* by stating whether they are used correctly in the following sentences. Mark each sentence R (Right) or W (Wrong). If wrong, explain why and write a new sentence to show how the words should be used.

1. It was one of the best hotels we'd ever stayed at. It was really **disgusting**. ______
2. I've got a History **assignment** to complete by the end of next week. ______
3. He's very fit and usually **recycles** to and from work. ______
4. The present government had brought the country to the **edge** of economic disaster. ______
5. They were very poor, so could only afford to live in a **mansion**. ______
6. He was arrested and charged with possessing a **fake** passport. ______
7. 'Ooh! What a **cute** baby! Can I hold her?' James said to his best friend. ______
8. The goal was **rejected** by the referee. ______
9. His arguments were very **persuasive**. I couldn't really disagree with anything he said. ______
10. It gives us great pleasure to **denounce** the engagement of our daughter, Maria. ______

186 Focus on British and American English

In the text *Cars are Disgusting!* some American English words were used which have different words in British English, namely:

American English	British English
gas	petrol
parking lot	car park
candy bar	chocolate bar

There are lots of differences like these, so it's well worth learning some of the most common ones. Fill in the missing American words in the sentences below. To help you, the equivalent British words are given in brackets. Choose from the following:

bill	diapers	freeway	restroom	subway
cab	drapes	janitor	sidewalk	truck
cellphone	elevator	pants	stand in line	vacation
cookie	fall	purse	streetcars	
deck	flashlight	realtor	street light	

1. What do you think of my new ______? They're really cool, aren't they? (trousers)
2. I have a 12-month contract on my ______ . (mobile phone)
3. He handed the ______ driver a $10 ______ and told him to keep the change. (taxi, note)

4 We can play poker if someone has a ____________ of cards. (pack)
5 Joanna drew the ____________ and switched the light on. (curtains)
6 The car mounted the ____________ and crashed into a ____________. (pavement, lamppost)
7 We looked on our map to find the nearest ____________ station. (underground)
8 Would you like a ____________ with your coffee? (biscuit)
9 I'm afraid Mr Silverberg's on ____________ this week. Somewhere in Florida, I think. But he should be back next week. (holiday)
10 It's dark in the woods, so take a ____________ with you. (torch)
11 My birthday's in the ____________ – on October 14th to be exact. (autumn)
12 We went to the ____________ to see what houses were for sale. (estate agent)
13 There are still lots of ____________ in San Francisco. (trams)
14 We'll have to use the stairs, I'm afraid. The ____________ isn't working. (lift)
15 When do babies usually stop needing to wear ____________? (nappies)
16 She opened her ____________ and took out a comb and a lipstick. (handbag)
17 My uncle's a ____________ at a high school in Houston. (caretaker)
18 We had to ____________ for two hours to get tickets for the concert. (queue)
19 There was an accident on the ____________ this morning in which two cars and a ____________ were involved. (motorway, lorry)
20 Excuse me, where's the nearest ____________, please? (toilet)

187 Let's talk!

What's your opinion?

Work in two groups – A and B (2–3 people per group). Group A looks at this page. Group B turns to page 300.

Below are ten sentences to read out to group B. They also have ten sentences to read out to you. But you yourselves decide which sentence to talk about each time by choosing a number between 1–10. Say to Group B: *Read out sentence (3).* Then cross the number out so you don't ask for the same sentence again!

Take it in turns to read out a sentence and answer. When you answer, one person can start by giving his/her opinion, then the rest of the group can join in. *Your group starts by asking for a number.*

Look at Resource Section p. 146 for phrases you can use when discussing things.

1	2	3	4	5	6	7	8	9	10

1 It's better to take any job rather than be unemployed.
2 You should look after your parents when they're old, even if this means one or more of your parents living with you.
3 It's impossible to have a successful career and a successful family life. You have to choose one or the other.

4 It's an advantage to be an only child.
5 Watching violent films and TV programmes or playing violent computer games makes young people aggressive.
6 Smoking should be made illegal like other drugs.
7 Pop music is mainly for young people.
8 All forms of censorship, whether it's books, films, the Internet, etc. is wrong.
9 The future is frightening rather than exciting.
10 There's too much money in sport nowadays – especially when it comes to the Olympics.

188 Parts of a car

Work in pairs. Do you know what the various parts of a car are called in English? Here's your chance to find out. Your teacher will give you more information.

189 Writing

James Hoff is strongly against cars. Find an issue that engages you and write a letter to the editor. See Resource Section on page 138.

Make use of Peer response – writing in Resource Section on p. 127.

WSM: SOME GENUINE INSURANCE CLAIMS

FOCUS ON GRAMMAR

	Grammar	Interactive exercise
Conditional clauses	p. 327	
The Passive	p. 328	
Question tags	p. 328	

CONVENIENCE FOOD (page 92)

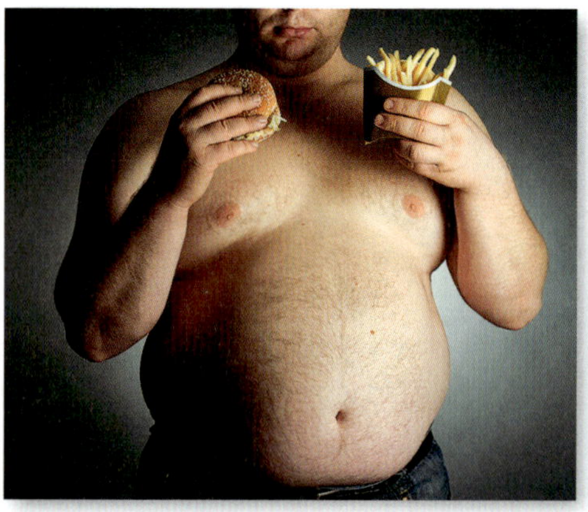

190 Starter

Here's a list of food items. Mark with a cross any that you've eaten in the past two weeks.

1 a meal at a hamburger restaurant ☐
2 a Chinese takeaway ☐
3 a Thai takeaway ☐
4 a sandwich from a sandwich bar ☐
5 a pizza ☐

6 a hot dog ☐
7 a kebab ☐
8 a falafel ☐
9 a ready made microwave meal ☐
10 a meal you cooked yourself ☐

Now work in groups of 3–4 and compare your answers. What have many of these meals in common?
How often do you eat meals cooked by yourself or a member of your family?

191 Textwork

Read *Convenience Food*. Then fill in the missing information or choose the correct answer (a, b or c). The sentences are in no special order.

1 The book this extract is taken from is for people who *a) are good at cooking b) are interested in making complicated meals c) don't normally enjoy cooking.*
2 Many years ago, it was very ________________ to see an overweight child.
3 Tables in fast food restaurants are usually ________________ .
4 In the 1960s people were a lot slimmer than they are now. *a) True b) False*
5 ________________ is/are an example of a 'flavour of the month' food.
6 Convenience food *a) takes just as much effort as cooking your own dinner b) saves a lot of time c) takes a while to eat.*
7 Often eating fast foods leaves you longing for something ________________ to eat and also feeling ________________ .
8 The meals in the book can be made *a) quickly b) without cooking them c) with almost no fat, sugar or salt content.*
9 The least healthy foods are usually the cheapest. *a) True b) False*
10 Eating potatoes, puddings and pies is all right as long as you also remember to eat some ________________ too.

192 Interact

1 If fast food is part of your diet, why is that so? Give reasons.
2 Why do you think healthy food has become so popular lately?
3 Are there any good health cafés where you live? What do they serve?
4 What's your idea of a healthy diet?

Practise the vocabulary in Wordmatch/Spelling

193 Vocabulary: Fill in the gaps

Fill in the missing words in the sentences below. Choose from the following words, taken from the text. Then make up your own sentences for the four words that are left over.

apparently	deprive	occasional	resort
commercially	in vain	packaging	skinny
convenient	involves	rejected	unfamiliar
craving	obesity	remove	virtually

1 More than 30% of the cost of our food goes on ________________ . What a waste!
2 A diet that's high in fat can lead to ________________ .
3 Buying things online is a very ________________ way to shop.
4 "You should eat more, Sophie. You're far too ________________ ," my grandmother told me when I last went to visit her.
5 When my wife was pregnant, she developed a ________________ for strawberry ice-cream.
6 So far, I've been ________________ by two of the universities I've applied for. I'm starting to lose hope.
7 The red squirrel has become ________________ extinct in most parts of the country.
8 The young, inexperienced teacher tried ________________ to control the noisy class.
9 You can ________________ a red wine stain from a carpet by sprinkling salt over it.
10 Running your own business usually ________________ working long hours.
11 The union achieved their demands without having to ________________ to calling the workers out on strike.
12 There's usually quite a lot of fat, sugar and salt in ________________ prepared food.

194 One word only

Read the following text about a dinner party and write **ONE** word in each gap. The word you write must make sense in the text and be grammatically correct.

The Dinner Party

I don't know (1)____________ the following story is true or not but, according to a friend of (2)____________ , it happened to her sister a couple of years ago.

My friend's sister worked for an advertising agency and one particular evening had invited her boss and (3)____________ important clients home for a meal.

She wanted to make a good (4)____________ and one of the things she intended to make was a salmon mousse. She had just finished cleaning the fish and left it on the kitchen table (5)____________ she gathered up the rest of the ingredients. However, while her back was turned her cat (6)____________ onto the table and started eating the fish. Fortunately, she heard it purring and quickly chased it away. At the same time she though to herself, "Well, (7)____________ will know that the cat has nibbled the fish." Consequently, she washed and cleaned it again and got on with her preparations.

The dinner party was a great (8)__________ and as the guests left they thanked her very much and were especially complimentary (9)__________ the salmon mousse. As she was closing the gate after the last car had left she suddenly (10)__________ in the flower-bed near the front door her cat. It was very stiff and very dead!

"Oh, my God!" she thought. "The fish. It (11)__________ have been contaminated!"

In desperation she rushed to the phone and called all her guests to (12)__________ what had happened and to advise them to visit the doctor immediately. Needless to say, they were not particularly (13)__________ to know that she had given them food that the cat had chewed.

Just after she'd made the last phone call the doorbell rang. It was her next-door neighbour looking very nervous. He explained that (14)__________ that evening he had unfortunately run over her cat in his drive. He was very sorry but he'd been in a desperate hurry at the time as he was on his way to meet a train. He'd rung the doorbell a few times but unfortunately couldn't make anyone hear above the noise of the dinner party. Instead he'd (15)__________ the cat by the front door. Had she found it yet?

195 **Writing: My favourite recipe**

What's your favourite recipe? Try and write it out in English.
Present it to a small group or the class.
See Resource Section on page 134 on how to write instructions.

WSM: MCDONALD'S – A BRIEF HISTORY

SURRENDER TO PEACE (page 92)

196 **Starter**

Which of the following have you heard of? Who are/were they?

Yoko Ono	Joan Baez	Bob Dylan	Donovan
John Lennon	Pete Seeger	Joni Mitchell	Frank Zappa

197 Textwork

Work in pairs. Read through the text *Surrender to Peace*. Take turns to ask and answer the following questions.

1. Give an example to show that Yoko Ono was a peace activist.
2. Name one way that Yoko has commemorated her husband since his death in 1980.
3. Which new country did they announce in 1972 and who could be a citizen of it?
4. What did Nutopia's white flag represent?
5. Why did they want to take Nutopia's flag to the United Nations?
6. Why didn't people at this time like the term "surrender"?
7. What do you think a 'macho radical' is?

198 Interact

1. Have you ever publicly protested against anything? If so, what?
2. Do you like the idea of the country called Nutopia? Why? Why not?
3. What peace movements have you heard of?

Practise the vocabulary in Wordmatch/Spelling

199 Vocabulary: Words of similar meaning

Complete the pairs of words below with another word that is similar in meaning. Choose from the following words, all taken from the text.

announce	concept	maintenance
citizen	found	radical
commemorate	macho	surrender

1. idea, notion, ____________
2. capitulate, give up, ____________
3. national, subject, ____________
4. manly, masculine, ____________
5. celebrate, mark, ____________
6. care, upkeep, ____________
7. declare, state, ____________
8. extremist, revolutionary, ____________
9. establish, set up, ____________

200 **Vocabulary Bank: Useful nouns 2**

Put the correct noun into each sentence. Choose from:

explanation   opinion   superstition   trial   vehicles

1 Several __________ were involved in the accident on the M4 earlier this morning. *(fordon)*
2 There's still no reasonable __________ for quite a number of UFO sightings. *(förklaring)*
3 Millions of people followed the O. J. Simpson murder __________ on television. *(rättegång)*
4 'If I want your __________ I'll ask for it, all right!' he snapped. *(åsikt)*
5 People in Britain say that breaking a mirror will bring you seven years' bad luck. Do you have the same __________ in your country? *(vidskepelse)*

Now turn to page 309 in Vocabulary Bank and do *Useful nouns 2*

IMAGINE (page 94)

201 **Starter**

Work in pairs or groups of three.

1 Talk about any pop songs that have made a strong impression on you – especially the song's lyrics. Explain why.
2 Almost every year someone compiles a list of the 10 best pop songs ever. How about you? Working together, try and compile such a list.

1 ______________________________
2 ______________________________
3 ______________________________
4 ______________________________
5 ______________________________
6 ______________________________
7 ______________________________
8 ______________________________
9 ______________________________
10 ______________________________

When you've finished, find another group. Compare your selections. How many were the same?

Practise the vocabulary in Wordmatch/Spelling

202 **Textwork**

Without looking back at the lyrics for the John Lennon song *Imagine*, try and fill in the 16 missing words. Choose from these:

brotherhood	dreamer	hard	peace	sky
countries	easy	hell	possessions	today
die	greed	join	religion	world (x 2)

Imagine by John Lennon

Imagine there's no heaven
It's (1)___________ if you try
No (2) ___________ below us
Above us only (3) ___________
Imagine all the people living for (4) ___________

Imagine there's no (5) ___________
It isn't (6) ___________ to do
Nothing to kill or (7) ___________ for
And no (8) ___________ too
Imagine all the people living life in (9)___________

You may say
I'm a (10) ___________, but I'm not the only one
I hope some day you'll (11) ___________ us
And the (12) ___________ will be as one

Imagine no (13) ___________
I wonder if you can
No need for (14) ___________ or hunger
A (15) ___________ of man
Imagine all the people sharing all the (16) ___________ .

REPEAT "You may say..."

Now check your answers by looking at the lyrics again on page 94.

203 **Focus on musical genres**

A Work in pairs or groups of three. Here are 30 different types of musical genres. How many are you familiar with? Which ones have you never heard of? Test yourself on some of them by matching ten of them to the definitions below.

Acid rock	Electronica/Dance	Jazz	Rock
Alternative	Folk	Latin	Rockabilly
Blues	Funk	New Age	Rock 'n' roll
Boogie-woogie	Gospel	Pop	Skiffle
Calypso	Grunge	Punk	Soul
Country	Hardcore	Rap	World
Disco	Heavy metal	Reggae	
Easy Listening	Hip hop	Rhythm and Blues (R & B)	

1 A type of popular music originating in Jamaica in the 1960s, characterized by a strongly accentuated offbeat. ____________

2 A type of loud, aggressive and often offensive rock music popular in the late 1970s and early 1980s. ____________

3 Rock music from the late 1960s and early 1970s with a repetitive beat and lyrics that suggest psychedelic experiences. It usually featured distorted guitar playing.

____

4 A type of music in the style of the traditional music of the southern and western United States. ____________

5 A type of loud rock music, and a fashion for untidy clothes which was popular in the early 1990s. ____________

6 A type of music created by African-American musicians in New Orleans around 1900 in which the players often improvise. ____________

7 A style of music with a strong loud beat played on guitars and drums, which first became popular in the 1950s. ____________

8 Popular dance music (especially in the late 1970s) which was melodic with a regular bass beat; intended mainly for dancing at discotheques. ____________

9 A type of slow, sad music, originally from the southern US, in which the singer typically sings about their difficult life or bad luck in love. ____________

10 A type of music born in the late 1960s with a very strong beat played very loud on electric guitars, often with male lead singers with unnaturally high-pitched voices.

____

B Are there any other musical genres that have been left out? Which are your favourites? Which genre is normally associated with these singers/groups?

1 The Clash ____________
2 One Direction ____________
3 The Rolling Stones ____________
4 Bob Marley ____________
5 Pink Floyd ____________
6 Lady Gaga ____________
7 Swedish House Mafia ____________
8 Jay-Z ____________

204 **Project**

Find the English lyrics of a pop song that means a lot to you. Make copies, hand it out to a group or the whole class and explain why it means so much to you. If you like, play the song too.

WSM: MARK DAVID CHAPMAN - THE MAN WHO KILLED JOHN LENNON

LISTENING: THE FINAL CURTAIN

205 **Starter**

What do you know about Michael Jackson?

206 **Listen and recall**

Listen to the text *The Final Curtain* and choose the best answer (a, b or c). Before you start, read through the sentences and check the words in the word list.

1 There were *a) half a million b) over a million c) three quarters of a million* tickets available for the Michael Jackson O2 concerts.
2 He *a) was b) wasn't* intending to do his famous 'moonwalk' during these concerts.
3 He was intending these concerts to be *a) ones where he'd perform mostly new songs b) the last time he'd perform live c) concerts to celebrate his 50th birthday.*
4 Michael had never really enjoyed touring with his brothers. *a) True b) False*
5 In order to get fit for the concerts, Michael trained *a) once b) twice c) three times* a week with Lou Ferrigno, the star of *The Incredible Hulk.*
6 Michael was hoping to become muscular like Lou Ferrigno. *a) True b) False*
7 During his training, Michael *a) ate a lot b) only ate one meat dish a day c) ate only vegetarian food.*
8 While training, Michael always wore *a) pyjamas b) a suit jacket c) a tracksuit.*
9 Seven days before he died, there were rumours circulating that *a) the O2 concerts wouldn't take place b) Michael was mentally ill c) he had decided to quit singing.*
10 Cherilyn Lee, a Californian registered nurse advised Michael to *a) go to hospital b) rest for a week c) not take a sedative called Dipriva.*
11 The day before his death, Michael *a) rehearsed for three hours b) seemed to be having problems with his new dance routines c) was dancing almost as well as the younger dancers around him.*
12 Conrad Murray was Michael Jackson's *a) doctor b) personal trainer c) best friend.*

Practise the vocabulary in Wordmatch/Spelling

207 Vocabulary: Unscramble the letters

Unscramble the letters to find a word that fits into the sentence. All the words are taken from the listening text *The Final Curtain*. To help you, the first letter of the word is given.

1	cocanut	She gave a thrilling a____________ of her life in the jungle.
2	alaycult	Did he a____________ hit you or just threaten you?
3	lacered	Severe flooding has prompted the governor of Louisiana to d____________ a state of emergency.
4	adlye	He decided to d____________ his decision until he'd seen the full report.
5	axseedhut	By the time they reached the summit of the mountain they were completely e____________ .
6	albaletfin	Have you ever tried exercising with an i____________ exercise ball?
7	muroru	The band denied a r____________ that they were going to split up at the end of the year.
8	scudheel	The Foreign Secretary took time out of his busy s____________ to give an interview to the BBC.
9	prcas	The government has been forced to s____________ its plans for a rise in the basic rate of income-tax.
10	asidevet	Cherilyn Lee refused to give Michael Jackson a powerful s____________ called Dipriva.
11	coincunsous	She was hit on the head by a stone and knocked u____________ .
12	creampenfro	Although the team lost 2–1, the manager said that he was impressed by their p____________ .

208 Speaking

Search the web for information about the death of Michael Jackson. What sources do you find trustworthy? Do they all give the same account of his death? Evaluate your sources.

See Resource Section p. 123 for further information on critical reading.

Looking at word-building 2

In Unit 7 you practised changing verbs and nouns into adjectives. Here's further practice at changing nouns and verbs into adjectives.

Changing verbs and nouns into adjectives

The word in **bold** type at the end of each of the following sentences can be used to form a word that fits suitably in the blank space. Fill each blank in this way. Change nouns into adjectives for 1–10 and verbs into adjectives for 11–20.

1 What a lovely painting! Your daughter must be very ______________, Mrs Green! **art**
2 My new car is far more ______________ than the one I had before. **economy**
3 There's no need to worry about the dog. He won't bite. He's perfectly ______________. **harm**
4 Oh, grow up, David! Stop being so ______________! **child**
5 Being on board a car ferry when a fire broke out was one of the most ______________ experiences of my life. **fright**
6 I took the computer back to the shop because it was ______________. **fault**
7 His parents wouldn't let him have a motorbike. They thought it was too ______________ and that he'd end up killing himself. **danger**
8 Thank you for everything you've done. You've been most ______________. **help**
9 A desert can be a dangerous and ______________ place. **friend**
10 The song she wrote was so ______________ that she decided to give up her job and become a full-time songwriter. **success**

Change verbs into adjectives.

11 The temperature is very ______________ at this time of year. **vary**
12 If you're going to the supermarket, don't forget to get a packet of ______________ peas. **freeze**
13 I can think of ______________ reasons for not getting married, but even so, I still want to one day. **count**
14 In this essay you've said the same thing several times. It's very ______________. **repeat**
15 I couldn't help feeling ______________ when he offered me £250 to help him carry his bags through customs. **suspect**
16 The earthquake caused ______________ damage. **extend**
17 The team were very ______________ when they lost 2-0 in the semi-final of the FA Cup. **disappoint**
18 Don't ask Paul to do it, he's so ______________. You just can't trust him. **rely**
19 I think toy guns and other weapons should be banned as they're quite ______________ for children. **suit**
20 It was a really ______________ evening. Everyone had a wonderful time. **enjoy**

WSM: THE EARLY LIFE OF MICHAEL JACKSON

Read the following text about the early life of Michael Jackson. A number of words have been left out. Below you will find four alternatives for each gap. Choose the **best** alternative and write your choice, A, B, C or D in the appropriate box below.

Michael Joseph Jackson was born on August 29, 1958 in Gary, Indiana. His middle name was his father's. He was the seventh of nine children. In 1963, at the age of 5, he joined his brothers as the "Jackson Five" and began playing at local clubs. The brothers were coached and __**1**__ by their steelworker father, himself a guitar player.

When Michael was six the group __**2**__ various talent contests. The Jackson Five came through as a very professional group, thanks __**3**__ to their father. He never left anything to chance. Everything was well-prepared and well-designed. Their clothes, their hair, their shoes, their movements – everything had to be perfect!

From Gary they moved on to Chicago, where they made five nightly performances, six nights a week. Quite a different world for a family __**4**__ as Jehovah's Witnesses! When Michael was ten they recorded their first record, *Big Boy*. A short while __**5**__ , the group won a major talent contest at the Apollo Theater in New York City. The only thing missing now was a major record contract with Motown.

Eventually Motown called them and the family __**6**__ off to Detroit for an audition. It has been said that Michael got really nervous just before the audition. But __**7**__ being sympathetic, his father got really angry and made it clear to the 10-year-old Michael that he'd better behave himself if he ever wanted to see his eleventh birthday! Fortunately, everything went well and Motown signed them up. Their three first singles __**8**__ the charts. They moved to California and stayed with Diana Ross. The group became very successful.

1	A recommended	B encouraged	C persuaded	D convinced
2	A took part in	B entertained	C performed	D got away with
3	A as a rule	B strangely	C generally	D largely
4	A trained	B risen	C brought up	D looked after
5	A before	B following	C subsequently	D later
6	A moved	B headed	C travelled	D reached
7	A instead of	B because of	C although	D in spite of
8	A succeeded	B made up	C topped	D played

1	2	3	4	5	6	7	8

WHO CAN YOU TRUST? (page 96)

210 **Starter**

The Internet is an enormous meeting place for people. What precautions can you take to be safe on the net? Give each other advice.

211 **Textwork**

Read the text *Who Can You Trust?* and match the opening sentences (1–13) with the correct endings (a–m). They're in no special order.

____	1 She tried eating a hot dog	a) was in the basement.
____	2 She was told that in America	b) wasn't a blood relative.
____	3 She moved to the USA	c) and tried to molest her.
____	4 Her bedroom	d) but didn't really like it.
____	5 Her uncle's neighbours thought he	e) living in Maine.
____	6 Most of her family thought	f) she left without a word.
____	7 Her uncle came to her bedroom	g) had eaten all the squirrels.
____	8 She was going to live with	h) didn't know much about Africa or black people.
____	9 After her uncle's sexual advances,	i) you had to learn to give and take.
____	10 There weren't many black people	j) with her uncle and family.
____	11 Her uncle	k) all Americans owned guns.
____	12 At first, she felt really at home	l) a relative living in Maine.
____	13 The girls at the community college	m) from Lagos.

212 **Interact**

1 She says she won the 'American visa lottery'. What does she mean by this?
2 What intentions do you think this man had with the girl?
3 What do you think will happen to her?

Practise the vocabulary in Wordmatch/Spelling

Another exercise on the words in the word list

213 Vocabulary: Choose the meaning

The following words and expressions in **bold** are all found in the text. Mark the alternative (a, b, c or d) that best corresponds to the meaning of the words and expressions as they are used in the text.

1 They **trooped into** the room in Lagos...
a) *rushed inside* b) *walked in one behind the other* c) *walked slowly in*
d) *gathered there in a group*

2 ... lived with your father and mother and three **siblings**.
a) *brothers and sisters* b) *grandparents* c) *cousins* d) *uncles and aunts*

3 ... because they were desperately trying to look **diverse**.
a) *dynamic* b) *clever* c) *different* d) *generous*

4 You gave up a lot but you **gained** a lot, too.
a) *picked up* b) *got* c) *expected* d) *hoped for*

5 They **gawped at** your hair.
a) *laughed at* b) *made fun of* c) *pulled at* d) *stared rudely at*

6 ... a mixture of **ignorance** and arrogance, he called it.
a) *lack of knowledge and understanding* b) *rudeness*
c) *feeling you're better than someone else* d) *inexperience*

7 ... into the **cramped** basement where you slept...
a) *smelly* b) *uncomfortable* c) *damp* d) *very small*

8 ...pulled you forcefully to him, squeezing your **buttocks**...
a) *breasts* b) *thighs* c) *either side of your bottom* d) *lips*

214 Speaking/Writing: Ambiguous headlines

The following three newspaper headlines are all ambiguous – in other words they have two different meanings – one rather unexpected and totally different from the intended one.

BREAST CANCER LINKED TO SMOKING IN A STUDY
(Unexpected meaning: If you smoke in a study you could get breast cancer.)

TWO THUGS EAT THEN ROB RESTAURANT OWNER
(Unexpected meaning: Two thugs eat the restaurant owner before they rob him.)

WE SAW MANY BEARS DRIVING THROUGH YELLOWSTONE PARK.
(Unexpected meaning: We saw many bears who were driving (their own cars) through Yellowstone Park.)

So how would you rewrite the above to get rid of any ambiguity? Here's one solution.

IN A RECENT STUDY, SMOKING HAS BEEN LINKED TO BREAST CANCER.
AFTER HAVING A MEAL AT A RESTAURANT, TWO THUGS THEN ROBBED THE OWNER.
WHILE WE WERE DRIVING THROUGH YELLOWSTONE PARK, WE SAW MANY BEARS THERE.

Work in pairs. Now it's your turn to see if you can rewrite five more headlines so that they're no longer ambiguous. Your teacher will give you more information.

215 **Useful expressions: Idioms 4**

A Complete the definitions below with a suitable idiom. Choose from these. To help you, a Swedish translation is given in brackets.

bark up the wrong tree
be like a bear with a sore head
butter someone up
cook the books
get a move on
go Dutch
have the gift of the gab
Keep it under your hat!
make a bomb
tighten one's belt

1 To ________________ means to make a lot of money. *(tjäna massor med pengar)*
2 To ________________ is to flatter someone – usually for your own ends. *(smickra någon)*
3 To ________________ is to share the costs, especially at a restaurant. *(betala var och en för sig)*
4 If you tell someone to ________________ , then you want them to hurry up. *(skynda på, lägga på ett kol)*
5 To ________________ is to have the wrong idea of how to get or achieve something. *(vara inne på fel spår)*
6 To say to someone, '________________' means that what you've just told them is a secret, and that they shouldn't tell anyone else about it. *(hålla tyst om något)*
7 To ________________ is to spend less money than you did before because you've got less money now. *(dra åt svångremmen)*
8 To ________________ is to be in a bad mood which causes you to treat other people badly and complain a lot. *(vara vresig, retlig)*
9 If you ________________ , then you're able to speak easily and confidently in a way that makes people want to listen to you and believe you. *(vara vältalig)*
10 To ________________ is to change numbers dishonestly in the accounts of an organization – especially in order to steal money from it. *(fiffla med räkenskaperna)*

B Now complete the sentences using seven of the idioms from A.
Make any necessary changes.

1 Something must have upset our teacher. She's ________________ this morning.
2 Now remember, this is a surprise party, so ________________ !
3 Most students and young couples ________________ nowadays when they go out for a drink or a meal.

4 I've just lost my job, so I'm going to have to ______________ until I find another one.
5 Don't take any notice of him, Cathy. He's only trying to ______________ you ______________ so that you'll buy something off him.
6 My sister ______________. She'd make an excellent politician.
7 We'd better ______________ if we're going to catch that train!

C Now write your own sentences for the three idioms left over.

____

____

____

216 Sum up and comment

1 What hot issues are being discussed at the moment? Which one do you think is the most important?
2 What did you learn by using *Peer response – writing*? How did it improve your letter?
3 What did you learn from critically reading articles about Michael Jackson's death?

217 Books to read and enjoy

Clarkson, Jeremy: *Driven to Distraction*
Cox, Brian: *Wonders of Life*
Gordimer, Nadine: *The Pickup*
Hiaasen, Carl: *Nature Girl**
Mohammadi, Kamin: *The Cypress Tree*
Moore, Michael: *Downsize This!; Capitalism: A Love Story*
Muchamore, Robert: *Man vs Beast**
Shriver, Lionel: *We Need to Talk about Kevin*

*teenage fiction or less advanced books

9 HORROR

THE COLLECTOR

- [ ] Starter
- [ ] Act it out
- [ ] Interact
- [ ] One word only

FOCUS ON GRAMMAR

DEAD MEN TALK

- [ ] Starter
- [ ] Textwork
- [ ] Interact
- [ ] Vocabulary: Fill in the gaps
- [ ] Focus on crime words

WSM: SUICIDE OR MURDER?

COUNTERFEIT PROTECTION

- [ ] Starter
- [ ] Textwork
- [ ] Interact
- [ ] Writing
- [ ] Vocabulary Bank: Useful nouns 3

WSM: COMMON INTERNET SCAMS – AN OVERVIEW

LISTENING: THE YEAR WE DISAPPEARED

- [ ] Starter
- [ ] Listen and recall
- [ ] Vocabulary: Which word ...?
- [ ] Interact

WSM: FACE TRANSPLANTS – A SHORT HISTORY

HUSH, HUSH

- [ ] Starter
- [ ] Interact
- [ ] Vocabulary: Definitions
- [ ] Writing
- [ ] Act it out
- [ ] Looking at word-building 3

- [ ] Fun with vocabulary 5
- [ ] Sum up and comment
- [ ] Books to read and enjoy

THE COLLECTOR (page 100)

218 **Starter**

Read the following plot of the film, *The Collector* and write **ONE** word in each gap. The word you write must make sense in the text and be grammatically correct.

Frederick Clegg is a nerdy, rather lonely bank clerk (1) __________ only pleasure seems to be collecting butterflies. One day, he (2) __________ a large sum of money on the Football Pools. With the money, he buys a large, fairly isolated country house and (3) __________ up its cellar with all the comforts of home. When the house is ready, he then puts into practice his (4) __________ to kidnap Miranda Grey, an art student he has long fancied and has been stalking, but has always been (5) __________ shy to speak to.

One day, after Miranda has finished her classes for the day, he follows her in his van. He grabs her (6) __________ her flat, chloroforms her, then loads her unconscious (7) __________ into the back of his van and drives to his house, locking her in the cellar that he's prepared for her.

When Miranda (8) __________ up, Frederick confesses his love for her, and explains that he only wants time for her to get to know him. Naturally, she isn't (9) __________ keen on this, and demands to be released. But she later agrees to stay for four weeks, but (10) __________ if he gives her his word that he'll let her go at the end of that time.

Four weeks go by, (11) __________ which Frederick discovers and prevents a number of clever escape attempts by Miranda. On the night of her promised release, Frederick surprises Miranda with a formal dinner and champagne in the main house. He presents her with a wedding (12) __________ and asks her to marry him. When Miranda agrees, Frederick becomes suspicious of her motives. They argue, and he chloroforms her and locks her in the (13) __________ again.

During her next outing to the main house, Miranda (14) __________ to seduce Frederick. He's appalled, and tells her he's lost all respect for her, and he can't allow her to leave. While being taken back to the cellar in the rain, she (15) __________ a shovel and hits Frederick over the head with it. He's wounded, but he manages to pull her back into the cellar. Frederick then drives to a nearby hospital for treatment, (16) __________ Miranda remains locked in the cold cellar, soaking wet.

Frederick (17) __________ a few days later to find Miranda terribly ill, and he goes into town to get a doctor. But instead of finding one, he returns alone with just (18) __________ medicine for her. But he's too late. He enters the cellar only to find that Miranda is already (19) __________.

He buries her body in the grounds and decides that Miranda wasn't the right person for him after all. She was far too clever and from a different social background. So he decides that he needs to find someone simpler and more common that he can "teach" and who will really (20) __________ him.

The final scene from the film shows Frederick back behind the wheel of his van - this time stalking a young nurse.

219 **Act it out**

Work in groups of three. One person plays Miranda, one person plays Clegg while the third person is the director. Working together, practise and then act out one of the scenes. It's up to the director to try and get the best out of the two actors. Your teacher will give you copies of scripts to use.

220 **Interact**

1. Why do you think the film (and the book) is called *The Collector*?
2. What do you think is wrong with Clegg?
3. Are there any other films you've seen where kidnapping is a main theme?
4. Unfortunately abduction takes place in real life? What cases have you heard of?

Practise the vocabulary in Wordmatch/Spelling

FOCUS ON GRAMMAR

	Grammar	Interactive exercise
Word order	p. 329	
Prepositions of place (in, on, at)	p. 332	
Prepositions of time (in, on, at)	p. 333	

DEAD MEN TALK (page 105)

221 Starter

Jigsaw reading

Here are two short news extracts relating to crime. Unfortunately, they're mixed up. Try to sort them out. Number the first 1-9 and the second 10-16. To help you, the first part of each story is already marked.

__10__ George Cabaso, 27, had a heavy meal at a restaurant in Baguio City in the
_____ believe the man was 21. The robber swore he was, but still the clerk refused.
_____ twenty-one. As soon as he left, the cashier called and gave the police the
_____ money from the cash register. After the cashier put the money in the bag as
_____ was arrested two hours later.
_____ a complaint. He was caught in the act by restaurant staff, who summoned the
_____ set free.
__1__ A man walked into the corner store with a shotgun and demanded all of the
_____ a nine-inch snake into a bowl of soup, hoping to get a free dinner by lodging
_____ swallowed the snake and said, 'Where is your evidence now?' Cabaso was
_____ instructed, the man demanded the bottle of Scotch he saw behind the
_____ Finally, the robber handed over his ID and proved that he was indeed
_____ police. But while a policeman was taking down Cabaso's statement, he
_____ Philippines, in October 1984. Then he walked into the kitchen and dropped
_____ counter. The cashier refused to hand over the Scotch because he didn't
_____ name and address of the man who had just robbed the store. The suspect

222 Textwork

Here are the answers to twelve questions. Read the text *Dead Men Talk* and try to write a question for each answer.

1 ______________________________?
Yes, at Clonard Street, Balbriggan.

2 ______________________________?
For less than a year.

3 ______________________________?
No, it wasn't. It was murder.

4 ______________________________?
She'd been strangled by Colin.

5 ______________________________?
He'd had a long relationship with an older woman.

6 ____?

To escape from being abused sexually and physically by Colin.

7 ____?

Websites to find out the best way to asphyxiate someone without leaving any marks on the victim's neck.

8 ____?

How serial killers evaded detection for long periods.

9 ____?

To get the money from a £400,000 life insurance policy he had taken out on himself and his wife.

10 ____?

No, he didn't. He disappeared while he was still on bail.

11 ____?

Colin's car plus his clothes.

12 ____?

He's in prison serving a life sentence for murder.

223 Interact

1 What strategies do con men use to fool women into believing they love them?
2 What strategies can the police use in order to catch criminals? Give examples.
3 If you witnessed a serious crime would you consider being a witness in court? Why/Why not?

Practise the vocabulary in Wordmatch/Spelling

224 Vocabulary: Fill in the gaps

Fill in the missing words in the sentences below. Choose from the following words, taken from the text. Then make up your own sentences for the four words that are left over.

abandoned	choked	distraught	jurisdiction
abuse	confirm	emergency services	lengthy
apparently	convinced	evade	obstacles
callous	dispose of	forensic	trace

1 If there's a fire or you see a crime being committed, you should phone the __________ immediately.
2 In general, the British courts have no __________ to deal with crimes outside the UK.
3 One major practical problem of killing someone is how to __________ the body afterwards.
4 Colin Whelan's car, together with his clothes, were found __________ at the cliffs in Howth in Dublin.
5 Many airline passengers face __________ delays because of the strike by baggage handlers.

6 He grabbed her around the neck and __________ her to death.
7 Colin had a history of sexual and physical __________ towards his first wife.
8 A __________ examination revealed a large quantity of poison in the dead man's stomach.
9 There are still a number of __________ in the way of a lasting peace settlement in the Middle East.
10 The missing child's __________ parents made an emotional appeal for information on TV.
11 "I'll just call the hotel and __________ our reservations," said Jake to his wife.
12 It might sound __________ , but I don't care if he *is* homeless. He's definitely not coming to live with us!

225 **Focus on crime words**

A Work in pairs. Here are 28 different crimes arranged alphabetically. How many of them do you know? Use a dictionary if necessary. Test yourself on some of them by matching ten of them to the definitions below.

arson, assault, assassination, bigamy, blackmail, bribery and corruption, burglary, drug trafficking, embezzlement, espionage (spying), forgery, fraud, hijacking, kidnapping, libel, manslaughter, mugging, murder, perjury, rape, robbery, shoplifting, slander, smuggling, theft, treason, trespassing, vandalism

1 __________ is the crime of copying things such as banknotes, letters, official documents, etc.
2 __________ is the crime of deliberately damaging public property, e.g. telephone kiosks, usually just for the fun of it.
3 __________ is the crime of deliberately setting fire to a building, etc. often for the insurance money.
4 __________ is the crime of attacking someone, often in a public place such as a park or a street, in order to rob them.
5 __________ is the crime of lying in court while giving evidence, when you've promised to tell the truth.
6 __________ is the crime of stealing from someone's home.
7 __________ is the crime of demanding money from someone by threatening to reveal a secret about them.
8 __________ is the crime of betraying your own country to help its enemies.
9 __________ is the crime of printing or publishing something which is untrue and which damages another person's reputation.
10 __________ is the crime of taking a person hostage, usually in order to demand money in exchange for releasing them.

B Now make up your own definitions for five of the words that are left over. Read them out to another pair and see if they can guess which words you've defined.

COUNTERFEIT PROTECTION (page 109)

226 **Starter**

1. In what situations do you have to be extra careful with your bank card?
2. Have you heard of ways in which criminals try to get hold of people's bank cards, pin codes, etc?
3. What can you do to protect yourself from scams?

227 **Textwork**

Show that you have understood the text *Counterfeit Protection* by completing the statements below with information from the text. Sometimes one or two words are enough. The sentences are in no special order.

1. There are several stages involved in the printing of banknotes, including ___________ and ___________ .
2. To beat counterfeiters, the main weapon used by governments nowadays is to ___________ .
3. If you hand in a counterfeit note to a bank, it ___________ .
4. Two details on portraits in banknotes are difficult to copy – namely ___________ and ___________ .
5. It's a lot more difficult to spot a counterfeit note when ___________ .
6. The $100 dollar bill has the words "___________" along Benjamin Franklin's coat lapel.
7. To make notes difficult to reproduce, some countries have introduced innovative devices such as ___________ .
8. The front of a £20 note shows ___________ or ___________ depending on the angle you view it.
9. The paper for the $100 bill is made of ___________ .
10. One reason why banknote counterfeiting remains a problem is because people can now buy ___________ .
11. Fully printed banknotes have existed since the ___________ century.
12. Australian banknotes are more difficult to copy because ___________ .

228 **Interact**

1. What's the easiest way of keeping tabs on your finances – by having cash or by using a bank card?
2. What are the advantages of using cash instead of bank cards?
3. Will bank notes disappear in the future? What do you think?

Practise the vocabulary in Wordmatch/Spelling

Another exercise on the words in the word list

229 Writing

Imagine if Twitter had been around in the past. What tweets would people have been posting then? Here are six situations from the past. Choose two and post a tweet for each – but don't forget, no more than 140 characters long!

1 You're Christopher Columbus and it's 1492. You've just reached the West Indies. Post a tweet telling people that the world is round after all. Also mention a rather strange plant you've found that the natives dry and then put in a pipe called a 'tobaco' to inhale the smoke. You're thinking of trying it yourself.
2 It's 1602 and you've just been to the Globe Theatre in London to see a play called *Hamlet*. Although you'd never heard of the author, William Shakespeare, before, you really enjoyed the evening and think that this guy Shakespeare may well have a future in the theatre. Post a tweet telling everyone about it.
3 It's 1969 and you've just turned on the television. There are some rather unclear black and white images of someone walking around in a strange grey landscape beside an American flag. He's saying something about 'a giant leap for mankind.' You realize you're watching the first man on the moon, Neil Armstrong. Post a tweet about what you're watching.
4 You're in Dallas in 1963 watching President J F Kennedy's procession through the city. His car has just passed you when suddenly there's a shot and lots of people start running around and shouting. You hear the words, 'The President's been shot!' Post a tweet about the incident.
5 You're in Italy in 1609 and have just been introduced to Galileo who, like you, is very interested in the stars and planets. He takes you to his studio to show you some wonderful new tube which will enable you to see the stars as you've never seen them before. Post a tweet describing what you've seen.

230 Vocabulary Bank: Useful nouns 3

Put the correct noun into each sentence. Choose from:

courage desire equality experience gratitude

1 Probably the only time there could be true __________ between men and women is if men could become pregnant and give birth to children. *(jämlikhet)*
2 It took __________ for the Prime Minister to admit publicly that he was wrong. *(mod)*
3 Our new neighbours didn't seem to show a lot of __________ for all the help we'd given them. *(tacksamhet)*
4 In working life, __________ is often more important than qualifications. *(erfarenhet)*
5 Her one __________ in life was to get married and have children. *(önskan)*

Now turn to page 310 in Vocabulary Bank and do *Useful nouns 3*.

LISTENING: THE YEAR WE DISAPPEARED

231 **Starter**

Why is plastic surgery such big business today? What's your opinion about it?

232 **Listen and recall** To listen, follow this link

Listen to *The Year We Disappeared* and choose the best answer (a, b or c). Before you start, read through the sentences and check the words in the word list.

1. The operation his father went through was *a) to reconstruct his body b) done at a hospital in Texas c) experimental.*
2. His lower jaw was removed when he was shot in the head with *a) a shotgun b) a rifle c) a pistol.*
3. Before his operation, he couldn't *a) read b) write c) speak.*
4. The man who'd been shot had *a) three b) two c) four* children.
5. In the comic book, her oldest brother had shown her a skeleton that *a) carried around a big gun b) was very kind c) did bad things.*
6. Their father had been *a) a police officer b) a soldier c) a firefighter.*
7. *a) The family b) The town of Falmouth c) A charity* would have to pay for the operation.
8. The day of the fund-raiser was *a) warm and sunny b) very windy c) hot and humid.*
9. Her favourite dessert was *a) vanilla ice-cream b) chocolate chip cookies c) chocolate pudding.*
10. You could buy *a) one b) two c) three* cookies for fifty cents.
11. When she told the women her name, she got the cookies for *a) nothing b) 25 cents c) 15 cents each.*
12. The woman gives the girl *a) a kiss b) some money c) a hug.*
13. Someone wanted to *a) hurt b) kill c) make fun of* their father.
14. In the end, the family *a) were sent to stay with a relative in the south b) were moved to another town where no one knew them c) were lucky not to be moved to a different town.*

Practise the vocabulary in Wordmatch/Spelling

233 Vocabulary: Which word...?

Here are some words found in the listening exercise *The Year We Disappeared.*

bequeath	fund-raiser	lose one's mind	shotgun
braids	gums	muggy	surgeon
comic book	in the line of duty	pull through	wink
courage	jaw	respond	

Which of the above...

1 are part of your mouth? ___________
2 is another word for 'to answer'? to ___________
3 has something to do with hair? ___________
4 is someone who works in a hospital? ___________
5 is another word for 'bravery'? ___________
6 is part of your face? ___________
7 means to go mad? ___________ .
8 do you do with your eyes? ___________
9 means to officially leave something to somebody after your death? ___________
10 fits into this sentence? *We all hoped he would* ________ *the operation.*
11 can help to get money for a good cause? ___________
12 is a type of weapon? ___________
13 describes weather that's unpleasantly warm? ___________
14 can you read? ___________
15 fits into this sentence? *The police officer died* ________ .

234 Interact

1 Why do you think someone wanted to kill the police officer?
2 What dangers do police officers face?
3 What can force a person to live using a hidden identity?

WSM: FACE TRANSPLANTS - A SHORT HISTORY

When was the first face transplant involving a human?
In November 2005, surgeons in Amiens, France, performed the first partial face transplant for Isabelle Dinoire, 38. Her nose, lips, chin and parts of her cheeks had been removed after she was bitten by her dog in May that year. The operation involved transplanting facial material from a dead 46-year-old woman. A report by the surgical team on Dinoire's progress 18 months later suggested she was "very satisfied".

When was the first in the United States?
In December 2008 at the Cleveland Clinic, Ohio. In a 22-hour operation, Connie Culp had most of her face replaced five years after her husband turned a shotgun on her, shattering her nose, cheeks, the roof of her mouth and an eye. In May 2009 she revealed how she could talk, smile, smell and taste her food again. It was the most elaborate operation so far – and the fourth in all.

Where and when was the first full facial transplant?
In Barcelona, Spain, in March 2010. A Spanish farmer, known as Oscar, who was unable to breathe or eat on his own after accidentally shooting himself five years before, underwent a 24-hour operation. Doctors lifted an entire face, including jaw, nose, cheekbones, muscles, teeth and eyelids, from a donor and placed it mask-like on Oscar.

And in the US?
Dallas Wiens, who had been left blind, without lips, nose or cheeks after being burnt by a high-voltage wire while painting a church in 2008, had his transplant at Brigham and Women's hospital, Boston, in March 2011. His sight could not be restored.

What about in the UK?
None yet. Peter Butler, a leading proponent of such surgery, was given the go-ahead for the first in Britain in 2006, and has assessed patients for combined face and hand transplants.

What problems are there for potential patients?
Despite huge advances by surgeons in facial reconstruction, many hurdles must be overcome. Apart from finding the right surgical match from deceased donors and the difficulties in returning full form and function to new faces, patients can expect to take immuno-suppressant drugs for the rest of their lives. These increase the risk of infection and cancer and generally weaken muscles and bones. China's first transplant patient died in 2008, two years after the operation, apparently having given up his immuno-suppressant drugs and turning to herbal medicine instead.

From The Guardian

HUSH, HUSH (page 112)

235 **Starter**

Work in pairs or small groups. When choosing a book to read, it's common to read the blurb first - which is a brief summary of the book's plot - and is usually found on the back of the book. It's intended to make you want to buy the book.

Here's the 'blurb' for the book *Hush, Hush.* Read it and then decide whether it would make you want to buy or read it.

FALLING IN LOVE WAS NEVER SO EASY... OR SO DEADLY.

For Nora Grey, romance was not part of the plan. She's never been particularly attracted to the boys at her school, no matter how much her best friend, Vee, pushes them at her. Not until Patch came along. With his easy smile and eyes that seem to see inside her, Nora is drawn to him against her better judgement.

But after a series of terrifying encounters, Nora's not sure who to trust. Patch seems to be everywhere she is, and to know more about her than her closest friends. She can't decide whether she should fall into his arms or run and hide. And when she tries to seek some answers, she finds herself near a truth that is way more unsettling than anything Patch makes her feel.

For Nora is right in the middle of an ancient battle between the immortal and those that have fallen – and, when it comes to choosing sides, the wrong choice will cost her life.

236 **Interact**

1 The ending to this extract is rather dramatic. Why do you think the old lady was shot?
2 Why do you think young adult paranormal romance novels such as *Hush, Hush* are so popular?
3 Who do you think they appeal to most - boys or girls or both?
4 Here are some other young adult book series. Which ones have you heard of and which ones have you read?

- *Fallen* series by Lauren Kate
- *House of Night* series by P.C. Cast

- *The Hunger Games* series by Suzanne Collins
- *The Immortals* series by Alyson Noel
- *The Mortal Instruments* series by Cassandra Clair
- *The Twilight Saga* series by Stephenie Meyer
- *The Vampire Diaries* series by L.J. Smith
- *The Wolves of Mercy Falls* series by Maggie Stiefvater
- *Vampire Academy* series by Richelle Mead

Practise the vocabulary in Wordmatch/Spelling

237 Vocabulary: Definitions

Here are definitions of twelve words found in the text. Can you work out what they are? To help you, the first and last letter of each missing word is given.

1	To hold something tightly because you don't want to lose it.	c________h
2	You can wear these on your hands when it's cold.	m________s
3	Another word for 'disappear'.	v________h
4	If you describe something as ______, you mean it's unusual and attractive, especially in an old-fashioned way.	q________t
5	A small, round close-fitting hat.	b________e
6	A long narrow space between rows of seats in a bus, an aircraft, a cinema or a church.	a________e
7	A container made of wood, plastic or metal, especially one used for carrying bottles.	c________e
8	A narrow street between or behind buildings, not usually used by cars.	a________y
9	Something that's ______, is something that's been thrown away because it's no longer wanted or needed.	d________d
10	The American word for 'pavement'.	s________k
11	______ eyes are small, round, and shiny – used especially about someone you think looks dishonest or strange.	b________y
12	You use these to build walls and houses.	b________s

Now write your own definitions for <u>two</u> of the following words, again found in the text.

cackle derrière resemble tug

238 Writing

Using one of the series from exercise 237, write a summary of the plot of one or more of the books in the series.

239 Act it out

Try acting out the scene between Nora Grey and the woman. Your teacher will give you a copy of the script. You could try doing it in groups of three, with one person acting as the director.

240 Looking at word-building 3

Various changes

The word in **bold** type at the end of each of the following sentences can be used to form a word that fits suitably in the blank space. It could be an adjective, a verb, a noun or an adverb. Fill each blank in this way.

1 I'm sorry, I __________ with you completely. I don't think men and women can ever be equal. **agree**
2 There's been a lot of __________ in this area since the Honda factory closed last year. **employ**
3 It's __________ to study a language if you're never going to use it. **point**
4 I didn't think he'd pass his driving test, so I __________ him from trying it. **courage**
5 But how could you do it? Really, Ophelia, I feel quite __________ of you! **shame**
6 What a __________ dress you're wearing! It's really gorgeous! **beauty**
7 We could hear a dog barking __________ from inside the house as we knocked on the front door. **angry**
8 The __________ of the fire was welcome after our long journey through the snow. **warm**
9 His injury was clearly causing him a lot of __________ . **comfort**
10 Most people feel nervous if they have to make a __________ in public. **speak**
11 They said my illness was __________ . Don't they realise I'm in a lot of pain? **imagine**
12 For most families with children nowadays, both parents going out to work is a __________ . **necessary**
13 What sort of fish is this? It's completely __________! **taste**
14 There's a __________ of cheap accommodation in London and other major cities. **short**
15 The fire was caused by an __________ fault in the television. **electricity**
16 It was an incredible story, quite __________. **believe**
17 The sudden __________ of the chief cashier a few days after the bank robbery confirmed the police's suspicions that it was an inside job. **appear**
18 All the students agreed that this year's exam was __________ easy. **compare**
19 This job requires a working __________ of French and Spanish. **know**
20 Do you want to go to the pub or the cinema tonight? You decide. It's your __________ . **choose**

 Fun with vocabulary 5

A Homonyms

A homonym is a word that's spelt the same and sounds the same as another, but is different in meaning. For example, *We missed the last* ***train*** *home and had to walk. She went to London to* ***train*** *to be a nurse.*

Work in pairs. Read through the following pairs of sentences and try to decide which words are missing. The same word is used for both gaps but with two completely different meanings. When you've finished, translate the pairs of words into Swedish.

1 Let's go out tonight for a ________ . (*Sw:* ________)
The shopkeeper gave her £1.50 ________ . (*Sw:* ________)
2 This ________ contains a speling mistake. (*Sw:* ________)
The man was given a two-year prison ________ . (*Sw:* ________)
3 The FBI have uncovered a ________ to assassinate the President. (*Sw:* ________)
The film's special effects were excellent, but the ________ was really weak.
(*Sw:* ________)
4 He was offered the ________ in the new film. (*Sw:* ________)
There was a notice in the park saying: 'Dogs must be kept on a ________ at all times.'
(*Sw:* ________)
5 The doctor told her that her husband's condition was ________ . (*Sw:* ________)
We put the horse in the ________ for the night. (*Sw:* ________)
6 That's all the news we have at ________ I'm afraid. (*Sw:* ________)
I need to buy a birthday ________ for my girlfriend. (*Sw:* ________)
7 Her voice on the phone was so ________ that I could hardly hear what she was saying.
(*Sw:* ________)
It was so hot and stuffy on the underground that I thought I was going to ________ .
(*Sw:* ________)
8 The waiter was so friendly that I gave him a big ________. (*Sw:* ________)
It's only the ________ of an iceberg that's visible above the water. (*Sw:* ________)
9 The restaurant bill came to £40, including ________. (*Sw:* ________)
The funeral ________ will take place on Friday. (*Sw:* ________)
10 I've been working for this ________ for nearly fifteen years. (*Sw:* ________)
Doing these exercises will give you very ________ muscles. (*Sw:* ________)

B Homophones

A homophone is a word that sounds the same as another but is different in spelling and meaning. For example, *Tom, I'd like you to* ***meet*** *my brother, Brian. I don't eat* ***meat*** *– I'm a vegetarian.*

Work in pairs. Read through the following pairs of sentences and try to decide which words are missing. When you've finished, translate the pairs of words into Swedish.

1 If you drop that vase, it will ________ . (*Sw:* ________)
He put his foot on the ________ to slow down. (*Sw:* ________)
2 You can pay by ________ or credit card. (*Sw:* ________)
'Could you ________ this to make sure it's correct?' he asked. (*Sw:* ________)
3 During the fire, the ________ was filled with thick black smoke. (*Sw:* ________)
Prince Charles is ________ to the British throne. (*Sw:* ________)
4 The rail ________ to London from here is about £75. (*Sw:* ________)
She had long, ________ hair. (*Sw:* ________)
5 Japanese people usually ________ when they greet one another. (*Sw:* ________)
He hit his head on the ________ of the tree. (*Sw:* ________)
6 The letter was ________ by airmail. (*Sw:* ________)
Flowers are often chosen for their ________ as well as for the way they look. (*Sw:* ________)
7 The bride looked really lovely as she walked down the ________ . (*Sw:* ________)
The ________ of Wight is just off the south coast of England. (*Sw:* ________)
8 The polar ________ is a very big animal. (*Sw:* ________)
During the winter, all the trees were ________ . (*Sw:* ________)
9 The ________ of the holly tree is bright red. (*Sw:* ________)
Dogs love to ________ bones in the garden. (*Sw:* ________)
10 He ordered a plate of ________ at his favourite restaurant in Brussels. (*Sw:* ________)
You exercise lots of different ________ when you go swimming. (*Sw:* ________)

C Now make up your own sentences for the following pairs of homonyms and homophones.

leaves (verb) / leaves (noun)	allowed / aloud
date (noun, 2 meanings)	queue / cue
rule (verb) / rule (noun)	heard / herd
course (noun, 2 meanings)	cell / sell
sound (adjective) / sound (noun)	deer / dear

242 Sum up and comment

1 Crime doesn't pay or does it? Give your opinion.
2 What's been most interesting to read about in this textbook?
3 Time to finally assess your level of English! Turn to the Resource Section p. 122 and evaluate how you've progressed.

243 **Books to read and enjoy**

Busby, Colin and John: *The Year We Disappeared*
Connelly, Michael: *Lost Light*
Dexter, Colin: *The Way Through the Woods*
Finch, Janet: *White Oleander*
Fitzpatrick, Becca: *Hush, Hush**
Fowles, John: *The Collector*
Mina, Denise: *Gods and Beasts*
Pitcher, Annabel: *My Sister Lives on the Mantelpiece**
Robinson, Peter: *Watching in the Dark*
Rankin, Ian: *Standing in Another Man's Grave*

*teenage fiction or less advanced books

STUDENT B

034 **Let's talk!**

Twenty Questions (from page 166)
Below are ten questions to ask group A. They also have ten questions to ask you. But you yourselves decide which question to answer each time by choosing a number between 1-10. Say to Group A: *Ask us question (5).* Then cross the number out so you don't get the same question again!

Take turns to ask and answer. When you answer, one person can start and the rest of the group can join in. *Group A starts.*

1	**2**	**3**	**4**	**5**	**6**	**7**	**8**	**9**	**10**

1 What's the best holiday you've ever had and what made it so special?
2 If you won a lot of money in what ways would it change your present life and in what ways wouldn't it?
3 Which three human qualities *(e.g. honesty)* do you consider to be the most important?
4 What is the most important invention in the last 50 years and what makes it so important?
5 What are the best things about living in Sweden and what are the worst?
6 What's the most enjoyable family occasion (e.g. wedding, birthday, etc.) you can remember, and what made it so enjoyable?
7 How would you describe your 'perfect' job?
8 How would you describe your taste in clothes and what would you wear if you wanted to make a good impression at a job interview?
9 Who's the most interesting person you've ever met? What made him or her so interesting?
10 What's your idea of the perfect 3-course meal? Describe each course.

040 **The top 10 animal horrors** (from page 170)

These are 'The top 10 animal horrors' in order:

1. parasitic worms
2. snakes
3. bees
4. spiders
5. bats
6. great white sharks
7. grizzly bears
8. piranhas
9. mice
10. wolves

Just a minute! (from page 196)

You're going to be asked in turn to talk about a subject for one minute. Below are the subjects for group A. They also have subjects for you to talk about, but you yourselves decide on a subject by choosing a number between 1–10. The person who's going to talk says to Group A: *I'd like to talk about subject (8).* Then cross the number out so you don't get the same subject again!

One person in Group A will now read out the subject you asked for. Try and talk for one minute. (Someone in Group A will tell you when to stop!) If you manage to do it, your team scores 1 point. *Group A starts.*

1	**2**	**3**	**4**	**5**	**6**	**7**	**8**	**9**	**10**

Subjects for group A

1 A happy memory.
2 The future.
3 Pets.
4 My last holiday.
5 Friendship.
6 Space travel.
7 My favourite relative.
8 People who have influenced history.
9 How to enjoy yourself.
10 Pop music.

Group B

Below are ten sentences to read out to group A. They also have ten sentences to read out to you. But you yourselves decide which sentence to talk about each time by choosing a number between 1–10. Say to Group A: *Read out sentence (2).* Then cross the number out so you don't ask for the same sentence again!

Take it in turns to read out a sentence and answer. When you answer, one person can start by giving his/her opinion, then the rest of the group can join in. *Group A starts by asking for a number.*

Look at Resource section p. 146 for phrases you can use when discussing things.

1	**2**	**3**	**4**	**5**	**6**	**7**	**8**	**9**	**10**

1 You can tell a lot about a person from the clothes he or she wears.
2 We should try to cure criminals not punish them.
3 Generally speaking, getting married and having children is less important for a man than it is for a woman.
4 When you speak a foreign language, it doesn't matter if you make mistakes, as long as people understand you.
5 It's better to grow up in the country than in a town or city.
6 Marriages don't often work when couples are from different backgrounds, race and religion.
7 Men and women can never really be equal, no matter how much we try.
8 Having fun is more important than having a career.
9 In the future, governments will try to censor the Internet more and more.
10 It's socially acceptable for a man to marry a women much younger than himself, but not for a woman to marry a man much younger than herself.

VOCABULARY BANK

Useful verbs, adjectives and nouns

1	Useful verbs 1	☐
2	Useful verbs 2	☐
3	Useful verbs 3	☐
4	Useful adjectives 1	☐
5	Useful adjectives 2	☐
6	Useful adjectives 3	☐
7	Useful nouns 1	☐
8	Useful nouns 2	☐
9	Useful nouns 3	☐

1 Useful verbs 1

Complete each sentence by choosing the correct verb from the list.
Make any necessary tense changes.

achieve	cause	envy	hitchhike	replace
annoy	charge	exaggerate	inherit	resign
ban	defeat	force	interrupt	surround
blush	drizzle	frown	predict	tempt

1 I really ________ my neighbour. He's just bought a brand-new BMW. *(avundas)*
2 They still don't know what ________ the recent train accident. *(orsaka)*
3 The Government's decided to ________ smoking in all public places. *(förbjuda)*
4 'Don't ________, Bill! You didn't walk 30 kilometres on Saturday. It was only 10!' *(överdriva)*
5 'Sorry to ________ you, but you're wanted on the phone.' *(avbryta)*
6 It started to ________, so we ran into a doorway to shelter. *(duggregna)*
7 The soldiers ________ the village. *(omringa)*
8 She ________ £400,000 when her mother died. *(ärva)*
9 If the goods are faulty, the company will have to ________ them. *(ersätta)*
10 What sort of things ________ you? *(förarga, irritera)*
11 Sally tended to ________ when she was embarrassed. *(rodna)*
12 The sun shining in her eyes made her ________. *(rynka pannan)*
13 She ________ because of ill health. *(avgå)*
14 It's very difficult to ________ someone to do something – especially children when it comes to eating vegetables. *(tvinga)*
15 'Could I ________ you to another piece of cake?' she asked. *(fresta)*
16 We've decided to ________ across Europe this summer. *(lifta)*
17 'Who did Nelson ________ at the Battle of Trafalgar?' *(besegra)*
'I'm not sure. Napoleon, maybe?'
18 Manchester United have ________ a lot in the past ten years. *(prestera, åstadkomma)*
19 'How much do you ________ for cleaning windows?' he asked. *(ta betalt)*
20 Do you believe that some people can ________ the future? *(förutsäga)*

2 Useful verbs 2

Complete each sentence by choosing the correct verb from the list.
Make any necessary tense changes.

appreciate	confirm	hug	pat	rely
assure	contain	impress	persuade	reveal
cancel	convince	occur	pity	sacrifice
challenge	fail	participate	rape	suffocate

1 The mother told her young daughter to __________ her friend's dog. *(klappa)*
2 After the driving test, the examiner told Margaret that she had __________ . *(misslyckas)*
3 It was quite a shock for many of his fans when the teenage pop star __________ that he was married. *(avslöja)*
4 He bought an expensive Rolex watch - just to __________ people. *(imponera på)*
5 Henry's mother tried to __________ her son to give up smoking. *(övertala)*
6 A near miss by an asteroid __________ more often than we think. *(hända, förekomma)*
7 He __________ him to a duel. *(utmana)*
8 He __________ his girlfriend when she got out of the train. 'I missed you so much!' he whispered. *(krama)*
9 This book __________ lots of good advice for staying healthy. *(innehålla)*
10 'I don't hate you - I just __________ you!' Jane said to her ex-boyfriend. *(tycka synd om)*
11 Ask James to do it, you know you can __________ on him! *(lita /på/)*
12 Thanks for your help. I really __________ it! *(uppskatta)*
13 A famous pop star has been accused of trying to __________ a fan. *(våldta)*
14 He asked the travel agent to __________ the booking in writing. *(bekräfta)*
15 'I __________ you, the Government is doing all it can to improve the National Health Service in this country,' the Prime Minister said to the reporter. *(försäkra)*
16 They had to __________ the planned open air concert because of bad weather. *(inställa)*
17 The woman told the police that the man had tried to __________ her. *(kväva)*
18 It took Ed a long time to __________ his girlfriend that he hadn't been seeing another girl behind her back. *(övertyga)*
19 Over 10,000 athletes __________ in the 2012 Olympic Games in London. *(delta)*
20 Many parents __________ their own lives for the sake of their children. *(offra)*

3 Useful verbs 3

Complete each sentence by choosing the correct verb from the list.
Make any necessary tense changes.

abandon	deceive	hijack	prosecute	sue
abstain	despise	limp	shrink	supply
affect	distinguish	overhear	skid	underestimate
betray	extinguish	prohibit	sneak	volunteer

1 He __________ for several weeks after the accident. *(halta)*
2 'Don't __________ them,' the coach told his players. 'Don't forget, they beat Brazil 2-0 last month.' *(underskatta)*
3 I __________ to babysit so my sister could go out with her friends. *(ställa upp som frivillig)*
4 Because of protests from local people, they have __________ their plans to build a new motorway. *(överge)*
5 Smoking is __________ on planes nowadays. *(förbjuda)*
6 It took the firefighters three hours to __________ the blaze. *(släcka)*
7 Pilots must __________ from alcohol for 24 hours before flying. *(avstå /ifrån/)*
8 He tried to __________ out of the house without his parents noticing. *(smyga)*
9 'I can never forgive him. I __________ him now!' June said to her best friend. *(förakta)*
10 Can you __________ between an American and a Canadian accent? *(skilja mellan)*
11 They signed an agreement not to __________ weapons to Iraq. *(förse med)*
12 The car __________ on the icy road. *(sladda)*
13 They __________ her for attempted murder. *(åtala)*
14 Arthritis is a crippling disease which __________ people all over the world. *(påverka)*
15 Jeans sometimes __________ when you wash them. *(krympa)*
16 She only found out after the divorce that her husband had __________ her for years. *(bedra)*
17 She threatened to __________ the newspaper if they printed a story about her being a drug addict. *(stämma)*
18 'How do you know Brian fancies me?'
'Because I __________ him telling Peter he'd love to go out with you.' *(råka höra)*
19 News is just coming in that three armed men have __________ an aeroplane on its way from Cuba to London. *(kapa)*
20 I could never be a traitor. I could never __________ my country. *(förråda)*

4 Useful adjectives 1

Complete each sentence by choosing the correct adjective from the list.

absent-minded	envious	mature	prejudiced	sensible
affectionate	greedy	mean	reliable	stubborn
ambitious	imaginative	nosy	responsible	vain
bossy	impatient	patient	ruthless	weird
creative				

1 He was very ________ and always wanted more than other people. *(girig)*
2 My sister's so ________. She just can't pass a mirror without taking a look at herself. *(fåfäng)*
3 I hate ________ people! *(dominerande)*
4 Brian's very ________ and hopes to be Prime Minister one day. *(ärelysten)*
5 Alan never buys anyone a drink. He's so ________ ! *(snål)*
6 Are Swedes ________ towards foreigners? *(fördomsfulla)*
7 To be successful in business, you often have to be ________ . *(skoningslös)*
8 Writers are usually very ________ and ________ people. *(fantasifulla / skapande)*
9 You have to be very ________ to be a driving instructor. *(tålmodig)*
10 At 13, girls are usually more ________ than boys. *(mogna)*
11 My husband's very ________ and often buys me flowers and tells me he loves me. *(tillgiven)*
12 We're looking for a ________ person to work in the sales department. *(ansvarsfull)*
13 'What do you think of Walter?'
'I'm not sure. He's a bit ________ , isn't he?' *(konstig, underlig)*
14 You can trust Maria to do it. She's very ________ . *(pålitlig)*
15 Our new neighbour's very ________ . She always wants to know other people's business. *(nyfiken)*
16 Do you think girls are more ________ than boys? *(förnuftiga, förståndiga)*
17 'I've never met such a ________ person as you!' she cried. *(envis)*
18 Timothy was ________ of his brother's success. *(avundsjuk)*
19 I could never be a teacher – I'm far too ________! *(otålig)*
20 He was a typical professor – scruffy, brilliant and ________ . *(tankspridd)*

5 Useful adjectives 2

Complete each sentence by choosing the correct adjective from the list.

artificial	conscious	filthy	significant	valid
average	delayed	peculiar	spacious	voluntary
bilingual	delicious	precious	urgent	vulnerable
compulsory	disgusting	rare	vacant	well-off

1 People with high blood-pressure are particularly __________ to diabetes. *(sårbara, utsatta)*
2 They announced that the flight was __________ by more than twenty-five minutes. *(försenad)*
3 Could you reply to this letter, please. It's rather __________ ! *(brådskande)*
4 The __________ salary in this country is about £26,000 a year. *(genomsnittliga)*
5 Mmm! This food is really __________ ! *(utsökt, läcker)*
6 You don't have to do it – it's completely __________ . *(frivilligt)*
7 The sign on the toilet said '__________'. *(ledig)*
8 The flat was really __________ . *(rymlig)*
9 Your train ticket is __________ for two months. *(giltig)*
10 She was very __________ of her height and never wore high heels when she went out dancing. *(medveten)*
11 He had a very __________ way of walking. *(egendomligt)*
12 She's __________ and can speak English and Spanish equally well. *(tvåspråkig)*
13 Bob comes from a very __________ family. *(välbärgad)*
14 This kitchen is __________ ! When was the last time you cleaned it? *(mycket smutsigt)*
15 It's very __________ to see badgers during the day. *(sällsynt)*
16 You have to do it – it's __________ . *(obligatoriskt)*
17 The room they gave us at the hotel was so __________ that we refused to stay there. *(äckligt, vidrigt)*
18 This crown is made out of __________ jewels. *(dyrbara)*
19 There's been a __________ increase in the number of people trying to seek asylum this year. *(betydande, markant)*
20 These flowers aren't real – they're __________ ! *(konstgjorda)*

6 Useful adjectives 3

Complete each sentence by choosing the correct adjective from the list.

accurate	gloomy	incredible	mutual	prone
annual	harmless	independent	numerous	sufficient
domestic	ignorant	inevitable	outstanding	unwilling
fragile	inconvenient	insufficient	portable	vivid

1 He gave us a ______ account of his trip across China. *(livlig)*
2 Singapore's been ______ for quite some time now. *(självständigt)*
3 'I hate you!'
'That's all right. The feeling's ______!' *(ömsesidig)*
4 Help yourselves! There should be ______ food for everyone. *(tillräckligt med)*
5 Be careful with that vase – it's very ______! *(bräcklig, skör)*
6 He tried to reassure people that his experiments using animals were quite ______. *(ofarliga)*
7 People like using laptops because – unlike desktop computers – they're ______. *(bärbara)*
8 She was able to give the police an ______ description of her attacker. *(exakt, noggrann)*
9 The murderer was described as an ______ and uneducated man. *(okunnig)*
10 The Eurovision Song Contest is an ______ event. *(årlig)*
11 'Excuse me, which terminal do ______ flights go from?' *(inrikes-)*
'Terminal 2.'
12 When I saw their ______ faces I knew that something was wrong. *(dystra)*
13 'I hope I haven't arrived at an ______ moment?' she said to her best friend and her boyfriend kissing on the sofa. *(olämpligt)*
14 'Do you know Pete Smart?'
'Oh yes. I've met him on ______ occasions.' *(talrika, många)*
15 She seemed ______ to join in with us. *(motvillig)*
16 Daniel Day-Lewis's performance in the film *Lincoln* was quite ______ and he fully deserved to win an Oscar. *(enastående)*
17 This breed of dog is particularly ______ to arthritis – especially in its hind legs. *(benägen /att/; ha anlag för)*
18 There was ______ evidence to convict the man the police had arrested. *(otillräckliga)*
19 Some people believe that a Third World War is ______ *(oundvikligt)*
20 It's quite ______ that wasps, mosquitoes and ants always seem to know where people are going to have their picnics! *(otroligt)*

7 Useful nouns 1

Complete each sentence by choosing the correct noun from the list.

abbreviation	charity	emergency	intention	pollution
advantage	circumstances	environment	investigation	reputation
ancestors	conclusion	government	lack	shortage
bargain	disadvantage	incident	origin	voyage
challenge	election			

1 BMW has a __________ for making quality cars. *(rykte)*
2 In the past, the __________ to Australia could take more than 6 weeks. *(båtresa)*
3 The __________ 'p.t.o.' means 'please turn over'. *(förkortning)*
4 Do you think there will be a change of __________ at the next __________? *(regering / val)*
5 Do you think it's an __________ or a __________ to be an only child? *(fördel / nackdel)*
6 Did you know that Clive's __________ came from Iceland? *(förfäder)*
7 Do you ever give money to __________? *(välgörenhet)*
8 It only cost £4. It was a real __________! *(fynd)*
9 There's a serious __________ of teachers in many of the major cities in Britain. *(brist, underskott)*
10 After discussing the matter for several hours, they still failed to reach a satisfactory __________ . *(slutsats; beslut)*
11 'I'm sorry, Pam. It wasn't my __________ to upset you.' *(avsikt)*
12 The police __________ is taking longer than expected. *(undersökning)*
13 Some people are very good in an __________ . Others are hopeless and go to pieces. *(kris, nödläge)*
14 The police had to drop the charges for __________ of evidence. *(brist)*
15 Do you know the __________ of the word 'sellotape'? *(ursprung)*
16 According to the police, the __________ took place outside the Pitcher & Piano pub in Wind Street late on Saturday night. *(händelse)*
17 The man was found dead in very suspicious __________ . *(omständigheter)*
18 Most people like a __________ , don't they? *(utmaning)*
19 We must do all we can to protect the __________ . *(miljö)*
20 In most countries, __________ is a serious problem. *(föroreningar)*

8 Useful nouns 2

Complete each sentence by choosing the correct noun from the list.

abundance	detour	hostage	predecessor	ransom
appearance	equivalent	interest	profit	recognition
assassination	expenditure	novel	proprietor	subscription
commuters	extent	precaution	publisher	turnover
currency	hospitality			

1 The magazine ________ was £35 a year. *(prenumeration)*
2 My cousin's just finished writing a ________, so she's looking for a suitable ________ now. *(roman / förläggare)*
3 There's an ________ of heather on the mountains in Scotland. *(överflöd)*
4 There's no true ________ of the word 'lagom' in English. *(motsvarighet)*
5 On our way to Ludlow, we decided to take a ________ through the village of Luston. *(omväg)*
6 A company's ________ is now a measure of its eventual ________ . *(omsättning / vinst)*
7 'Which restaurant do you work at?'
'My own! I'm the ________!' *(ägare)*
8 'This is Mrs O'Sullivan, my ________.' *(företrädare)*
9 This bank account will give you 4% ________ . *(ränta)*
10 The kidnappers demanded a ________ of $500,000 to return their daughter safely. *(lösensumma)*
11 'What's the ________ of Pakistan?'
'The Pakistani rupee?' *(valuta)*
12 Most people remember the ________ of President John F. Kennedy in 1963. *(mord)*
13 We thanked them for their ________ . *(gästfrihet)*
14 Between 8 o'clock and 9 o'clock in the morning, the London Underground is full of ________ . *(pendlare)*
15 Although he was famous all over the world, in his own country he never really got the ________ he deserved. *(erkännande)*
16 The journalist who was recently taken ________ in Mali has now been released. *(gisslan)*
17 James took the ________ of insuring his digital camera and camcorder before taking them with him on holiday. *(försiktighetsåtgärd)*
18 To what ________ can parents be blamed for their children's behaviour? *(omfattning)*
19 She was a vain person who was always very concerned about her ________ . *(utseende)*
20 I wonder how much the total ________ on defence is for all the European countries? Do you think it's more than for education? *(utgifter)*

9 Useful nouns 3

Complete each sentence by choosing the correct noun from the list.

ability	awe	consolation	honour	prejudice
achievement	bliss	despair	jealousy	recovery
admiration	confusion	destiny	obsession	responsibility
anguish	connection	disgust	poverty	stamina

1 Winston Churchill was convinced that it was his __________ to be a great leader. *(öde)*
2 Mike certainly has the __________ to pass his exams, but as he does so little work, he may well fail them. *(förmåga)*
3 We were filled with __________ at his achievements. *(beundran)*
4 Golf isn't just a game to my cousin – it's an __________ with him! *(fix idé, besatthet)*
5 The tennis star made a quick __________ after his injury. *(tillfrisknande)*
6 It's an __________ to play for your country – especially in the World Cup. *(ära)*
7 The language used by the comedian was very offensive, so half the audience left in __________ . *(avsmak, avsky)*
8 Cathy's drug addiction has driven her parents to __________ . *(förtvivlan)*
9 I didn't get the job, but it was some __________ to me that I'd been selected for the final interviews. *(tröst)*
10 The main reason for their divorce was her husband's constant __________ . *(svartsjuka)*
11 It's quite an __________ to win a gold medal at the Olympics. *(insats, prestation)*
12 Because Sir Paul McCartney is so famous, we were all in __________ of him when we met him at the opening of his Art Exhibition. *(djup respekt, vördnad)*
13 You could see the look of __________ on his mother's face when the police told her that her son had been arrested for drug-pushing. *(vånda)*
14 My idea of __________ is to lie in a hot bath with classical music playing in the background. *(lycksalighet, lycka)*
15 Nowadays, although everyone must know the __________ between lung cancer and smoking, more and more young people are starting to smoke now than ever. *(samband)*
16 Is a child – once it leaves home – still its parent's __________? *(ansvar)*
17 Running a marathon requires a lot of __________ . *(uthållighet, kraft)*
18 Many people in the developing countries live in great __________ . *(fattigdom)*
19 A fire broke out at the prison, and in the __________ , three of the inmates escaped. *(förvirring)*
20 There's still quite a lot of __________ towards foreigners in Britain – especially towards black people and Muslims. *(fördomar)*

GRAMMAR

NOUNS

Nouns are e.g. people and animals (*boy, girl, cat*), things (*chair, pen, car*) and feelings (*love, fear, despair*). Nouns also include people's names and places such as Kate and England.
There are nouns in the singular and in the plural.

Nouns in the plural

Most words form the plural with *–s* or *–es*, e.g. **a** film/two film**s, a** glass/two glass**es**.

-ies
If the word ends in a consonant (b, d, f, etc.) + *y* change the *-y* to *–ies*, e.g. baby/bab**ies**.

-oes
A few common words ending in *–o* have the plural ending *-oes.*

potato**es**
tomato**es**

f **changes to *-ves***

life	li**ves**
wife	wi**ves**
scarf	scar**ves**

The same in the singular and in the plural

sheep	**sheep**
salmon	**salmon**
crayfish	**crayfish**

Special plural forms
Learn these by heart!

child	**children**
foot	**feet**
goose	**geese**
man	**men**
mouse	**mice**
tooth	**teeth**
woman	**women**

Remember: *Women and children first! Then the men!*

Always plural meaning

cattle (singular: a cow, a bull)
people (singular: a person)
police (singular: a police officer)

Always plural form

binoculars (a pair of binoculars)
glasses (a pair of glasses)
jeans (a pair of jeans)
pyjamas (a pair of pyjamas)
scissors (a pair of scissors)
trousers (a pair of trousers)

Countable/Uncountable Nouns

A **countable** noun can be singular (e.g. bus) or plural (buses). We can say **a** bus, **one** bus, **two** buses or **some** buses. But you can't put **a/an** in front of **uncountable** nouns (e.g. butter) and they cannot be plural.

a singer, a choir of fifty singer**s** — *en kör med femtio sångare*

Uncountable both in Swedish and English

butter	*smör*	some butter	*lite smör*

Countable (i.e. singular and plural**) in Swedish but uncountable in English**

news	*nyhet*	(–) good news	*en bra nyhet*
weather	*väder*	(–) terrible weather	*ett fruktansvärt väder*
traffic	*trafik*	(–) terrible traffic	*en fruktansvärd trafik*
progress	*framsteg*	(–) great progress	*stora framsteg*
advice	*råd*	(–) good advice	*ett gott råd*
furniture	*möbel, möbler*	our new furniture	*våra nya möbler*
homework	*läxa, läxor*	too much homework	*för många läxor*
information	*upplysningar*	look for information	*söka upplysningar*
money	*pengar*	Where <u>is</u> my money?	*Var är mina pengar?*
bread	*bröd*	Buy some bread/ (a) loaf of bread, please	*Köp bröd/Ett bröd, tack.*

Some phrases to use with uncountable nouns

a glass of beer**, a bottle of** milk, **a bucket of** water, **a cup of** tea, **a loaf of** bread, **a jar of** coffee, **a spoonful of** sugar, **a piece of** advice, **a slice of** cheese, etc.

The Genitive

's

When you want to show that somebody, usually a person or an animal, owns something then you add an **'s** to the word. You attach the **s** with an apostrophe (').

Henry's (*Henrys*) jeans.

s'

When there are several owners and the noun is in the plural e.g. girls just add an apostrophe without any extra s.

The **girls'** (*flickornas*) jeans.

For irregular plurals follow this pattern:

The **children's** toys.
The **men's** changing rooms.

of

When the 'owner' is not a person or an animal but a thing use the *of*-construction.

Red is **the colour of** love. *Röd är kärlekens färg.*

The Indefinite Article

A or **an**?

A is used:
with singular nouns that start with a consonant (b, c, d, j, p, etc.).

a **b**oy, a **d**og, a **p**icture, a **t**able.

with nouns that start with 'u' or 'eu' when it sounds like 'you' [j].

a **u**niversity, a **Eu**ropean

An is used:
with singular nouns that start with a vowel (a, e, i, o, u)

an **a**pple, an **e**ngineer, an **i**sland, an **o**range, an **u**mbrella

with nouns that start with a silent letter h:

an **h**onest politician, an **h**onour to meet you, it lasted an **h**our (But a <u>h</u>appy man, a holiday, a horror film)

You use **a** or **an:**
to refer to a person or thing you are mentioning for the first time.

The house has **a** big garden. Sally bought **a** skirt and **a** blouse in the sale.

when saying what jobs or professions people have.

My brother's **a** doctor and my sister's **an** accountant.

in definitions or general statements in the singular.

A spider is **an** insect that has eight legs. **A** gun is **a** dangerous weapon. **A** poodle is **a** type of dog.

with prices, how often we do things and how fast.

£3 **a** kilo, three times **a** week, forty kilometres **an** hour

with hundred, thousand, million and billion.

a hundred, **a** thousand, **a** million, **a** billion

The Definite Article

Use **the**:

when the person, place or thing is unique – there is only one.

The Moon is 250,000 miles away.

when you talk about a person, place or thing for the **second** time or when you're talking about something that your listener knows about.

Compare:

I borrowed **a** CD from Peter.	This is **the** CD I borrowed from Peter.
There's **a** good film on this week.	**The** film I told you about is on TV tonight.

with most geographical names (rivers, mountain ranges, plural place names, plural band names).

The Thames flows through London. We went skiing in **the** Alps. **The** Rolling Stones.

with musical instruments. (UK)

Paul plays **the** piano. Sheila plays **the** trumpet.

with many job titles.

I'd like to see **the** manager. Who's **the** director of the film?

PRONOUNS

Pronouns are used instead of nouns e.g. *Henry = he, him*   *Kate = she, her*
Steve and Jenny = they, them, My family and myself = we, us

The Possessive Pronoun

A possessive pronoun shows who the owner is.

I like **my** earrings (*mina örhängen*). The earrings are **mine**. (*mina*)

my, your, his, her, its, our, their are ALWAYS followed by a noun.
mine, yours, his, hers, its, ours, theirs are NEVER followed by a noun.

Isn't that **my** coat? It looks like **mine**! (= It looks like **my coat**.)

The Reflexive Pronoun

A reflexive pronoun is "the same person twice".
"**I** looked at **myself** in the mirror." ("I" and "myself" are the same person.)
Reflexive Pronouns always end in:

-**self** (my, your, him, her, its) or
-**selves** (our, your, them).

The Relative Pronoun

A relative pronoun refers back to something mentioned earlier in the sentence.
Who refers back to people.
Which refers back to animals, things and issues and sentences.

who	It was <u>**Brad Pitt who**</u> ordered the cheeseburger.
which	Cinderella has a <u>**mink coat which**</u> is brand new.

The Indefinite Pronoun

The indefinite pronoun refers to any thing or any person 'not defined'. Common indefinite pronouns are *some, any, something, anything, nothing, somebody, anybody, nobody, all, etc.*

Some and Any

You can use **some** and **any** with both countable and uncountable nouns.

Uncountable: I've got **some water** but I haven't got **any cola.**

Countable: There are **some bottles** but there aren't **any cans**.

Use **some**:

in positive statements.

We need **some** more glasses. I'd like **some** apples, please.

when you make an offer or a request.

Would you like **some** coffee? Do you want **some** more to eat?

Can you give me **some** information?

Other words that are used like **some** are:

someone, somebody, something and *somewhere*

Use **any**:

in negative statements.

We haven't got **any** coffee. I haven't got **any** brothers or sisters.

in questions.

Have we got **any** homework tonight? Are there **any** glasses on the table?

Other words that are used like **any** are:

anyone, anybody, anything and *anywhere*

Four other useful words are:

no one *(not anyone)*, **nobody** *(not anybody)*, **nothing** *(not anything)* and **nowhere** *(not anywhere)*

There is (There's)... / There are...

Det finns ..., Det står ..., Det ligger ... can be translated as There is (There's) or There are.

There's/There is milk in the kitchen. *Det finns mjölk i* köket.

There are 366 days in a leap year. *Det finns/är 366 dagar på ett skottår.*

It is (It's)...

Det är in Swedish is normally It is/It's ... in English.

It's hot. *Det är varmt.*

It's nice. *Det är trevligt.*

It's a long way. *Det är långt.*

ADJECTIVES

Adjectives describe people and things. The form of the adjective never changes.

a **happy** boy   two **happy** boys
an **old** coin   several **old** coins

You put an adjective *before* a noun.

I saw a **handsome** man. They had a very **big** garden.

An adjective can stand alone after the verbs *be, feel, look, taste, smell* and *sound.*

The man was **handsome**. Their garden was **big**.
I feel **hungry**. Cathy looks **happy**. This spaghetti tastes **wonderful**. That cheese smells **horrible**. That song sounds **familiar**.

Comparative and Superlative

Adjectives are used to compare things.

Base form	Comparative	Superlative
short adjectives*	**+er**	**+est**
old	older	/the/oldest
*long** adjectives*	**more +**	**most +**
intelligent	more intelligent	/the/most intelligent

* With one or two syllables.
Long adjectives usually have at least three syllables and are compared with **more and **most**.

ADVERBS

Adverbs describe **how** someone or something does something. In other words an adverb usually tells us more about a verb. The adverb is usually placed after the verb.

Peter **plays** the piano **beautifully**. ('Beautifully' describes how Peter plays.)
My uncle always **drives** very **carefully**. ('Carefully' describes how my uncle drives.)

You form regular adverbs by adding –**ly** to the adjective e.g. beautiful and beautiful**ly.**

If an adjective ends with –**y**, the adverb ends with –**ily,** happy and happ**ily.**

If an adjective ends with –**ble**, the adverb ends in –**bly,** horrible and horri**bly.**

Some adverbs are irregular. You have to learn these by heart. Here are some common ones.

good	**well**	hard	**hard**
fast	**fast**	late	**late**

Some words change their meaning when ending in **-ly**

I haven't seen Barbara **lately** *(nyligen)*.
He was so exhausted he could **hardly** *(knappt)* speak.

It can sometimes be difficult to tell the difference between an adjective and an adverb. By translating the sentence into Swedish and changing it into the plural you can work out if it's an adverb or an adjective. Only adjectives change in the plural.

She's beautiful. *Hon är vacker.*
They're beautiful. *De är vackra.*

She sings beautifully. *Hon sjunger vackert.*
They sing beautifully. *De sjunger vackert.*

Adverbs of manner (quickly, slowly, hard, etc.)
Adverbs which tell us how people do things are called **adverbs of manner**. Here are some common ones: angrily, badly, beautifully, carefully, carelessly, dangerously, efficiently, fast, happily, hard, late, loudly, quickly, quietly, slowly, terribly, well.

Adverbs of frequency (always, often, never, etc.)
Adverbs of frequency tell you how often people do things.

The most common ones are:

0 %	never	*aldrig*
5 %	hardly ever	*nästan aldrig*
10 %	rarely, seldom	*sällan*
30 %	sometimes/occasionally	*ibland/då och då*
70 %	often	*ofta*
80%–90 %	normally/usually	*normalt/vanligtvis*
100 %	always	*alltid*

The percentages are of course approximate!

VERBS

A verb tells you what someone or something does, is, has or will become.
A verb tells you what someone or something

- did five minutes ago/yesterday
- has done some time in the past
- will do in the future
- could do/have done

You recognize a verb by placing "to" in front of the base form: *to dance* (this form is called the infinitive).

The three verb forms

You have probably conjugated a verb many times, "play - played - played" and "go - went - gone" no doubt sound familiar.
It's well worth learning three verb forms by heart because with them you can construct all the other verb tenses.

Main verbs have three basic forms: the **base form**, the **past tense** and the **past participle** form.

For **regular verbs** add **-ed** to the base form to construct the other two forms.

Base form	**Past tense**	**Past participle**
laugh	laughe*d*	laughe*d*

There are also **irregular verbs** such as:

Base form	**Past tense**	**Past participle**
go	went	gone

These irregular verbs you have to learn by heart - see pages 330-332.

The Present Simple

Use the Present Simple:
about things that happen regularly (habits and routines).

Charles **plays** tennis every Friday. I always **walk** to school.

about facts.

Water **boils** at 100º Centigrade. Helen **doesn't speak** Spanish.

-s after 3rd person singular
After **he**, **she** or **it** you always add an -**s** to verbs in the present simple.

he talk**s**..., the boy play**s**..., she cycle**s**... Ruth like**s**... it rain**s**... the dog bark**s**...

The Present Continuous

Use the Present Continuous:

about temporary things, that are happening now, at the time of speaking.

The bus **is coming**. Sweden **are leading** 2-1 against England.

about things that continue for a limited period of time around now, e.g. holidays, visits, temporary jobs, courses.

I'**m learning** Spanish at the moment. I'**m getting on** quite well.

These verbs are not normally used in the Present Continuous:

believe, hate, know, like, love, mean, remember, understand, want

The Past Simple

Use the Past Simple:

for a finished action or event in the past, with or without a time expression such as *ago, last month, this morning, yesterday, at 4 o'clock, in 1997,* etc.

She **got married** in 1998.

He **locked** the door and **left** the house.

The Past Continuous

Form

was/were + the -ing form of the verb.

I **was having** lunch. The children **were playing** in the park.

Use the Past Continuous:

to talk about an action or situation that began before and continued after a particular time in the past (e.g. at 7 p.m., last weekend, in 1990).

I **was driving** home from work at 6.30 last night. **I was eating** breakfast at 7.30 yesterday morning.

about an action that was in progress when something else happened.

I **was having** a bath when the phone **rang**. It **was raining** when we **left** the party.

The Perfect Simple

Use the Perfect Simple:
to talk about completed actions or events but not about when they happened.

Her son **has passed** all his exams. The Browns **have come** home.

for a completed action with just, already, yet, not yet, ever and never.

We'**ve** just **finished** doing our homework. They'**ve** already **had** breakfast.

The Past Perfect

Form the Past Perfect with **had** + the **past participle** of the verb.

I **had lost** my passport. He **hadn't remembered** to pay the telephone bill.

Use the Past Perfect:
for a past action which happened *before* another past action. It is often used with *because, after* and *just.*

I couldn't buy a ticket because I **had left** my wallet at home.

and in reported speech.

She told the doctor that she **had suffered** from hay fever for years.
He informed us that he **had booked** tickets for the show.

The Future

Be going to
Use be going to:
about things you've decided or planned to do in the future.

I'**m going to visit** my grandparents this weekend. We'**re going to see** the new James Bond film tonight. Trevor and Susan **are going to move** to York later this year.

Will
Use will:
about future facts and things you think or believe will happen in the future.

Simon **will be** fifty next week. One day people **will live** on the moon.

when you make a decision to do something at the time of speaking. (Not something previously planned.)

(The telephone rings) **I'll** answer it!
'Does anyone want to go to the cinema tonight?' 'Yes, **I'll** come.'
'What would you like to drink?' '**I'll** have a Coke, please.'

Present tenses: Is...? Are...? Do... Does...?

1 The verb 'to be'

Singular		*Plural*	
Am I	hungry?	**Are** we	lost?
Are you	late?	**Are** you	tired?
Is he/she	a teacher?	**Are** they	French?
Is it	Tuesday?		

2 The Present Simple

Singular		*Plural*	
Do I	snore?	**Do** we	know you?
Do you	speak Spanish?	**Do** you	play tennis?
Does he/she	eat meat?	**Do** they	live in Leeds?
Does it	snow a lot?		

3 The Present Continuous

Singular		*Plural*	
Am I	dreaming?	**Are** we	going now?
Are you	coming?	**Are** you	staying in?
Is he/she	sleeping?	**Are** they	driving home?
Is it	still raining?		

Past tenses: Was...? Were...? Did...?

The verb 'to be'

Singular		*Plural*	
Was I	rude?	**Were** we	too early?
Were you	upset?	**Were** you	at home last night?
Was he/she	awake?	**Were** they	hungry?
Was it	cold yesterday?		

The Past Simple

Singular		*Plural*	
Did I	upset you?	**Did** we	embarrass you?
Did you	phone me?	**Did** you	have a nice time?
Did he/she	walk home?	**Did** they	move abroad?
Did it	snow yesterday?		

The Past Continuous

Singular		*Plural*	
Was I	snoring?	**Were** we	making too much noise?
Were you	waiting long?	**Were** you	planning to visit us?
Was he/she	dreaming?	**Were** they	playing well?
Was it	raining yesterday?		

Perfect Tense: Have you...? Has she...? etc.

Have I told you lately that I love you?
Have you posted the letter yet?
Has Susan gone home?

The Future: Are you going to...? Will you...?

be going to

Am I **going to** be rich and famous one day?
Is he/she **going to** come to the party?
Is it **going to** snow tonight?
Are you/we/they **going to** start learning Spanish?

will

Will they ever get married?
Will you promise to love me for ever?
Will he/she get the job?
Will it ever happen?
Will we/they ever find a cure for the common cold?

Verb + to / Verb + -ing

Verb + to

The first form of the verb in English, the base form, often has the word 'to' in front it, e.g. Do you want **to marry** me?

Common verbs followed by *to + base form.*

agree	fail	mean	seem
can't afford	happen	offer	tend
choose	have to (= must)	plan	

I can't **afford to go** on holiday this year.
We **have to be** there by 6.30.

Verb + -ing

Here are some of the most common verbs followed by the *–ing form.*

admit	carry on	fancy	keep on	resent
avoid	consider	finish	mention	risk
be used to	deny	give up	mind	stop

Paul **stopped smoking** two months ago.
He **kept on asking** lots of questions.

Can, can't, could, couldn't, would, wouldn't
- are never used with do
- have only one form *I can, she can, they can*

Use can and can't:
about things you are able or unable to do generally.

James **can** ski really well. Pamela **can't** swim.

about things you are able or unable to do *at the moment*.

I **can** see the moon.
It's too cloudy. I **can't** see the moon or the stars tonight.

to talk about what is allowed in general.

In Britain you **can** drive from the age of seventeen, but you **can't** vote until you're 18.

to ask permission and make requests.

Can we go now?
Can you help me?

NOTE: **Could** is more formal than can in requests.

Could I have a word with you, please?
Could I use your phone, please?

Use could and couldn't:
about things you were able to do generally in the past.

I **could** run a 1000-metre race in under 5 minutes when I was younger.

Do *not* use could
about things achieved in the past with difficulty or with effort

After walking for days **they managed/were able** to reach the oasis. ... *kunde de nå fram till ...*

Use would and wouldn't:
to describe wishes.

I **would** like to be rich and famous one day.
I **would** prefer to stay at home this evening.

for a refusal.

I offered her the job but she **wouldn't** take it.
I switched on the computer but it **wouldn't** start.
I **wouldn't** marry you even if you were the only person left on Earth!

Would often translates into *skulle*. **Would like** translates into *skulle vilja*.

I **would like** (I'd like) to speak to Tom Hanks, please.

Must, mustn't, have to, needn't, don't have to, should, shouldn't

Must is only used in the present tense and translates into *måste/är tvungen*.
For other tenses use **have to**.

I **had to** get up early this morning.
Tomorrow I'**ll have to** get up even earlier.

Måste inte translates into **don't have to / doesn't have to**.
You **don't have to** stay if you don't want to.

Use needn't or don't have to:
to say that something is not necessary.

We **don't have to** go to school tomorrow. It's Saturday.
You **needn't** buy any milk – I'll go shopping later.

Should translates into *borde*.
Use should and shouldn't:
to give advice or to say what is good or bad for you to do.

Everybody over the age of 30 **should** make a will.
You **should** weigh your bag before leaving for the airport.

Conditional clauses

A conditional clause expresses a condition followed by a result, e.g. if you run fast (*the condition*) you will win (*the result*). In other words, these clauses consist of an **if-clause** – if you run fast – and a **main clause** – you will win.

There are three basic patterns:

1st conditional: If-clause – present tense, main clause – will (or 'll).

If the weather **is** nice tomorrow, **we will** *(we'll)* **go** to the beach.
He will *(he'll)* **phone** us **if** the train **arrives** late.

2nd conditional: If-clause – past tense, main clause – would (or 'd).

If he **got** more exercise **he would** *(he'd)* **feel** a lot better.
If Shakespeare **was** alive today **he would** *(he'd)* probably **write** for films and TV rather than for the stage.

3rd conditional: If-clause – past perfect tense, main clause – would have (or 'd have)

If you **had** (*you'd*) **called** me, I **would** (*I'd*) **have picked** you up at the station.
If we **had** (*we'd*) **gone** by train we **would** (*we'd*) **have been** there by now.
If I **had** (*I'd*) **worked** harder at school, **I would** *(I'd)* **have got** a better-paid job.

The Passive

Active: John Lennon *wrote* **the song *Imagine*.**
Passive: **The song *Imagine*** *was written* by John Lennon.

The two sentences have the same meaning.
In the active sentence 'the song *Imagine*' is the object. In the passive sentence, 'The song *Imagine*' is the subject.

Summary of verb tenses

We form the Passive with a tense of **'be'** + **past participle**.

Tense	Active	Passive
Present Simple	makes (sing.), make (plur.)	**is/are** made.
Present Continuous	is/are baking	**is/are being** baked
Past Simple	wrote	**was/were** written
Past Continuous	was singing	**was/were being** sung
Perfect Simple	has/have destroyed	**has/have** been destroyed
Past Perfect Simple	had eaten	**had been** eaten
Future	will direct	**will be** directed
Modal verbs	must make	**must be** made
	should eat	**should be** eaten
	may take	**may be** taken
	can repair	**can be** repaired

Question tags

Question tags are questions attached to the end of a sentence and correspond to the Swedish *... eller hur, ... väl, ... ju.*

A positive clause is followed by a question tag with *not*.

"You **miss** me, **don't you**?"
Expected answer: "Yes, I do."

A negative clause is followed by a positive question tag.

"You **didn't miss** me, **did you**?"
Expected answer: "No, I didn't."

Auxiliary verbs are repeated in the question tag. (*be, have, can,* etc).

"You **must** leave, **mustn't you**?"
"He **was** there, **wasn't he**?"
"You **can't** swim, **can** you?"

Other verbs are followed by a form of do.

You **invent** things, **don't you**? (present tense)
You **broke** the glass, **didn't you**? (past tense)

Word order

To understand how English word order works you need to know what the subject and what the predicate is in a sentence.

Henry went to the airport.
SUBJECT PREDICATE

The person who performs an action in this sentence is *Henry,* so Henry is the **subject**.
The action he performs *went* is called the **predicate**.
Subject followed by the predicate is the usual word order in English.

Swedish differentiates between *'rak'* and *'omvänd'* word order. This is unusual in English. English puts the subject before the predicate in both these cases. Compare:

Katie worked yesterday. *Katie arbetade igår.*
Yesterday **Katie worked**. *Igår arbetade Katie*.

Word order with adverbs of frequency

The adverb is placed before the main verb:

My father **always drives** to work.
Cathy **never remembers** her dreams.
The children **usually cycle** to school.

The adverb is placed before the verb (as above) but **after auxiliary verbs**. (be, have, will, would, must, might, shall, should, can, could, etc.)

Jeremy **is often** late for school.
You **should never** go swimming after eating a heavy meal.
My parents **have always** lived in Wales.

awake, awoke, awoken väcka (vakna), väckte, väckt
be, was/were, been vara, var, varit
bear, bore, born bära, bar, burit
beat, beat, beaten slå, slog, slagit
become, became, become bli, blev, blivit
begin, began, begun börja, började, börjat
bend, bent, bent böja, böjde, böjt
bet, bet, bet slå, slog, slagit (vad)
bind, bound, bound binda, band, bundit
bite, bit, bitten bita, bet, bitit
blow, blew, blown blåsa, blåste, blåst
break, broke, broken bryta, bröt, brutit
bring, brought, brought ta, tog, tagit (med)
burn, burnt, burnt brinna, brann, brunnit
burst, burst, burst brista, brast, brustit
buy, bought, bought köpa, köpte, köpt
catch, caught, caught fånga, fångade, fångat
choose, chose, chosen välja, valde, valt
come, came, come komma, kom, kommit
cost, cost, cost kosta, kostade, kostat
creep, crept, crept krypa, (smyga), kröp, krupit
cut, cut, cut hugga (klippa), högg, huggit
do, did, done göra, gjorde, gjort
draw, drew, drawn rita, ritade, ritat
dream, dreamt (dreamed), dreamt (dreamed) drömma, drömde, drömt
drink, drank, drunk dricka, drack, druckit
drive, drove, driven köra, körde, kört
eat, ate, eaten äta, åt, ätit
fall, fell, fallen falla, föll, fallit
feed, fed, fed mata, matade, matat
feel, felt, felt känna, kände, känt
fight, fought, fought slåss, slogs, slagits
find, found, found hitta, hittade, hittat
flee, fled, fled fly, flydde, flytt
fly, flew, flown flyga, flög, flugit
forget, forgot, forgotten glömma, glömde, glömt
freeze, froze, frozen frysa, frös, frusit
get, got, got få, fick, fått
give, gave, given ge, gav, givit
go, went, gone gå, gick, gått
grow, grew, grown växa, växte, vuxit

hang, hung, hung hänga, hängde, hängt
have, had, had ha, hade, haft
hear, heard, heard höra, hörde, hört
hide, hid, hidden gömma, gömde, gömt
hit, hit, hit slå, slog, slagit
hold, held, held hålla, höll, hållit
hurt, hurt, hurt skada, skadade, skadat
keep, kept, kept hålla, höll, hållit
know, knew, known veta, visste, vetat
lay, laid, laid lägga, lade, lagt
lead, led, led leda, ledde, lett
lean, leant (leaned), leant (leaned) luta sig, lutade, lutat
leap, leapt, leapt hoppa, hoppade, hoppat
learn, learnt, learnt lära sig, lärde, lärt
leave, left, left lämna, lämnade, lämnat
lend, lent, lent låna (ut), lånade, lånat
let, let, let låta, lät, låtit
lie, lay, lain ligga, låg, legat
lose, lost, lost förlora, förlorade, förlorat
make, made, made göra, gjorde, gjort
mean, meant, meant mena, menade, menat
meet, met, met träffa, träffade, träffat
pay, paid, paid betala, betalade, betalat
put, put, put ställa, (sätta, lägga) ställde, ställt
read, read, read läsa, läste, läst
ride, rode, ridden rida, red, ridit
ring, rang, rung ringa, ringde, ringt
rise, rose, risen stiga, steg, stigit
run, ran, run springa, sprang, sprungit
say, said, said säga, sade, sagt
see, saw, seen se, såg, sett
seek, sought, sought söka, sökte, sökt
sell, sold, sold sälja, sålde, sålt
send, sent, sent skicka, skickade, skickat
set, set, set sätta (ställa), satte, satt
sew, sewed, sewn sy, sydde, sytt
shake, shook, shaken skaka, skakade, skakat
shine, shone, shone skina, sken, skinit
shoot, shot, shot skjuta, sköt, skjutit
show, showed, shown visa, visade, visat
shut, shut, shut stänga, stängde, stängt
sing, sang, sung sjunga, sjöng, sjungit

sink, sank, sunk sjunka, sjönk, sjunkit
sit, sat, sat sitta, satt, suttit
sleep, slept, slept sova, sov, sovit
slide, slid, slid glida, gled, glidit
smell, smelt (smelled), smelt (smelled) lukta, luktade, luktat
speak, spoke, spoken tala, talade, talat
spell, spelt, spelt stava, stavade, stavat
spend, spent, spent tillbringa, tillbringade, tillbringat
spread, spread, spread sprida, spred, spridit
stand, stood, stood stå, stod, stått
steal, stole, stolen stjäla, stal, stulit
stick, stuck, stuck fastna, fastnade, fastnat
strike, struck, struck slå, slog, slagit
swear, swore, sworn svära, svor, svurit
sweep, swept, swept sopa, sopade, sopat
swim, swam, swum simma, simmade, simmat
swing, swung swung svänga, svängde, svängt
take, took, taken ta, tog, tagit
teach, taught, taught lära (ut), lärde, lärt
tear, tore, torn riva, rev, rivit
tell, told, told berätta, berättade, berättat
think, thought, thought tänka, tänkte, tänkt
throw, threw, thrown kasta, kastade, kastat
understand, understood, understood förstå, förstod, förstått
wake, woke, woken vakna, vaknade, vaknat
wear, wore, worn bära (ha på sig), bar, burit
weep, wept, wept gråta, grät, gråtit
win, won, won vinna, vann, vunnit
wring, wrung, wrung vrida, vred, vridit
write, wrote, written skriva, skrev, skrivit

PREPOSITIONS

Prepositions of place

In, at, and **on**

Use **in** with enclosed spaces (e.g. rooms, buildings) and also with towns, parks, countries, continents and containers.

My sister's **in** the bathroom washing her hair.

'Where's Tom?' 'He's still **in** bed.'

Use **on** with surfaces (e.g. walls, shelves, floors) and lines (e.g. paths, coasts, the equator).

Please don't walk **on** the grass.

He has a flat **on** the fourth floor.

Use **at** with a place or a building.

We waited for ages **at** the bus stop.

Jill and Ken spent the evening **at** home.

Prepositions of time

In, at, and **on**

Use **in** with parts of the day (morning, evening, etc.) and with months, seasons, years and centuries.

in the morning, **in** January, **in** the spring, **in** 1944, **in** the 19th century, **in** the 21st century, etc.

Use **on** with days and dates.

on Monday, **on** Christmas Day, **on** December 10th (Say 'on December **the** tenth' or 'on **the** tenth **of** December').

Use **at**

for times of the day and with meals and mealtimes.

at 11.30, **at** three o'clock, **at** breakfast

and with these words:

at night, **at** midnight, **at** the weekend, **at** Easter, **at** Christmas, **at** Midsummer, **at** the moment, **at** the end of the week/month/year

WORD LISTS

1 GET DOWN TO IT

THE RIGHT LEVEL

level nivå
attend gå på
political science statskunskap
short story novell
memoir självbiografi, memoar
depict skildra
divorce skilsmässa
publish publicera, ge ut
explore utforska
ambivalent kluven, vacklande
marriage äktenskap
get settled komma till rätta
shameless oblyg, fräck
grade årskurs
patent leather lack(skinn)
ability förmåga
humiliating förnedrande, förödmjukande
entire hel
semester termin
memorize lära sig utantill
flash cards bildkort
hammer down *h.* spöregna; hamra ner
geek tönt
oral muntlig
in my opinion enligt min åsikt
select välja (ut)
endive endiv (en slags sallad)
saunter strosa, flanera
smugly självbelåtet
peer jämlike
swiftly snabbt
evident tydlig, uppenbar
barely nätt och jämt
rapid-fire kulsprutesnabb
apparently uppenbarligen
fluent flytande
gasping for air kippa efter luft
wobbling osäkra, darriga
scurry rusa, kila
plump mullig, rund

LOSING MY VIRGINITY

virginity oskuld
chairman ordförande
educate utbilda; gå i skola
found grunda
mail order postorder
retailer återförsäljare
autobiography självbiografi
short-sighted närsynt
deem anse
accurately exakt
prep(aratory) school (privat) förberedande skola
confuse blanda ihop
intuitive intuitiv**,** *ung.* att gå på känsla
proposal förslag
dwell dröja vid, älta
grasp fatta tag i; begripa
expand utveckla, vidga
saving grace min räddning
overestimate överskatta
public school privatskola för 13 – 18 år
bully mobba
master lärare
fail bli underkänd
intensely ytterst
keen angelägen
excel vara bäst, utmärka sig
cup pokal
sprinting sprinterlopp
hurdling häcklöpning
long jump längdhopp
soar sväva
marquee stort tält
Victor Ludorum mästartitel
defender försvarare
score a goal göra mål
boot sparka
bounce studsa
floor somebody slå omkull
sliding tackle glidtackling
ghastly hemsk, fasanfull
a split second en bråkdel av en sekund
twisted vriden
angle vinkel
matron husmor
agony svåra plågor
cartilage brosk
general anaesthetic narkos
unconscious medvetslös
evacuate evakuera
recover återhämta sig
mantelpiece spiselhylla

PHENOMENAL WOMAN

phenomenal enastående
cute söt
reach räckvidd

span omfång
hip höft
stride kliv
curl krökning
scholarship stipendium
drop out hoppa av skolan
cable car AmE spårvagn
playwright dramatiker
civil-rights activist medborgarrättsaktivist
producer producent
director regissör

ROCK WHAT YOU'VE GOT

rock skaka, sätta i gungning
rock what you´ve got använd det du har
various olika slags
issue fråga
body image kroppsuppfattning
disgusting motbjudande; äcklig
confident säker; självsäker
self-worth självförtroende
sibling syskon
self-defeating självförgörande
pity party "tycka synd om" party
self-loathing självleda
assure försäkra
blessed välsignad
comfort trösta
awkward besvärlig
high chair barnstol
self-esteem självkänsla
reinforcement förstärkning
insecurity osäkerhet
admittedly onekligen
fourth grade tredje klass
chubby knubbig, rund
pencil thin smal som ett streck
awareness medvetenhet
inexplicably oförklarligt
puberty pubertet
cruising altitude marschhöjd
sob snyfta; snyftning
weeping gråt
catch a breath hämta andan
barely nätt och jämt
asset tillgång, fördel
perceive uppfatta
flaw brist, fel
articulate artikulera, uttala
average medel-, genomsnittlig
advanced avancerad
distinction särskiljande
separation frånskiljande
implement genomföra
solidify befästa
achieve one's goals uppnå sina mål
reassuring lugnande
announce meddela
remarkably anmärkningsvärt
pressure stress, press

LISTENING: FREEDOM WRITERS DIARY

diary dagbok
at-risk students riskelever
undertake företa; sätta igång med
odyssey resa
encourage uppmuntra
among others bland andra
record *h.* skriva ner; återge
entry anteckning
out of touch hänger inte med
preppy snobbig
expectation förväntning, förhoppning
gated community inhägnat och bevakat bostadsområde
dub döpa till; kalla för
gangsta-rap en slags hiphopmusik
depiction skildring
warped snedvriden
perception uppfattning
LBC Long Beach California
bulletproof vest skottsäker väst
utopia idealstat
blow something out of proportion överdriva
reputation rykte
desirable åtråvärd
hood stadsdel
shore kust
projects miljonprojekt
within the confines of inom gränserna för
quad fyrkantig skolgård
Rodney King offer för polisbrutalitet 1991
riot upplopp
tension spänning
due to på grund av
bussing bussning
demographics befolkningsstatistik
the student body eleverna
naïve aningslös
saunter släntra
bounce studsa
disciplinary disciplinär
transfer omplacering
precede föregå; komma före
previous tidigare
showdown uppgörelse
sole enda
butt skottavla
antics upptåg
caricature karikatyr (förlöjligande bild)
exaggerated överdriven
façade *h.* utsida; fasad
go ballistic bli rasande

the Holocaust förintelsen
timidly blygt
meticulously noggrant
core kärna
curriculum kursplan
field trip studieresa

CHEAT!

cheat fusk; fuska
snap fotografera
official tjänsteman
strategy strategi, taktik
frontier gränsområde
defeat besegra
gum tuggummi
disguise dölja
accomplice medbrottsling
recessed nedsänkt
desktop dataskrivbord
screen skärm
scratch paper kladdpapper
turn in lämna in
proctor skrivvakt
suspicious misstänkt
evidence bevis
associate dean biträdande fakultetschef
enrolled inskriven
crackdown hårdare kontroll
eternal ständig; evig
temptation frestelse
cut and paste klippa och klistra in
extent omfattning
appear förefalla, verka
widespread omfattande, utbredd
survey enkät, undersökning
average medeltal
assignment beting, uppgift
anti-plagiarism antiplagiering
require kräva
submit lämna in
booming blomstrande
business affärsverksamhet

2 MAKE IT HAPPEN

LISTENING: DOWN THE NIAGARA FALLS

barrel tunna
be ashamed skämmas
feat bragd, prestation
be a bit bruised ha lite blåmärken
attempt försök
cramped trång
strap rem
cushion dämpa, mildra
impact stöt, sammanstötning
trial run provtur
confident säker
the Civil War inbördeskriget
unsettled rastlös
daredevil våghals, dumdristig person
tightrope spänd lina
old hat ute, omodern
shoot the rapids kasta sig utför forsarna
take the full plunge ta steget fullt ut
head sätta kurs
upstream uppåt floden
anxious orolig, rädd
plummet rasa
edge kant
rescue boat räddningsbåt
up your sleeve på lut, på gång
broke pank, barskrapad
fine böter

FRY AND JOBS – STEPHEN MEETS STEVE

broadcaster mediepersonlighet
recently nyligen
audio book ljudbok
novel roman
screenplay filmmanus
established erkänd, etablerad
encounter möte
innovator nyskapare, innovatör
showman estradör
overseer förman
visionary visionär
opportunist opportunist, ngn som drar nytta av eller utnyttjar ett tillfälle
insistence krav, hävdande av
finish fulländat utförande
ease of use användarvänlighet
reliability driftsäkerhet; pålitlighet
turtleneck sweater polotröja
impostor bedragare, skojare
impart ge, skänka
delicacy skörhet
William Hurt am. skådespelare
ledge *h.* ledig yta; fönsterbräde
slide show bildspel
grin flin
patient tålmodig
amusement nöje; munterhet
abashed generad
product launch produktlansering
the liberal arts humaniora
intersection korsning
commerce handel
commercial affärsmässig
concede medge
starting point utgångspunkt

pleasure glädje
Winnie the Pooh Nalle Puh
bundle sampacka
unaffected naturlig
lectern läspulpet; vinklat ställ
profound omvälvande
that rings a bell det låter bekant
device grej
immersive AmE absorberande
emerge komma ut ur
scare chock
obituary dödsruna
curtain ridå
fitting passande
career karriär
respond to reagera på
peep kika
slip holder skyddsfodral
sigh suck
snarl morra
wrestle kämpa, brottas

ENCOUNTERS

encounter möte; träffa på
lizard ödla
creature varelse
unlikely föga lovande
quest jakt; sökande
cougar puma
head sätta kurs
species art
modest anspråkslös
entrance ingång
immaculately perfekt
peacock påfågel
strut stoltsera
roam ströva omkring
walkway trädgårdsgång
admission fee inträdesavgift
reptile kräldjur
enclosure område
glisten glänsa
variety mängd; variation
external yttre
feces AmE avföring
shed skin ömsa skinn
leave unattended lämna utan skötsel
announce meddela
PA (public address system) högtalaranläggning
saltie *h.* saltvattenkrokodil
the dawn of time tidernas början
ancient gammal
solid kraftig, stark
appear verka, tyckas
wristwatch armbandsur
wrist handled
approachable åtkomlig, tillgänglig
casually *h.* avspänt
lunge out störta upp ur
snap hugga
territorial revirbevakande
nail nagla fast
excude utstråla
big-note framhäva
connected besläktad
kindred spirit själsfrände

LISTENING: ENCOUNTERS CONT.

topic ämne
courting ritual uppvaktningsritual
nudge puffa
receptive mottaglig
affection ömhet, kärlek
murky dunkel, mörk
erupt välla fram, brytas
neatly ordentligt
deposit lägga, anförtro
reverberation eko
rifle report gevärssmäll
fence stängsel, inhägnad
scare the daylights out of sb skrämma ngn från vettet
subadult halvvuxen
rule regel
tacker *h.* rackare; häftpistol
pose utgöra
naughty elak, stygg
dinghy jolle, räddningsbåt
capture fånga in
captivated fängslad
detail redogöra för i detalj
accomplish uträtta
candlepower normalljus
reveal avslöja
idle gå på tomgång
leap hoppa
scruff of the neck nackskinn
thrashing piskande
dislodge rubba
snag uppstickande trädstam
pin down kila fast
snapping huggande
a piece of cake lätt som en plätt
incredible otrolig, fantastisk
overwhelming överväldigande

3 CROSSING LINES

SO WHERE YOU FROM?

small talk kallprat, småprat
utter yttra
grocery store speceriaffär
cashier kassörska
prompt framkalla, orsaka
beat a hasty retreat hastigt ta till reträtten
rude ohövlig, oförskämd
insufferable odräglig, olidlig
ungrateful otacksam
contagious smittsam
opt välja
anonymity anonymitet
fresh off the boat *ung.* just anlänt
dread bäva, fasa
to make matters worse till råga på allt
cooped up inburad
detect upptäcka
undeterred inte avskräckt
lawyer advokat
soften the blow mildra slaget
chuckle småskratta, skrocka
anonymous anonym
occupation yrke
reveal avslöja
offend förolämpa, såra
stiff stel
assure försäkra
ruin förstöra

LISTENING: WHERE ARE THEY?

chicken chunks kycklingbitar
chase jaga
kitten kattunge
examination undersökning
it's my treat jag bjuder
starter förrätt
famished utsvulten
venison rådjurskött
sea bass havsabborre
ridiculous löjlig
parking fine parkeringsbot
clamp *h.* använda hjullås
stunning jättesnygg
groom brudgum
stunned paff, alldeles lamslagen
establish fastställa
fair share beskärda del
apparently uppenbarligen
do the washing-up diska
feel run down känna sig trött och nere
blood pressure blodtryck
sleeve ärm
prescription recept (av tandläkare)
charity välgörenhet
exhausted utmattad
robbed rånad
robbery rån
duck pond ankdamm
bench bänk
marketing marknadsföring
Lithuanian litauiska
qualification merit
work experience arbetslivserfarenhet
speed-limit hastighetsbegränsning
built-up area tättbebyggt område
junction korsning

WATCH YOUR STEP

law degree juristexamen
extract utdrag
debut collection debutsamling
elegy sorgesång; klagan
Easterly namn på stad
view syn; åsikt
lightning blixt
festering varig
boil böld
bottom ända
fluff hår; fjun
put a spell on förhäxa
sorcery trolldom, häxeri
peek kika, titta
stye vagel
fate öde
proof bevis
reverse ta tillbaka; vrida tillbaka
wail tjuta, klaga högt
sniffle (snuffle) snörvla
elbow armbåge
obey lyda
cross one's fingers hålla fingrarna i kors
have nings on upphäva ngt

OCD

OCD tvångssyndrom
obsessive överdriven; abnorm
compulsive tvångsmässig
disorder störning, sjukdom
fizzy drinks läsk
fridge kylskåp
label etikett
straighten rätta till
anxiety ångest
unbearable outhärdlig
paranoid drabbad av förföljelsemani
go mental bli galen
crippling förlamande
psychiatrist psykiater

behaviour beteende, uppförande
compulsion tvång
covert *h.* dold; maskerad
compelled tvingad
prayer bön
sufferer lidande person
accidentally oavsiktligt
harm skada
overt öppen
germ bakterie
continually ständigt
hoard samla på hög; lagra
irrational oförnuftig, orimlig
incapable oförmögen
in spite of trots
charity välgörenhetsorganisation
tendency *h.* anlag; tendens
trigger utlösa, sätta igång
in response to som svar på
imbalance obalans
tend tendera, visa en tendens
in their late teens sent i tonåren
severe svår, allvarlig
cripple förlama, förstöra
weird underlig
support organization stödorganisation
booklet broschyr
assess bedöma, analysera
cognitive behavioural therapy (CBT) KBT
anti-depressants antidepressiva medel
mess up stöka till
gain control bemästra; ta kontroll
back on track tillbaka på banan
screw up förstöra, sabba

SEXY

non-fiction facklitteratur, sakprosa
fictional uppdiktad
adult vuxen
creative writing litterär gestaltning
varsity team skollag
sophomore andraårsstuderande
tease reta
go red in the face bli röd i ansiktet
glower blänga
grungy sjaskig
reversed bakvänd
sweatshirt collegetröja
frayed nött, fransig
cuff mudd
rotted sönderfallande
stained fläckig
size-eleven storlek 45
in a hot mood upprörd
erupt slå ut
upper back övre del av ryggen
flare blossa upp
itch klia
hives nässelutslag
unmistakably uppenbart, utan tvekan
jock sportig typ
struck blank helt tom
moth nattfjäril
blush rodna
mumble mumla
charge up ladda
explode explodera
hot *sl.* kåt
hard on "stånd"
intrude tränga sig på
lowlife "dräggigt"
trashy "billigt"
fussy petig, noga
construction byggarbete
county kommun
casual ledig, avspänd
trailer trash husvagnspack
manners uppförande
quaver skälvning
exchange utväxla, utbyta
glance ögonkast
shrug axelryckning
humor sb göra som ngn vill
no-nonsense *ung.* rak, rättfram
reproduction fortplantning
species mänskligheten
adaptation anpassning
spiritual beings andliga varelser
linger dröja sig kvar
add up to gå ut på
startled förvånad

4 MOVING ON

LEAVING HOME

graduate ta akademisk examen
unexpected oväntad
angle synvinkel, sida
attention uppmärksamhet
unglamorous inte tjusig
outsider särling
fiction skönlitteratur
scrunched-up ihopknycklad
kerchief snusnäsduk
rough sträv
translator översättare
colloquial vardaglig, talspråklig
blackboard svarta tavlan
school yard skolgård
fence staket

leather cap skärmmössa i skinn
seriously allvarligt

BEIJING TO LONDON

UFO = unidentified flying object ufo
indifference likgiltighet
long-distance långdistans-
confusing förvirrad
doubt tvivla, misstänka
fake förfalskad
noble fin, ståtlig
Ministry of Foreign Affairs utrikesdepartementet
request begära, uppmana
civil civil
authorities myndigheter
afford erbjuda
in case of need vid behov
desert öken
diploma akademisk examen
tiny liten
suburb förort
gift present

LISTENING: TAPAS & TEARS

on exchange på utbytesresa
dead cheap jättebilligt
count me in räkna med mig
parental consent forms blankett för föräldrasam-tycke
put someone up ta emot, hysa
commitment åtagande
Wicked! *sl.* Toppen!
bags me pax för
sternly strängt
keep an eye on hålla ett öga på
universal allmän
groan stön
ripple sprida sig i vågor
as far as I'm concerned för min del
push-over tönt, mes
try it on testa henne
cut them down to size sätta dem på plats
stick tjafs
bitchy elak, spydig
mess with bråka med
keep on a tight rein hålla i strama tyglar
to a degree till viss del
be slammed into detention åka på kvarsittning
naughty *h.* busig; elak
a goody two shoes superpräktig tjej
by nature till sin natur
hasten skynda sig
draw attention to dra uppmärksamhet till
supplies (= supply teachers) vikarier
staff personal
unfair orättvis
assembly morgonsamling
parents' evening föräldramöte
misery elände; kval
make small talk kallprata
excursion utflykt

SINGAPORE AND BACK

in earnest på allvar
courtyard gårdsplan
option alternativ, valmöjlighet
originally ursprungligen
average genomsnittlig
apparently uppenbarligen
playschool lekskola
pay attention bry sig om
with certainty med säkerhet
head off to sticka till, dra till
tourist trail turiststråk
advertising agency reklambyrå
by today's standards med dagens mått mätt
determined fast besluten
salesman försäljare
commercials reklaminslag
career ladder karriärstege
crap skit
struck out of struken från
team reckoning laguppställning
sidelines åskådarplats
ferry someone around transportera ngn runt
heater värmare
unload lasta av
spot a fake urskilja en bluffmakare
confide in sb anförtro sig åt ngn
pretty skint rätt pank
plush *sl.* flott, lyxig
expat (expatriate) utvandrad; landsflyktig
wages lön
walk-up apartment lägenhet utan hiss
childminding barnpassning
novelty nyhet, ovanlighet
discover upptäcka
pride stolthet
publicity tour reklamturné

5 IN REAL LIFE

MOVIE REVIEW – THE HUNGER GAMES

anticipate se fram emot
theatre *h.* biograf; teater
lead character huvudperson
entire hel
letdown besvikelse
involve omfatta
futuristic futuristiskt; framtida

society samhälle
be confined to vara instängd
reality type show en slags dokusåpa
emerge komma fram
select välja, utse
volunteer anmäla sig som frivillig
groom träna; göra fin
contest strid, tävling
competition tävling
contestant tävlande
impact effekt
occur inträffa
intense kraftig, intensiv
it all boils down to det hela går i korthet ut på
subject matter ämne
off-putting frånstötande
diluted urvattnad
casting rollbesättning
storyline handling
performance prestation
one dimensional endimensionell (*ung.* utan djup)
eccentric original, särling
facilitate underlätta
emotional bond känsloband
be rated vara klassad
profanity svordomar
in years past förr i tiden
off limits förbjudet
fair game lovligt villebråd
cast rollbesättning
score poängsätta
non-playful *ung.* allvarsam
trilogy trilogi
partly delvis

LISTENING: THE REAPING

reaping skördande
mandatory obligatorisk
official tjänsteman
be on death's door ligga för döden
imprison spärra in
surround omge
despite trots
banner fana; banderoll
grimness grymhet
perch sitta uppflugen
buzzard vråk
file in gå in en och en
keep tabs on hålla ögonen på, kolla
be herded bli drivna
perimeter *h.* ytterkanten; omkrets
at stake *h.* i riskzonen; stå på spel
slip smyga
refuse vägra
racketeer skojare, svindlare
in charge i ansvarig ställning
claim hävda, påstå
claustrophobic hemskt trång; klaustrofobisk
adjacent närliggande
clump klunga, grupp
terse fåordig
temporary tillfällig
podium podium; upphöjning
balding tunnhårig
escort ledsagare
concern oro
Panem namn på landet
drought torka
encroaching inträngande
sustenance föda
Capitol *jmf.* Capitolium i Washington
prosperity välstånd
uprising uppror
defeat besegra
obliterate utplåna
the Treaty of Treason avtalet om förräderi
punishment bestraffning
participate delta
vast vidsträckt
wasteland ödemark
at their mercy i deras våld
rebellion uppror
sacrifice offra
spot få syn på
in his favour till hans fördel
slip papperslapp
draw breath hämta andan
nauseous illamående
smooth släta ut

BOLLYWOOD PEOPLE AND PLOTS

plot intrig, handling
efficient effektiv
courage mod, tapperhet
villain bov, skurk
opponent motståndare
well-established väl inarbetad
pattern mönster
narrative berättelse
provide sörja för, ge
punch-up slagsmål
charismatic karismatisk, stark personlig utstrålning
stunt director stuntregissör
flatten slå ner
climax höjdpunkt
beat someone to a pulp slå någon sönder och samman
essential nödvändig, oumbärlig
recurrent återkommande
obstacle hinder
aplenty i överflöd
in their path på deras väg

jilted nobbad
heroine hjältinna
envious avundsjuk
devious oärlig, bedräglig
vanquish besegra
united förenad
trauma skada genom yttre våld
myriad oräknelig
land-owning jordägande
rapist våldtäktsman
scheming beräknande
lecherous liderlig
landowner jordägare
thwart motarbeta
repressive undertryckande
caste kast (social indelning)
intermingling umgänge
issue fråga
scenario scenario
unscrupulous samvetslös
gold-digger person ute efter pengar
considerable betydande, större
approval godkännande

INSTANT MILLIONAIRE

quiz show frågesportprogram
immediate omedelbar
dimmed dämpade
illuminate upplysa
revolving chair snurrfåtölj
semicircular halvcirkelformig
booming dånande
fade out tona bort
contestant tävlande
selected utvald
at random på måfå
a big round of applause en kraftig applåd
diversity mångfald
scowl at blänga på
script manus
vibe *sl.* bubbla
host vara värd för
rule regel
quit sluta
either.. or antingen...eller
stage stadium, steg
Lifeboat *h.* livlina
available tillgänglig
screen pairings matchning av par i film
blockbusting film dundersuccé
betrayal förräderi, svek
suspense spänningsfylld
superimpose lägga ovanpå
crescendo växande (ton)stryka
flash blixtra, flamma upp
commercial break reklampaus

PUBLIC, PRIVATE

joyful lycklig
celebration firande
discovery avslöjande
hurtle around virvla runt
segment avsnitt
The X Factor X Factor, *titel på TV-program*
wilt slappna, sloka
be due to ska (enligt avtal)
recklessly obetänksamt
opt välja
much-lauded mycket lovordade
rustle up fixa
hearty närande
BlackBerry mobiltelefon
chop hacka
management företagsledning
chuckle småskratta
cautiously försiktigt
claim påstå
pregnant gravid
scan *h.* ultraljud; scanning
ridiculous löjlig, skrattretande
numb stel
faint svimfärdig, matt
obviously självklart
confirm bekräfta
a load of rubbish en massa struntprat
flatly direkt
usher visa in
settle hjälpa till rätta
pop on slänga på
get away with komma undan med
flustered nervös, upphetsad
dash rusa
front cover omslagets framsida
literally rent av
editor utgivare; redaktör
urgently ivrigt
face to face ansikte mot ansikte
splash göra feta rubriker av
flushed blossande röd
admit medge
infringement kränkning
brim over flöda över
solemnly allvarligt
help yourselves to ta för er av

6 CITY LIFE

THE BIG APPLE

ingredients inslag; ingrediens
derive from komma från
participate in delta i

a big apple h. en stor belöning
consist of bestå av
borough stadsdel
domestic inhemsk
source of income inkomstkälla
ferry färja
surrounded by omgiven av
fairly easy ganska lätt
destroy förstöra
commemorate hedra minnet av
exhibition utställning
stock exchange börsen
suit kostym
tie slips
magnificent storslagen
gain access to få tillgång till
demolish förstöra
initiated by igångsatt av
commuter pendlare
headquarters högkvarter
recreation nöje, tidsfördriv
dedicated to tillägnad till
inhabitant invånare
predominately till övervägande del
reputation rykte
run down nedslitet
poverty-stricken utfattig
crime-ridden kriminellt belastat
designer product designvaror
reduced sänkt, lågt

LISTENING: WHICH CITY?

stare stirra
cheeky oförskämd
subway AmE tunnelbana
impressive imponerande
harbour hamn
fabulous toppen
St Patrick's Day irländsk högtid 17 mars
kilt yllekjol som män kan ha
draught vinddrag
bagpipe säckpipa
Maori ursprungsbefolkning i Nya Zeeland
cloud moln
according to enligt
dizzy yr
no end utan tvekan
handsome snygg
mountie ridande polis
sacred helig
holy helig
autorickshaw trehjulig taxi
cable car AmE spårvagn
The Caribbean Västindien
hurricane orkan
roam ströva omkring
bush vildmark
outback vildmark
top deck övre däck
moan beklaga sig

VERTICAL LIVING

manufacture tillverkning
lift hiss
high-rise building skyskrapa
improvement förbättring
megastructure stora byggnadsverk
superframe superbjälklag, superstomme
withstand stå emot
earth tremor jordskalv
foundation fundament, grund
soil jord
bedrock berggrund
spread footing typ av bred sula
caisson piles nedsänkta pålar
transmit sprida
concrete betong
evolve utveckla
geared to anpassad efter
environment miljö
core kärna
sustain lida, utstå
abutment pålverk
stairwell trapphus
provide ge
composed of ihopsatt av
skeleton skelettsystem
wind brace vindskyddsstag
shaft schakt
utility nödvändighet
lattice fackverksbalk
girder bärbjälke
cross-bracing tvärgående stag
rigidity styvhet
storey våningsplan
attach fastsätta
mainstay stöttepelare
perimeter ytterkant

IF MY DAD WERE STILL HERE

fifth grade fjärde klass
hang up lägga på
global infrastructure världsomspännande verksamhet
quote citera
chase jaga
surreal overklig
memorial service minnesgudstjänst
latch onto *ung.* spåra in på
coach träna
tremendously oerhört
decent skaplig
infant spädbarn

Jets ett amerikanskt fotbollslag från NYC
dwell on uppehålla sig vid
graduate ta examen
accomplishment prestation
valuable värdefull
hug krama
rejoice glädjas
closure slut
plot planera

THE BALLAD OF SONNY PAYNE

F-train en tunnelbanelinje i NYC
review recension
make it a point göra en poäng av
change växel
quarter 25 cents
adequate lämplig, tillräcklig
upgraded höjde
on average i genomsnitt
panhandling tiggande
dime 10 cents
nickel 5 cents
Pathmark mataffärskedja
Coinstar machine växelmaskin
exchange växla
be filled up vara mätt
give sb the shakes ge ngn skakningar
gracious behaglig
have access to ha tillgång till
rough svår, kärv
be laid off bli friställd
reverend pastor
range over sträcka sig över
leash koppel
tease reta
respond svara
gang up on gadda ihop sig
sigh sucka
a string of bad luck en period av otur
city-run shelter kommunalt härbärge
seemingly till synes
personable charmig
responsibility ansvar

NEW YORK, NEW YORK

stray ströva
heap hög
melt smälta
brand new helt ny

7 GET (DIS)CONNECTED

CHILDHOOD MEMORIES

poetry poesi, dikter
feature presentera
mess around gå och driva
stream å, bäck
kite drake
adult vuxen
coat cupboard kappskåp
tangled up tilltrasslad
pour vräka ner
dull matt
video case videokassett
board game sällskapsspel
spare extra
throughout under
sense känna
garlic vitlök
naïve barnslig; naiv
curtain gardin
nana mormor/farmor

LISTENING: THE STORY OF THE MAKGABE

apron förkläde
weave väva
jealous avundsjuk
including inklusive
splash plaska
emerge stiga upp
the loss of förlusten av
weep gråta
slither slingra sig
slime slem
fouled smutsig
approach närma sig
proposal of marriage frieri
chief hövding
comfortable nöjd och belåten

CAN YOU SEE ME?

enrol skriva in sig
master's program magisterprogram
weave väva
survivor överlevande
cope with klara av
delivery boy varubud
production uppvisande
wallet plånbok
greasy flottig
spring roll vårrulle
crowded fullpackad
skid kana
effort ansträngning
schmuck klantskalle
spanking flott
resemble likna
bootie stövelsko
clutch hålla fast vid
webbed shoe sko av sadelgjord

peel off ta av sig
decrepit skröplig, utsliten
awkward pinsam

PLAYING THE ENEMY

enemy fiende
senior överordnad
numerous otaliga
publication tidningar; publikationer
apartheid rasåtskillnadspolitik
cause anledning; sak (att kämpa för)
host vara värd för
remote avlägsen
capture fånga
unite ena
wholeheartedly helhjärtat
squad trupp
chant ropa taktfast
leafy lummig
suburb förort
anthem nationalsång
set an example vara en förebild
let sb down svika ngn
rehearse öva
pitch plan
strain ton
fall apart bryta ihop
crumble bryta samman
emotional rörd, känslosam
compared to jämfört med
reverberate eka, genljuda
fiancée fästmö
throat strupe
emotional känslomässig
brink gräns
dressing room omklädningsrum
the jumbo jet flyover överflygning av ett jetplan med texten Springboks
jersey tröja
the bowels det inre
recall komma ihåg
strapped up påklädd
tension spänning
supporter anhängare

LISTENING: AFTER THE GAME

invent uppfinna
instantly genast
enraptured hänryckt
touchline sidlinje; touchelinje
podium prispall
trophy pris
liberal frisinnad; fördomsfri
beer-bellied ölmagad
AWB types högerextremistiska typer
compatriot landsman
Boer nederländare och fransmän som utvandrat till SA
applaud applådera
memorable minnesvärd
impromptu improviserad
eloquence vältalighet
miss a beat darra på manschetten
battle kämpa
preserve bevara
sangfroid lugn
right-hand höger
shoot a glance kasta en blick
area område
hug krama
on such a scale i en sådan omfattning
sentiment uppfattning
trench dike; skyttegrav
self-denial självförnekelse
supped with the gods ätit med gudarna
anoint inviga
spiritual head andlig ledare
Afrikanerdom *ung.* det gamla SA
fond tillgiven, innerlig
gaze blick
chord sträng
response svar
script skriva (manus till)

8 HOT ISSUES

CARS ARE DISGUSTING!

disgusting motbjudande
assignment uppgift
persuasive övertygande
destroy förstöra
edge kant
brink rand
greenhouse gases växthusgaser
choke kväva; strypa
atmosphere atmosfär, luft
toxin giftämne
pollutant förorening
chip away "smådutta"
recycle återvinna
disastrous katastrofal
refreeze återfrysa
fearlessly utan fruktan
mind-set tänkesätt
gas bensin
exhaust avgaser
idle gå på tomgång
parking lot parkeringsplats
contain innehålla
cocoon kokong
Poland Spring water en slags mineralvatten

granola bar müslichoklad
insulation pod isoleringskapsel
delude lura
fake fejkad
candy bar godisbit
purify rena
reject förkasta
falsity lögnaktighet
lameness ofärdighet
denounce fördöma
vehicle fordon
crap skräp
simplicity of mind enkelspårighet
consumption konsumtion, köp
Target, Wal-Mart etc *olika affärer i USA*
unsustainable ohållbar
cute söt, gullig
lower-class underklass
upper-class överklass
mansion residens
gas-guzzling bensinslukande
minivan minibuss
pointlessly meningslöst
keep afloat hålla flytande

CONVENIENCE FOOD

convenience food snabbmat
convenient bekväm
remove avlägsna, ta bort
packaging emballage
pierce sticka hål
tray bricka
stir röra
scald skålla sig
in vain i onödan
gunk smörja
wolf glufsa
flat blankt, exakt
occur to falla in
justified motiverat
unhealthiest mest ohälsosamma
resort to bruka
reconstituted återskapad; återbildad
fizzy drink kolsyrad dryck
complicated invecklade
reject säga nej till
particularly särskilt
afford ha råd med
assume förutsätta, anta
unfamiliar okänd
recipe recept
involve medföra
contain innehålla
commercially kommersiellt, affärsmässigt
nutrient näringsämne
occasional sporadisk

continental *h.* utländsk; kontinental
Batchelor ett företagsnamn
savoury välsmakande
obsess hemsöka
effortlessly utan ansträngning
slim smal
apparently uppenbart
obesity sjuklig fetma
common vanlig
virtually praktiskt taget
rare ovanlig
skinny mager
chilly kylig
greens grönsaker
fast food hit snabbmatssuccéer
craving for längtan efter, begär efter
raging våldsam
thirst törst
current allmän
wheat grass kvickrot
alfalfa sprouts böngroddar
chain oneself kedja fast sig
deprive förvägra
drive sb around the bend driva ngn till vansinne

SURRENDER TO PEACE

surrender kapitulera, ge sig
commemorate hedra minnet
maintenance underhåll
fund finansiera
announce tillkännage
founding grundande
conceptual begreppsmässig
Nutopia ett påhittat land (ordlek utopia)
citizen invånare
airfield flygfält
joint gemensam
constitution grundlag
spirit anda
surrender kapitulation
concept begrepp, idé
founded grundad
radical radikal (ngn som söker förändringar)
defeat nederlag
for instance till exempel
waste of time slöseri med tid
macho supermanlig

IMAGINE

live for today leva för idag
possession ägodel
greed girighet
brotherhood brödraskap

LISTENING: THE FINAL CURTAIN

the final curtain *ung.* den sista showen
get underway komma i gång
insist insistera
run up "uppstart"
declare tillkännage
curtain call inropning
deep-down innerst inne
actually faktiskt
continual ständig
performance framträdande
one-off unik
improve förbättra
get fit komma i form
firm *h.* nära; fast
medical hälsoundersökning
pass klara
inflatable uppblåsbar
dumbbell hantel
suit jacket kavaj
delay skjuta upp
dress rehearsal genrep
rumour rykte
exhausting tröttsam
schedule schema
hint antydan
scrap skrota
spiritually själsligt
exhausted utmattad
registered nurse legitimerad sjuksköterska
sedative lugnande medel
chief executive direktör
super-charged superladdad
goose pimples gåshud
candy store godisaffär
home free *ung.* ha det på det torra
capture fånga
account berättelse
emerge dyka upp
unconscious medvetslös
pronounced dead dödförklarad

WHO CAN YOU TRUST?

divide between dela mellan
visa lottery möjligheten att få visa till USA
troop into marchera in
sibling syskon
be enough to go round vara så att det räcker
in comparison to i jämförelse med
minor smärre
get on your feet komma på fötter
mustard senap
nauseate göra illamående
average medel
salary lön
stock option aktieoption
look diverse visa upp en mångfald
unit avdelning
give-and-take ge och ta
gain vinna
apply for ansöka om
cashier job jobb som kassörska
enroll skriva in
community college *ung.* vuxenutbildning
thigh lår
nail polish nagellack
self tanner brun utan sol
gawp glo
braid fläta
tightly knappt
ignorance okunnighet
arrogance högmod
squirrel ekorre
Igbo ett språk som talas i Nigeria
garri en maträtt gjord på cassavarot
cramped trång
basement källare
carton kartong
buttock skinka
moan stöna
related släkt
baby fish fiskyngel
honk tuta

9 HORROR

THE COLLECTOR

draft utkast
revision omarbetning
cellar källare
gasp for breath kippa efter luft
screen skärm
tentatively trevande; exprimentellt
cereal flingor
the Ladies toalett; damrum
pipe ledning, rör
demand kräva
forcefully kraftfullt
oblige tvinga
preparation förberedelse
wardrobe garderob
ought to borde
intention avsikt
Mazarine Blue namn på en blå fjäril
Queen of Spain Fritillary en sorts gul fjäril med svarta prickar
for ages i evigheter
reassure lugna
scholarship stipendium
completely thrown *ung.* helt svarslös

the Job Centre arbetsförmedlingen
forced to tvungen till
obey orders lyda order
clutch at straws gripa efter ett halmstrå
headmaster rektor
a stand off dödläge
sarcastically spydigt
flustered nervöst
regain control återta kontrollen
ludicrous löjlig

DEAD MEN TALK

callous hjärtlös
encounter råka ut för
solicitor's clerk advokatbiträde
forthcoming stundande
ironic ironisk
newly-weds nygifta
apparently uppenbarligen
befall drabba
dressing gown morgonrock
cord skärp
distraught bestört
emergency services räddningstjänsten
convinced övertygad
investigating undersökande
gardai polis
concern intresse
grieving sörjande
investigation undersökning
pathologist obducent
upgrade uppgradera
strangulation strypning
choke kväva
ligature mark blåmärke
shield skydda
trawl sökande
unearth gräva fram
murky skum
lengthy långvarig; vidlyftig
physical abuse misshandel
trace spår
whereabouts vistelseort
victim offer
launch starta
reveal avslöja
the long game *ung.* ta det långsiktigt
reap få, bärga
financial rewards ekonomisk belöning
prowess skicklighet
forensic kriminalteknisk
asphyxiate kväva
access få tillgång till
scour söka överallt
evade undvika
detection upptäckt
dispose of göra sig av med
grizzly *h.* mörk; grå
divorcee frånskild, man eller kvinna
convenience bekvämlighet
heiress arvtagerska
insurance policy försäkringsbrev
spouse maka/make
obstacle hinder
inconvenient besvärlig
significant viktig
charged with anklagad för
stand trial stå inför rätta
the jurisdiction rättsväsendet
on bail frigiven mot borgen
abandoned övergiven
commit suicide begå självmord
impending trial förestående rättegång
dogged envis
sighting iakttagelse
confirm bekräfta
transpire visa sig
extradition warrant utlämningsorder
murder squad mordrotel
unexpectedly oväntat
plead guilty erkänna sig skyldig
convicted dömd
stupidity dumhet
trail spår

COUNTERFEIT PROTECTION

counterfeit förfalskning
banknote sedel
obvious självklar
target mål
render framställa
forge förfalska
range urval
technique teknik
innovative nyskapande
device uppfinning, grepp
hologram en typ av tredimensionellt foto
in ciculation i omlopp
feature särdrag
intaglio printing djuptryck
engraved graverad, ristad
metal plate metallplatta
raised upphöjd
add lägga till
plastic bill plastsedel
sophistication raffinemang
remain förbli
punish straffa
fines böter
in addition to som tillägg till
depict framställa
utilize använda

fluorescent ljus med lägre våglängd (syns inte för blotta ögat)
apparent synbar
embedded innesluten
dash streck
reverse motsatta sidan
denomination valör
coat lapel kavajslag
repeatedly gång på gång
pliable mjuk, smidig
ample riklig
incorporate innehålla
highlight framhäva
foil bakgrund
according to i enlighet med
be liable to riskera att bli
confiscate beslagta
be on guard vara på sin vakt

LISTENING: THE YEAR WE DISAPPEARED

suspect misstänka
surgeon kirurg
embark engagera sig i
experimental försöks-
surgery kirurgi
bequeath testamentera, efterlämna
facial reconstruction ansiktsrekonstruktion
jaw käke
removed *ung.* bortsliten
shotgun hagelbössa
gums tandkött
chin haka
connect förena
dangling dinglande
request önskemål
legal pad block med gult linjerat papper
surveillance övervakning
guard duty vakttjänst
snap fräsa
comic book serietidning
creepy läskig
incredibly otroligt
in the line of duty i tjänsten
reassemble sätta ihop
fund-raiser välgörenhetsbasar
inappropriately olämpligt
unseasonably onormalt
muggy kvav
dressy fin
apply gälla
bake-sale table bordet med bakverk
lose one's mind tappa förståndet
courage mod
respond svara
braids flätor
wink blink
awkward tafatt
curb trottoarkant
smear smeta ner
crumb smula
descend on the snacks ge sig på godsakerna
sick to your stomach känna sig illamående
stuff oneself with proppa i sig
thrust into tvinga in i
pleasantry trevligheter, lustigheter
unfortunate olycklig
relocate förflytta
undisclosed okänd
notoriety *ung.* uppmärksamhet
distraction avledare
pull through klara sig

HUSH, HUSH

hush tyst
reveal avslöja
apply the brakes bromsa
aisle gång
window paneling fönsterruta
survey inspektera
rough tuff
neighborhood grannskap
block kvarter
quaint gammaldags
barred up with iron med galler
sideway AmE trottoar
desolate folktom, öde
path stig
rattling skramlande
cart kärra
garbage skräp
wheel rulla
beady små och lysande
twitch rycka
predatory evaluation plundringsutvärdering
discreet försiktigt
clutch hålla fast
mittens vantar
cackle skratta högt
confidence tillit
elaborate gå in på detaljer
resemble likna, påminna om
knotted twig knotig kvist
encourage uppmuntra
chiding tillrättavisande
quilted vadderad
peel off slänga av sig
goose bumps gåshud
derriere bak
barter förhandla
shuck off kasta av sig
zip into dra igen blixtlåset
chatter skaka

additional fee extraavgift
tug rycka
beanie "potta" typ av hatt
alley gränd
incredulously tvivlande
shrug rycka på axlarna
brick tegelsten
cluttered with nedskräpad med
unrecognizable oigenkännlig
hump hög
discarded bortkastad
chain-link kedjeliknande
fence stängsel
span spänna över
flank omge
barred tillbommade
crate back
crunch knastra
dart slunga
vanish försvinna
slim to none lika med noll
sleek glänsande
intuition omedelbar "magkänsla"
crackle knaster
screech away tjuta
chest bröst

ACKNOWLEDGEMENTS

The editor and publishers are grateful to the authors, publishers and others who have granted permission to use copyright material in *Solid Gold 1*. It has not been possible to identify or reach the copyright owners of some extracts, and in such cases the publishers would welcome information from copyright owners.

The Right Level by Elizabeth Gilbert: © Elizabeth Gilbert, 2006, *Eat, Pray, Love*, Bloomsbury Publishing Plc.
Losing My Virginity by Richard Branson: From *Losing My Viriginity: The Autobiography* by *Richard Branson*. Published by *Virgin Books*. Reprinted by permission of The Random House Group Limited.
Phenomenal Woman by Maya Angelou.
Rock What You've Got by Katherine Schwarzenegger: From the book ROCK WHAT YOU'VE GOT by Katherine Schwarzenegger. Copyright © 2010 Katherine Schwarzenegger. Reprinted by permission of Hyperion. All rights reserved.
Cheat! Originally published in Current (March-April 2011).
The Freedom Writers Diary by Erin Gruwell: From THE FREEDOM WRITERS DIARY by The Freedom Writers with Erin Gruwell, copyright © 1999 by The Tolerance Education foundation. Used by permission of Doubleday, a division of Random House, Inc. Any third party use of this material, outside of this publication, is prohibited. Interested parties must apply directly to Random House, Inc. for permission.
Fry and Jobs – Stephen Meets Steve by Stephen Fry: From *On the Mothership* by Stephen Fry. Originally published by Time Magazine.
Encounters by Terri Irwin: From *Steve & Me* by Terri Irwin. Used by permission of Simon & Schuster UK Limited.
So Where You From? by Iva R. Skoch. Reprinted by kind permission of Iva R. Skoch.
Watch Your Step by Petina Gappah: From *Elegy for Easterly* by Petina Gappah, reprinted by permission of Faber and Faber Ltd.
OCD, originally published in Current (March-April 2011).
Sexy by Joyce Carol Oates: From *Sexy* (hardcover edition) by Joyce Carol Oates. Reprinted by permission of HarperCollins*Publishers*.
Leaving Home by Rose Tremain: From *The Road Home* by Rose Tremain. Published by Chatto & Windus. Reprinted by permission of The Random House Group Limited.
Beijing to London by Xiaolu Guo: From *A Concise Chinese-English Dictionary for Lovers* by Xiaolu Guo. Published by Chatto & Windus. Reprinted by permission of The Random House Group Limited.
Singapore and Back by Peter Crouch: From *My Story* by Peter Crouch. Originally published by Hodder & Stoughton, London, UK.
Tapas and Tears by Chris Higgins, Hachette Children's Books.
Movie Review – The Hunger Games by Jackie K Cooper. Originally Published by Opposing Views (www.opposingviews.com).
Bollywood People and Plots by Nasreen Munni Kabir.
Instant Millionaire by Vikas Swarup: From *Q & A* by Vikas Swarup. Published by Doubleday. Reprinted by permission of The Random House Group Limited.
Public, Private by Dannii Minogue: From *My Story* by Dannii Minogue. Used by permission of Simon & Schuster UK Limited.
The Reaping by Suzanne Collins: From *The Hunger Games* by Suzanne Collins. Copyright © 2008 by Suzanne Collins. Reprinted by permission of Scholastic Inc.
Vertical Living. From SCIENTIFIC AMERICAN'S HOW THINGS WORK TODAY
If My Dad Were Still Here by Max Giaccone. Reprinted by kind permission of Max Giaccone. Originally published in Newweek/The Daily Beast (www.thedailybeast.com).
The Ballad of Sonny Payne by Steven Kurutz: Extract from *New York Stories – The Best of the City Section of The New York Times*.
New York, New York by Fred Ebb and John Kander: Music and lyrics by John Kander and Fred Ebb. Copyright © Unart Catalog Inc. EMI Catalogue Partner. All rights reserved. International copyright secured. Reprinted by permission of Edition Wilhelm Hansen AS, København.
Childhood Memories by Gareth Eoin Storey: Extract from *Born In the 1980s* by Gareth Eoin Storey. Originally published by Route Online (www.route-online.com).
Can You See Me? by Nicole Krauss: From *The History of Love* by Nicole Krauss.
Playing the Enemy and **After the Game** by John Carlin: Copyright © 2008 Enobarbus S.L. Used by permission of the Penguin Press, a division of Penguin Group (USA) Inc. (print and web) and Anne Edelstein Literary Agency (audio). All rights reserved.
The Story of the Makgabe by Alexander McCall Smith: From *The Girl Who Married a Lion* by Alexander McCall Smith. Used by permission of Canongate Books (print and web) and David Higham Literature, Film and TV agents (audio).
Cars Are Disgusting by Blake Nelson: Extract from *Destroy All* Cars by Blake Nelson, originally published by Scholastic Inc.
Convenience Food by Gill Holcombe: From *How to Feed Your Whole Family a Healthy, Balanced Diet With Very Little Money* by Gill Holcombe. Used by permission of Constable & Robinson.
Surrender to Peace by Yoko Ono: Yoko Ono, *Surrender to Peace*. Copyright © 2013 Yoko Ono. Used by permission/ All rights reserved.
Imagine by John Lennon: Music and lyrics by John Lennon. © Lenono Music. For the Nordic countries and the Baltic countries: Universal Music Publishing AB. Used by permission of Gehrmans Musikförlag AB.
Who Can You Trust? by Chimamanda Ngozi Adichie. Originally published by HarperCollins*Publishers*.
The Final Curtain: Reproduced with the kind permission of Haynes Publishing and taken from *Jackson: Unveiled* by James Fletcher, Jan Disley and Ros Wynne-Jones (2009, Haynes Publishing, Sparkford, Somerset BA22 7JJ).
The Collector by John Fowles/Mark Haley: Extract from Mark Helay's adaptation of John Fowles' novel *The Collector*.
Dead Men Talk by Sandra Mara. Originally published by Poolbeg Press.
Counterfeit Protection: From SCIENTIFIC AMERICAN'S HOW THINGS WORK TODAY, edited by Marshall Editions Ltd, copyright © 2000 by Marshall Editions Developments Ltd. Used by permission of Crown Publishers, a division of Random House, Inc. Any third party use of this material, outside of this publication, is prohibited. Interested parties must apply directly to Random House, Inc. for permission.
Hush, Hush by Becca Fitzpatrick: From *Hush, Hush* by Becca Fitzpartick. Used by permission of Simon & Schuster UK Limited.
The Year We Disappeared: From *The Year We Disappeared* by Cylin Busby and John Busby. © Cylin Busby and John Busby, *The Year We Disappeared* and Bloomsbury Publishing Plc.